CONTENDING WITH

CHRISTIANITY'S

CRITICS

CONTENDING WITH

CHRISTIANITY'S

CRITICS

Answering New Atheists & Other Objectors

EDITED BY PAUL COPAN

WILLIAM LANE CRAIG

ACADEMIC

NASHVILLE, TENNESSEE

ISBN: 978-0-8054-4936-5

Published by B&H Publishing Group
Nashville, Tennessee

Dewey Decimal Classification: 239
Subject Heading: APOLOGETICS\BIBLE—EVIDENCES, AUTHORITY,
ETC.\THEOLOGY

Printed in the United States of America
3 4 5 6 7 8 9 10 11 12 • 17 16 15 14 13 12 11 10
VP

CONTENTS

PREFACE

We are living in a time when certain critics of Christianity have abandoned all delicacy and decorum in debate. Rather than sticking to rational, carefully reasoned arguments, they have taken off the gloves to launch angry, sarcastic, and sloppily argued attacks. They lob their rhetorical grenades in hopes of creating the (incorrect) impression that belief in God is for intellectual lightweights who believe ridiculous, incoherent doctrines and are opposed to all scientific endeavor and discovery. These objectors are writing books—indeed, best sellers—that tend to be more bluster and emotion than substance. This new tone of debate is characteristic of the New Atheists such as Richard Dawkins, Sam Harris, and Christopher Hitchens. On another front, textual critic Bart Ehrman misleadingly raises doubts about the New Testament text's reliability, while novelist Dan Brown's *Da Vinci Code* and Jesus Seminar cofounder John Dominic Crossan mislead many into thinking that various Gnostic Gospels give us more reliable information about the historical Jesus than do the canonical Gospels. From various angles the public is being told that we cannot trust what the New Testament, and the Gospels in particular, say about Jesus of Nazareth.

The Evangelical Philosophical Society (EPS), with its journal *Philosophia Christi*, is dedicated to (among other things) addressing these challenges.[1] Indeed, part of the EPS's mission is to help equip

[1] Check out the EPS Web site at www.epsociety.org.

the church to respond to these pressing challenges. In conjunction with its annual meetings, the EPS hosts annual apologetics conferences at local churches in different regions of the country. Since 2003, leading scholars in their various fields—philosophy, biblical studies, biblical history and archaeology, theology, religious studies, and ethics—have freely contributed to the rousing success of these conferences, which consistently draw large crowds. Without fail conference participants are evidently enthusiastic, engaged, eager to learn, and encouraged to defend the gospel winsomely and wisely. They come with great anticipation, and they leave with a renewed appreciation for the intellectual foundations for their faith and a rekindled vision for responding to its critics and questioners.

As part of an ongoing series in accessible, cutting-edge Christian apologetics, this volume is a successor to our previous B&H book, *Passionate Conviction*.[2] Both of these books are the fruit of the annual EPS conferences. The chapters of this book, with the exception of the more in-house debate regarding open theism, are dedicated to addressing challenges from the New Atheists and other contemporary critics of Christianity concerning belief in God, the historical Jesus, and Christianity's doctrinal coherence. We pray that this book, too, will encourage your faith, strengthen your mind, and embolden your witness.

Paul Copan
William Lane Craig
Reformation Day 2008

---

[2] P. Copan and W. L. Craig, eds., *Passionate Conviction: Contemporary Discourses on Christian Apologetics* (Nashville: B&H Academic, 2007).

Part 1

THE EXISTENCE
OF GOD

Chapter 1

DAWKINS'S DELUSION

William Lane Craig

Richard Dawkins has emerged as the *enfant terrible* of the movement known as the New Atheism. His best-selling book *The God Delusion* has become the literary centerpiece of that movement. In it Dawkins aims to show that belief in God is a delusion, that is to say, "a false belief or impression," or worse, "a persistent false belief held in the face of strong contradictory evidence."[1] On pages 157–58 of his book, Dawkins summarizes what he calls "the central argument of my book." Note it well. If this argument fails, then Dawkins's book is hollow at its core. And, in fact, the argument is embarrassingly weak.

It goes as follows:

1. One of the greatest challenges to the human intellect has been to explain how the complex, improbable appearance of design in the universe arises.
2. The natural temptation is to attribute the appearance of design to actual design itself.
3. The temptation is a false one because the designer hypothesis immediately raises the larger problem of who designed the designer.
4. The most ingenious and powerful explanation is Darwinian evolution by natural selection.
5. We don't have an equivalent explanation for physics.
6. We should not give up the hope of a better explanation arising in physics, something as powerful as Darwinism is for biology.

[1] R. Dawkins, *The God Delusion* (Boston: Houghton Mifflin, 2006), 5.

Therefore, God almost certainly does not exist.

This argument is jarring because the atheistic conclusion that "therefore, God almost certainly does not exist" seems to come suddenly out of left field. You don't need to be a philosopher to realize that that conclusion doesn't follow from the six previous statements.

Indeed, if we take these six statements as premises of an argument intended logically to imply the conclusion "therefore, God almost certainly does not exist," then the argument is patently invalid. No logical rules of inference would permit you to draw this conclusion from the six premises.

A more charitable interpretation would be to take these six statements not as premises but as summary statements of six steps in Dawkins's cumulative argument for his conclusion that God does not exist. But even on this charitable construal, the conclusion "therefore, God almost certainly does not exist" simply doesn't follow from these six steps, even if we concede that each of them is true and justified. The only delusion demonstrated here is Dawkins's conviction that this is "a very serious argument against God's existence."[2]

So what does follow from the six steps of Dawkins's argument? At most all that follows is that we should not infer God's existence on the basis of the appearance of design in the universe. But that conclusion is compatible with God's existence and even with our justifiably believing in God's existence. Maybe we should believe in God on the basis of the cosmological argument or the ontological argument or the moral argument. Maybe our belief in God isn't based on arguments at all but is grounded in religious experience or in divine revelation. Maybe God wants us to believe in Him simply by faith. The point is that rejecting design arguments for God's existence does nothing to prove that God does not exist or even that belief in God is unjustified. Indeed, many Christian theologians have rejected arguments for the existence of God without thereby committing themselves to atheism.

Dawkins's argument for atheism is a failure even if we concede, for the sake of argument, all its steps. But, in fact, several of these steps are plausibly false in any case. Take step 3, for example. Dawkins's claim

---

[2] Ibid., 157. Indeed, he fancies himself to have offered a "devastating" and "unrebuttable refutation" of God's existence.

here is that one is not justified in inferring design as the best explanation of the complex order of the universe because then a new problem
arises: Who designed the designer?

This objection is flawed on at least two counts.

First, in order to recognize an explanation as the best, one needn't
have an explanation of the explanation. This is an elementary point
concerning inference to the best explanation as practiced in the philosophy of science. If archaeologists digging in the earth were to discover things looking like arrowheads and hatchet heads and pottery
shards, they would be justified in inferring that these artifacts are not
the chance result of sedimentation and metamorphosis but products
of some unknown group of people even though they had no explanation of who these people were or where they came from. Similarly, if
astronauts were to come upon a pile of machinery on the back side of
the moon, they would be justified in inferring that it was the product
of intelligent, extraterrestrial agents even if they had no idea whatsoever who these extraterrestrial agents were or how they got there.

In order to recognize an explanation as the best, one needn't be
able to explain the explanation. In fact, so requiring would lead to an
infinite regress of explanations so that nothing could ever be explained
and science would be destroyed. In the case at hand, in order to recognize that intelligent design is the best explanation of the appearance of
design in the universe, one needn't be able to explain the designer.

Second, Dawkins thinks that in the case of a divine designer of the
universe, the designer is just as complex as the thing to be explained so
that no explanatory advance is made. This objection raises all sorts of
questions about the role played by simplicity in assessing competing
explanations—for example, how simplicity is to be weighted in comparison with other criteria like explanatory power, explanatory scope,
plausibility, and so forth. If a less simple hypothesis exceeds its rivals
in explanatory scope and power, for example, then it may well be the
preferred explanation despite the sacrifice in simplicity.

But leave those questions aside. Dawkins's fundamental mistake
lies in his assumption that a divine designer is an entity comparable in
complexity to the universe. As an unembodied mind, God is a remarkably simple entity. As a nonphysical entity, a mind is not composed of

parts; and its salient properties—like self-consciousness, rationality, and volition—are essential to it. In contrast to the contingent and variegated universe with all its inexplicable physical quantities and constants (mentioned in the fifth step of Dawkins's argument),[3] a divine mind is startlingly simple. Certainly such a mind may have complex ideas (it may be thinking, for example, of the infinitesimal calculus), but the mind itself is a remarkably simple entity. Dawkins has evidently confused a mind's *ideas*, which may indeed be complex, with a mind *itself*, which is an incredibly simple entity.[4] Therefore, postulating a divine mind behind the universe most definitely does represent an advance in simplicity.

Other steps in Dawkins's argument are also problematic; but I think enough has been said to show that his argument does nothing to undermine a design inference based on the universe's complexity, not to speak of its serving as a justification of atheism.

Several years ago my atheist colleague Quentin Smith unceremoniously crowned Stephen Hawking's argument against God in *A Brief History of Time* as "the worst atheistic argument in the history of Western thought."[5] With the advent of *The God Delusion* the time has come to relieve Hawking of this weighty crown and to recognize Richard Dawkins's accession to the throne.

---

[3] Otherwise known as the fine-tuning of the universe for life. The optimism expressed in step 6 of Dawkins's argument with respect to finding a physical explanation for the cosmic fine-tuning is baseless and represents little more than the faith of a naturalist. For discussion of the design argument from the fine-tuning of nature's constants and quantities, see W. L. Craig, *Reasonable Faith*, 3rd ed. (Wheaton, IL: Crossway, 2008), 157–79.

[4] His confusion is evident when he complains, "A God capable of continuously monitoring and controlling the individual status of every particle in the universe *cannot* be simple. . . . Worse (from the point of view of simplicity), other corners of God's giant consciousness are simultaneously preoccupied with the doings and emotions and prayers of every single human being—and whatever intelligent aliens there might be on other planets in this and 100 billion other galaxies" (*God Delusion*, 149). This conflates God with what God is thinking about. To say that God, as an immaterial entity, is extraordinarily simple is not to endorse Aquinas's doctrine that God is logically simple (rejected by Dawkins on 150). God may have diverse properties without having the sort of complexity Dawkins is talking about, namely "heterogeneity of parts" (ibid., 150).

[5] Q. Smith, "The Wave Function of a Godless Universe," in *Theism, Atheism, and Big Bang Cosmology* (Oxford: Clarendon Press, 1993), 322.

Chapter 2

AT HOME IN THE MULTIVERSE?
CRITIQUING THE ATHEIST MANY-WORLDS SCENARIO[1]

James Daniel Sinclair

The Copernican Principle

Far out in the uncharted backwaters of the unfashionable end of the Western Spiral arm of the Galaxy lies a small unregarded yellow sun. Orbiting this at a distance of roughly ninety-eight million miles is an utterly insignificant little blue-green planet whose ape-descended life forms are so amazingly primitive that they still think digital watches are a pretty neat idea.[2]

—*Douglas Adams*

I s the Earth an uninteresting speck in a mundane solar system, re-siding within a run-of-the-mill galaxy within a pointless universe? This is the Copernican Principle.

The principle, named after the fifteenth-century Polish astronomer Nicolaus Copernicus, is a philosophical outgrowth of his discovery of a heliocentric universe. The dominant scientific view at the time had Earth as the physical center of the universe. Subsequent folklore had it that the

[1] Abstract: The universe has the appearance of being extraordinarily finely tuned for life. This is problematic for a chance-driven explanation. In response many atheist thinkers have explored the possibility that an ensemble of universes, the multiverse, could be a plausible alternative to design. This paper explores the theoretical viability of the multiverse while providing an overview of the subject for the intelligent layman.

[2] D. Adams, *The Hitchhiker's Guide to the Galaxy* (New York: Crown Publishing Group, 2004).

geocentric view placed Earth (hence man) in an exalted position.[3] Thus Copernicus is said to have knocked man off his throne. The more mundane and unspectacular our little patch of the universe seems, the more it seems to support an accidental view of our origins. This anecdote (revisionist history included) underlies the Principle and fits with a Western philosophical movement called the Enlightenment. The Enlightenment was a thought system based on the view that outside reality can be objectively known and is ultimately discoverable. It also endorsed a materialistic view of the universe; this discovery is done through unfettered reason. The older view that scientific investigation should include consideration of a final cause, a purpose, was overthrown.

The Problem: Apparent Design

In the fall of 1973, the world's most eminent astronomers and physicists gathered in Poland to commemorate the 500th birthday of the father of modern astronomy, Nicolaus Copernicus. . . . Yet of the dozens of scientific lectures presented . . . only one would be remembered decades later. . . . The title of the paper was technical sounding and the tone of the presentation highly tentative: *"Large Number Coincidences and the Anthropic Principle in Cosmology."* For the insights he presented, 500 years after Copernicus's birth, spelled nothing less than the philosophical overthrow of the Copernican revolution itself. . . .

Carter called his notion the "anthropic principle" from the Greek word anthropos, "man." . . . The anthropic principle says that all the seemingly arbitrary and unrelated constants in physics have one strange thing in common—these are precisely the values you need if you want to have a universe capable of producing life.[4]

This quotation from Glynn's 1997 book, *God, the Evidence*, lays out the amazing endgame of five hundred years of Copernican speculation.

---

[3] Actually the geocentric (Ptolemaic) view was that Earth occupied the lowest position in the cosmos. This fits with the gnostic heresy that matter, the physical universe, is irredeemably corrupt.
[4] P. Glynn, *God, the Evidence* (Rocklin, CA: Prima Publishing, 1997), 22.

Since 1973, the Anthropic Principle has effectively supplanted Copernicus within the field of cosmology. Why has this happened, and what is driving the reconsideration of the Copernican Principle? In essence recent physical investigation has revealed the following four independent problems with a strictly materialist worldview:

1. Fine-tuning of constants in the laws of physics and the masses of the elementary particles[5]
2. Fine-tuning of Earth as a life site[6]
3. Form of the laws of physics, unreasonable simplicity and rationality[7]
4. The argument from reason, our ability to comprehend the universe.[8]

The laws of physics, even the "fortunate" circumstances of the Earth itself, seem contrived, *as if* there were a designer. The Earth may not be the *physical* center of the universe, but it does seem to be its *biological* center.

The Strong Anthropic Principle (SAP)

We take the side of science in spite of the patent absurdity of some of its constructs, in spite of its failure to fulfill many of its extravagant promises of health and life, in spite of the tolerance of the scientific community for unsubstantiated just-so stories, because we have a prior commitment, a commitment to materialism. It is not that the methods and institutions of science somehow compel us to accept a material explanation of the phenomenal world, but, on the contrary, that we are forced by our a priori adherence to material causes to create an apparatus of investigation and a set of concepts that produce material explanations, no matter how counterintuitive, no matter how mystifying to the uninitiated. Moreover, that materialism is absolute, for we cannot allow a Divine Foot in the door.[9]

[5] See J. Leslie, *Universes* (London: Routledge, 1996).
[6] See D. Brownlee and P. Ward, *Rare Earth* (New York: Copernicus Books, 2000); H. Ross, *The Creator and the Cosmos* (Colorado Springs, CO: NavPress, 2001).
[7] W. Bradley, "The 'Just So' Universe," in *Signs of Intelligence*, eds. W. Dembski and J. Kushiner (Grand Rapids: Brazos Press, 2001).
[8] V. Reppert, *C. S. Lewis's Dangerous Idea* (Downers Grove, IL: InterVarsity Press, 2003).
[9] R. Lewontin, "Billions and Billions of Demons," review of *The Demon-Haunted World: Science as a Candle in the Dark*, by C. Sagan, in the *New York Review of Books* (January 1997): 28–32.

The guiding principle of Enlightenment philosophy in its dealings with science is as given by Richard Lewontin above. God is ruled out a priori. It is a key tenet of Enlightenment thinking that religious speculation does not produce knowledge. Hence any theory of origins—no matter how complicated, convoluted, or counterintuitive—is to be preferred.

The initial response is to form a different interpretation of the Anthropic Principle. One starts with Carter's original formulation, now widely referred to as the "Weak" version:

> *The Weak Anthropic Principle* (WAP): The universe will be observed to be amenable to the existence of observers because otherwise we wouldn't be here.

Philosopher Richard Swinburne has offered a refutation of the viability of the WAP by itself.[10] Suppose I am put up against a wall to be executed by firing squad. I close my eyes; 12 rifles, aimed by expert marksmen, fire. I am still alive. What is the best explanation for my continued good health? Should I be satisfied with the WAP as an explanation? Or is it more likely I am popular with the firing squad?

Why do lotteries prevent their officials (and families) from participating? The probability of skullduggery is thought to be higher than the probability that a relative can win by pure chance. Clearly WAP is true but unhelpful. An atheist view needs something more. Hence the addition of Many Worlds to the WAP. This dual formulation is referred to as the Strong Anthropic Principle.

The Gambler's Fallacy Versus Russian Roulette

Ockham's Razor: It is vain to do with more what can be done with less.

—William of Ockham

Design or Many Worlds? Both have power to explain the type of phenomena that interests us. How to break the tie? We start with consideration of the power of prior knowledge in judging explanatory sufficiency.

Consider the following example. Suppose you are sitting on a jury during a murder trial. The evidence appears overwhelming. The DA

---

[10] R. Swinburne, *The Existence of God* (rev. ed.: Oxford: Oxford University Press, 1991).

presents DNA evidence that apparently links the defendant with the crime scene. An expert witness testifies that the probability that the DNA match could be a false positive is 1 in 1 followed by eighteen zeroes (10^{18}). This evidence alone should be enough to convict.

Suppose that the defense comes forward with a novel theory. This is not the only world, the defense attorney says. There are, in fact, 10^{18} parallel worlds out there. Probability shows, therefore, that there is at least one person in the universe who, at this moment, is on trial for this murder but is *definitely* innocent. This is reasonable doubt. How can you convict?[11]

Before you decide, we note that the trial is not yet over. The DA presents additional evidence. The defendant is the only one with a motive, he says. The defendant lacks an alibi, he says. An eyewitness indicates the defendant was close by near the time of the murder.

On further consultation with my expert scientists, says the defense attorney, it turns out there are more than 10^{18} parallel worlds out there. In fact, there are enough worlds to cover the DA's circumstantial case. If the DA comes forward with evidence tomorrow that shows the defendant is an additional 10^{100} more likely to commit the crime than anyone else, we can certainly "discover" 10^{100} new worlds.

As one can see from the apocryphal story, there is room for the Many Worlds theory to be vastly abused. The Many Worlds advocate is engaged in a problem called the Gambler's Fallacy. Suppose I flip a coin repeatedly. Heads, you pay me a dollar. Tails, I pay you a dollar. I win 10,000 times in a row. Should you be upset? Not to worry. I assure you that there are sufficient Many Worlds out there where coin flipping is going on, and those copies of yourself must surely be winning so as to even the odds. Feel better? I'll give you double or nothing on the next flip.

But let us make a contrast to bring home an important point. Suppose Earth will be destroyed by an unavoidable natural disaster. We have time to build one spaceship big enough to take one family. A raffle is arranged where there are one billion families with an average size of six. One billion tickets are issued. Should we be surprised that

---

[11] If only one innocent man is too few to convince, I can produce any number through suitable propagation of worlds. In fact, the number of worlds (and innocent men) could be infinite!

someone wins the raffle? No; it was guaranteed. Thus should the winner be surprised, similar to the example of the firing squad victim? No.

What is the difference between the raffle example, where Many Worlds works, and the Gambler's Fallacy, where it doesn't? In the former example I have explicit prior knowledge. The raffle tickets, which are analogous to Many Worlds, are known to exist. It is known that *someone* will definitely win. So if I can directly observe Many Worlds, or I can show inferentially that some mechanism will definitely extrapolate a life-amenable universe with a life site, then I have something. If I am simply inventing Many Worlds, then I am engaged in the fallacy.

Six Problems Facing the Multiverse

Problem 1. Demonstrating the Reality of Alternate Worlds
Multiverse Options

> *"When you have eliminated the impossible, that which remains, however improbable, must be the truth."*[12]

As we have seen, the question turns on whether we have independent evidence for the existence of alternate worlds. But this will face some significant problems. First, we live in this world and cannot directly observe others. Second, the current philosophy of science rules out design a priori. Although science normally operates according to Ockham's razor, in the case of God, it operates according to Holmes's dictum. The course of science will be to postulate the complicated and improbable because, given that there cannot be a God, the improbable *must* be true.

This is unfortunate because evidence for a multiverse must come *indirectly*. The multiverse must be a *natural* prediction of a theoretical framework which itself was constructed based on direct observables, but the philosophy of science militates against this. Instead a materialist answer will be the starting point, and investigation will proceed

---

[12] Sherlock Holmes in A. C. Doyle, *Sherlock Holmes: Selected Stories*, ed. S. C. Roberts (Oxford: Oxford University Press, 1998).

by asking what must be true to (force-)fit that framework. Hence we can't get a *natural* prediction for the truth of materialism because the reasoning would be circular unless a scientist is initially ignorant that his theory might have metaphysical import!

We will look briefly at three of the options available that postulate a multiverse.

1. Oscillating Universes: Ekpyrosis (Temporal Multiverse). One of the latest proposals for reincarnation is called the "ekpyrotic universe,"[13] a term drawn from the Stoic model of cosmic evolution in which the universe is consumed by fire at regular intervals and reconstituted out of this fire.

This is a good example of the philosophy of science in action. The model's authors knew that two (among many) problems must be solved for a materialist oscillating model to work. Entropy must build in any universe so you need someplace to put it. Second, if you have a universe where things happen, you need a source of energy, so the authors postulated an infinitely sized sheet (to store an infinite amount of entropy), which effectively is falling down a bottomless pit (to supply an infinite store of free energy).[14] The model avoids collecting the entropy at the Big Crunch by making the universe's rebounce occur as a collision with *another* universe in a higher dimension.[15]

They thereby get past the problems of earlier cyclic models. But instead of the model predicting these materialist features as a natural extrapolation, the authors chose these features as the starting point. This limits the evidential value.

But could we "see" the extra dimensions Ekpyrosis predicts? One way would be to test how gravity weakens as it radiates from a source. If we are limited to three space dimensions, it weakens as 1/(dis-

---

[13] J. Khoury, B. A. Ovrut, P. J. Steinhardt, and N. Turok, "The Ekpyrotic Universe: Colliding Branes and the Origin of the Hot Big Bang," *Physical Review* D 64 (2001), 123522, http://arxiv.org/abs/hep-th/0103239 (accessed Oct. 7, 2008). I note, for completeness, that one of the authors (P. Steinhardt) is actually a critic of anthropic thinking as a resolution of the universe fine-tuning problem.

[14] See the February 2004 issue of *Discover* (p. 35) for a full, popular-level description of this model. Energetically, what really happens is that the universe's state of gravitational potential energy can be reduced infinitely; the stopping point is a boundary at negative infinity.

[15] Our particular world sheet expands at a rate consistent with keeping the entropy density constant.

tance)2. If there are extra dimensions, it weakens at a faster rate with respect to distance from a source. To date, experimental tests have not seen a deviation for a 1/(distance)2 reality. In fact, these experiments have limited the possible size of an extra dimension to less than 55 micrometers.[16]

2. Flat and Open Inflationary Universes (Spatial Multiverse). What exactly does it mean to have a "flat" universe? We apparently live on the three-dimensional surface of a four-dimensional reality. This cannot be visualized, but the meaning of *flat* is fairly simple. The shortest distance between two points is a straight line. Parallel lines do not intersect.

But a flat or open (i.e., saddle-shaped) universe usually[17] has the feature that space itself is infinitely sized. If so, then perhaps we can think of the universe like a patchwork quilt. Each patch could effectively represent a different reality. The physical constants and particle masses could be different for each patch. There is a plausible mechanism available to produce this.[18] One also randomizes stars, galaxies, etc., so that one may imagine ultimately producing a life site akin to Earth.

I personally find that this option has some evidential value. It arises as a natural fallout from Einstein's general relativity as opposed to an initial materialist force-fit. Einstein wasn't thinking "multiverse" when he formed his theory (although he *was* thinking "steady-state" to avoid the theistic consequences of an origin). But most of the available evidence militates against this option avoiding the Gambler's Fallacy.

For example, we could start with the problem that, while it is possible to prove that the universe is *not* flat, it is not possible to prove that it is! A flat universe will be produced when the energy density (i.e., all the stuff in the universe—remember E=mc2) is at a critical value. Scientists call this value omega, or Ω. When Ω = 1.0, the universe is flat. But this must be known to infinite accuracy. Our science instruments are good but not *that* good.

[16] J. H. Adelberger, T. S. Cook, J. H. Gundlach, B. R. Heckel, C. D. Hoyle, D. J. Kapner, and H. E. Swanson, "Tests of the Gravitational Inverse-Square Law Below the Dark-Energy Length Scale, *Physical Review Letters* 98 (2007) 021101, http://arxiv.org/abs/hep-ph/0611184v1 (accessed Oct. 7, 2008).

[17] Except for exotic topologies.

[18] A. Guth, *The Inflationary Universe: The Quest for a New Theory of Cosmic Origin* (New York: Perseus Publishing, 1998).

If, however, we measure Ω to be greater than 1.0 and can place sound error bounds around this measurement which exclude $\Omega = 1$, then you have proven that there is enough energy in the universe to force it to be finite. So what is the current measurement? In 2003, in the first-year data of the Wilkinson Microwave Anisotropy Probe satellite (WMAP), Ω was estimated to be 1.02 ± 0.02.[19] By 2008, this was refined to 1.005 ± 0.0064.[20] So the universe appears to be finite. But a flat universe is still possible, as this would be at the edge of the error boundary.[21]

Then we have the argument of Roger Penrose.[22] To simplify things Penrose was wondering why the universe is not just a huge black hole. It desperately wants to be. If you consider all the different ways one can take basic building blocks (like Legos) and cobble together a universe, virtually all those configurations will produce variations on a huge black hole. Things want to be messy, not clean. Black holes are by far the messiest things that exist. So if things prefer to be messy, why aren't they? Penrose makes a calculation, considering just the matter in the universe that we can see. But he rightly notes that if the universe is like the patchwork quilt, then as the size of the universe approaches infinity (hence the number of particles approaches infinity) and the rest of the universe looks like ours (the Copernican Principle), the calculated probability for us seeing the universe in its present configuration approaches zero!

3. Everett Quantum Mechanics (Quantum Multiverse). If you haven't heard of this before, this is going to seem way out there. Quantum mechanics (the science of the very small) permits the outrageous possibility that the universe splits into alternate realities every time a choice is

---

[19] G. Ellis, U. Kirchner, and J.-P. Uzan, "WMAP Data and the Curvature of Space," *Monthly Notices of the Royal Astronomical Society* 344 (2003) L65, http://arxiv.org/abs/astro-ph/0302597 (accessed Oct. 7, 2008).

[20] C. L. Bennett, J. Dunkley, R. Greason, B. Gold, M. Halpern, R. S. Hill, G. Hinshaw, M. N. Jarosik, A. Kogut, E. Komatsu, D. Larson, M. Limon, S. S. Meyer, M. R. Nolta, N. Odegard, L. Page, D. N. Spergel, G. S. Tucker, J. L. Weiland, E. Wollack, E. L. Wright, "Five-Year Wilkinson Microwave Anisotropy Probe (WMAP) Observations: Data Processing, Sky Maps, and Basic Results," *Astrophysical Journal Supplement Series* (forthcoming) http://arxiv.org/abs/0803.0732 (accessed Oct. 7, 2008).

[21] These errors are "one sigma" values. To be truly confident in an error bound, scientists will usually use bounds that are three to five times larger. So we currently have only weak confidence of a closed universe.

[22] R. Penrose, *The Emperor's New Mind* (Oxford: Oxford University Press, 1989), 344.

possible. The science fiction series Sliders was based on this, as are two dozen episodes of *Star Trek* (all incarnations) and *Stargate SG-1.*

As is explained well in Zukav's *The Dancing Wu-Li Masters,*[23] one can question a key assumption of rationality called contra-factual definiteness. When one questions "definiteness," one constructs many worlds. Definiteness is a simple idea. It is as follows: if I choose option A, then option B does not happen. But what if there is not a definite outcome to choice? What if A and B both still happen but in different universes? This is the core of the Everett theory. Every time something happens (such as a quantum event at the atomic level), the universe itself splits into as many realities as cover all the possible outcomes. If the original Everett view is sound, then it does indeed contend powerfully against the Cosmological Design Argument. If the physical parameters in the Standard Model of physics (particle masses, force strengths) are set by symmetry-breaking events shortly after the big bang,[24] then it would seem that all of them have been tried, and by an observer selection effect we must exist within a patch that has life-amenable values for these parameters.

With regard to evidential value for Many Worlds, Everett has some; I find it to be the most compelling multiverse option. But cosmologists don't seem to employ Everett in this useful form. Rather, they employ variations that deconstruct the notion of time. For example some (David Deutsche, Julian Barbour) employ a literal interpretation of the "Wheeler DeWitt equation," which is a formulation that joins Einstein's general relativity to quantum theory by asserting the outright elimination of the notion of time. The consequence seems to be a form of solipsism, given that there are no true histories. Thus our memories are not records of an actual "past." Another consequence is that the multiverse would be an *actual* infinity of worlds rather than merely a *potential* infinity.[25] This invocation of "strong" multiverse theory can be problematic for the atheist, as we'll see later (in the section "Proof of a Transcendent Creator").

---

[23] G. Zukav, *The Dancing Wu Li Masters* (New York: Bantam, 1989), 302.
[24] See Guth, *The Inflationary Universe.*
[25] A potential infinity is a finite quantity that is increasing without bound. An actual infinity is just as it sounds, a truly infinite quantity.

Second, four possible interpretations of quantum phenomena can be true,[26] and falsifying any of them may be impossible (on strictly quantum grounds). All of them can account for observed experimental results.

Problem 2. Positive Proof of a Single Universe

The second problem for the atheist is the apparent emergence (as of this writing) of good evidence for a closed inflationary universe.[27] Remember that a finite universe would limit the number of possible planets in the universe. So if you have few planets, yet an extremely low probability that any particular planet would be a life site, this militates toward design. Hence you have a direct and simple way to refute at least some multiverse candidates.

Sky Map of the Cosmic Background Radiation[28]

Hot spots (color differences) represent infant galaxies in the early universe. Source: NASA/WMAP Science Team: http://map.gsfc.nasa .gov/m_mm/mr_limits.html

[26] Research on this matter will show that more than four are discussed, but most are weeded out if we assert (1) a correspondence theory of truth, (2) that "ordinary" logic applies (i.e., we respect notions such as the Law of Excluded Middle), (3) that current quantum theory is complete, (4) that we ignore FAPP (for-all-practical-purposes) or instrumental-only (nonrealist) interpretations, (5) that we are interested only in interpretations where "the universe" is a meaningful concept, and (6) that this "universe" is an objective, extramental reality (which likely excludes the "consistent" or "decoherent" histories approach). If so, then the four options are:
    1. No hidden variables (Copenhagen)
    2. Hidden variables (e.g., DeBroglie-Bohm)
    3. Choice has no consequences (Everett Many Worlds Interpretation)
    4. There is no choice (Superdeterminism)
[27] Which, due to the effect of dark energy will expand forever (i.e., no reincarnation).
[28] See http://cmb.phys.cwru.edu/boomerang/press_images/raw_images/model_maps.jpg for a depiction of how the CBR can help determine the "flatness" of the universe.

In addition to the evidence that the critical density parameter omega (Ω) is greater than one, other features of the Cosmic Background Radiation (CBR)—the heat left over from the big bang itself—may be inconsistent with a *perfectly* flat (hence infinite) universe.

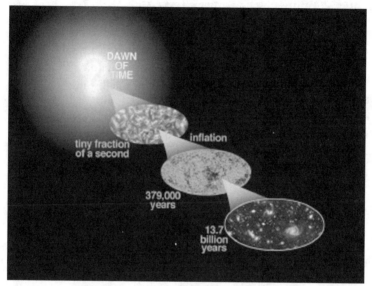

History of the universe: Source NASA / WMAP Science Team

Consider the following from the cover article in the October 9, 2003, issue of the journal *Nature*, from the research team of Luminet *et al.*:

> Temperature fluctuations on the microwave sky may be expressed as a sum of spherical harmonics, just as music and other sounds may be expressed as a sum of ordinary harmonics. A musical note is the sum of a fundamental, a second harmonic, a third harmonic, and so on. . . . Analogously, the temperature map on the microwave sky is the sum of spherical harmonics. *The relative strengths of the harmonic—the power spectrum—is [sic] a signature of the physics and geometry of the universe.*[29] [emphasis added]

[29] R. Lehoucq, J.-P. Luminet, A. Riazuelo, J. Weeks, J.-P. Uzan, "Dodecahedral space topology as an explanation for weak wide-angle temperature correlations in the cosmic microwave

In the words of Luminet, "In an infinite flat space, waves from the big bang would fill the universe *on all length scales*. . . . The first observable harmonic is the quadrupole."[30]

Luminet observes that the WMAP data shows an unusually weak signal in the CBR given a prediction that the universe is perfectly flat. The WMAP satellite has been used in recent times to study the CBR.[31]

> Cosmologists thus face the challenge of finding a model that accounts for the weak quadrupole while maintaining the success of the infinite flat universe model on small scales. . . .

> The low quadrupole implies a cut-off on the wavelengths of the 3-dimensional harmonics. Such a cut-off presents an awkward problem in infinite flat space, because it defines a preferred length scale in an otherwise scale-invariant space. *A more natural explanation invokes a finite universe*, where the size of space itself imposes a cut-off on the wavelengths. *Just as the vibrations of a bell cannot be larger than the bell itself, the density fluctuations in space cannot be larger than space itself.* While most potential spatial topologies fail to fit the WMAP results, the Poincaré dodecahedral space [Luminet's proposed model] fits them strikingly well. . . .

> WMAP found a quadrupole only about 1/7 as strong as would be expected in an infinite flat space. The probability that this could happen by mere chance has been estimated at about a fifth of one percent (Spergel et al., 2003).[32] The oc-

background," *Nature* 425 (2003) 593, http://arxiv.org/abs/astro-ph/0310253 (accessed October 7, 2008); G. Efstathiou, "Is the Low CMB Quadrupole a Signature of Spatial Curvature?" *Monthly Notices of the Royal Astronomical Society* 343 (2003) L95, http://arxiv.org/abs/astro-ph/0303127 (accessed Oct. 7, 2008). One should note that the authors do not probe (or endorse) the theistic implications of their research. See W. Hu and M. White, "The Cosmic Symphony," issue of *Scientific American* (February 2004): 44, which contains an excellent layman's level discussion of the CBR and what a scientist can learn from it.

[30] J.-P. Luminet, "The Shape and Topology of the Universe," Proceedings from the conference Tessellations: The World a Jigsaw (Leyden, the Netherlands), March 2006, http://arxiv.org/abs/0802.2236 (accessed Oct. 7, 2008).

[31] The following string of quotations is taken from Luminet's essay. All italics have been added.

[32] The specific reference cited here is: D. N. Spergel, L. Verde, H. V. Peiris, E. Komatsu, M. R. Nolta, C. L. Bennett, M. Halpern, G. Hinshaw, N. Jarosik, A. Kogut, M. Limon, S. S. Meyer, L. Page, G. S. Tucker, J. L. Weiland, E. Wollack, and E. L. Wright, "First Year Wilkin-

topole term, with wave number l = 3, is also weak at 72% of the expected value, but not nearly so dramatic or significant as the quadrupole.

The key is the statement that the probability that we could see what we are seeing and still have a perfectly flat universe "has been estimated at about a fifth of one percent." Combined with the critical density value and Ockham's razor, the most natural interpretation is a limited size universe. Some additional verification of this type of universe has recently come forward.[33] The best way to think of Luminet's universe[34] (given that one can't visualize higher dimensional space) is to think of a two-dimensional creature living on the inside surface of a soccer ball, similar to Edwin Abbott's *Flatland*.[35]

Imagine, for example, a star at the opposite side of the universe. (Let's stick with the unrealistic, but nonetheless easier-to-imagine, idea of living on the inside surface of a soccer ball.) It should be self-evident that light from that star can travel and reach us along many different paths, while for a perfectly flat (table-top) universe, there would be only one way for light to get here. The effect on the observer would be that she would see multiple images of the same star come in from many different directions (as long as there was enough time for light to

son Microwave Anisotropy Probe (WMAP 1) Observations: Determination of Cosmological Parameters," *Astrophysical Journal Supplement* 148 (2003) 175–94, http://arxiv.org/abs/astro-ph/0302209 (accessed Oct. 7, 2008).

[33] S. Bajtlik, M. Cechowska, B. Lew, A. Marecki, B. F. Roukema, "A Hint of Poincaré Dodeca-hedral Topology in the WMAP First Year Sky Map," *Astronomy and Astrophysics* 423 (2004) 821, http://arxiv.org/abs/astro-ph/0402608v4 (accessed Oct. 7, 2008); S. Bajtlik, M. Biesiada, H. Jurkiewicz, B. F. Roukema, A. Szaniewska, "A Weak Acceleration Effect Due to Residual Gravity in a Multiply Connected Universe," *Astronomy and Astrophysics* 463 (2007), 861, http://arxiv.org/abs/astro-ph/0602159v3 (accessed Oct. 7 2008); Z. Buliński, N. E. Gaudin, B. F. Roukema, A. Szaniewska, "The Optimal Phase of the Generalised Poincaré Dodecahedral Space Hypothesis Implied by the Spatial Cross-Correlation Function of the WMAP Sky Maps," *Astronomy and Astrophysics* 486 (2008), 55, http://arxiv.org/abs/0801.0006v2 (accessed Oct. 7, 2008); S. Caillerie, M. Lachièze-Rey, R. Lehoucq, J.-P. Luminet, A. Riazuelo, and J. Weeks, "A New Analysis of the Poincaré Dodecahedral Space Model," *Astronomy and Astrophysics* (forth-coming), http://arxiv.org/abs/0705.0217v2 (accessed Oct. 7, 2008); B. Lew, B. Roukema, "A Test of the Poincaré Dodecahedral Space Topology Hypothesis with the WMAP CMB Data," *Astronomy and Astrophysics* 482 (2008), 747–53, http://arxiv.org/abs/0801.1358v2 (accessed Oct. 7, 2008); J.-P. Luminet, "The Shape and Topology of the Universe."

[34] Luminet's dodecahedron is not the only possibility here. There are many more possible closed topologies.

[35] See http://abbott.thefreelibrary.com/Flatland for an online version of this book about a three-dimensional being visiting creatures that live in a two-dimensional "flat-land."

have traveled here along the possible path; hence there is a restriction on the size of the soccer ball). Something similar to this in our real universe is testable if it turns out the universe is small enough. One can search the oldest light in the universe, the CBR, to see if there are pattern matches in different sections of the sky.

As indicated above, there is some preliminary indication that such a pattern match has been found. If this model is correct, it implies:

- Inflation is true, not Ekpyrosis. Hence there is not even a debate as to whether the universe has recycled. We live in a finite-age, one-time-only universe.
- This is the only patch in the quilt; there are no infinite number of worlds out there with different physical constants, masses, life sites, etc.
- But quantum multiverse models would still be on the table.

Problem 3. Tiebreaker A: Boltzmann's Blunder

Suppose now that there really is a multiverse. It turns out that this is only "necessary but not sufficient" to defeat teleology (design). The Strong Anthropic Principle only gets one as far as explaining why one observer exists in the present. This puts it on par with a design theory, but other criteria can break this tie.

There is an issue called "Boltzmann's Blunder," named after the nineteenth-century physicist Ludwig von Boltzmann. To explain the low entropy state of the early universe, Boltzmann proposed that, however unlikely, the universe must occasionally fluctuate back to a low entropy state. Given infinite time, any nonzero probability of a "rebounce" will do.

John Barrow and Frank Tipler explain his mistake:

> The physicist Richard Feynman, in a 1965 lecture, leveled an objection to the fluctuations theory which is sufficiently general to apply against any size anthropic argument. He called the anthropic fluctuation theory "ridiculous" on the grounds that a fluctuation much smaller than the entire visible universe would account for the existence of an inhabited planet,

and thus it is most unlikely that the entire visible universe would be in an improbable state as it is observed to be.[36]

Roger Penrose explains the problem in relation to his earlier arguments in regard to the universe's low entropy state:

> The particular universe that we actually observe ourselves to inhabit is selected from among all the possible universes by the fact that we observe it! . . . However, the argument can get nowhere close to the needed figure of $10^{(10^{123})}$, for the "specialness" of the big bang. . . . By a very rough calculation *the entire solar system together with all its inhabitants could be created simply from the random collisions of particles* much more "cheaply" than this, namely with an "improbability" of "only" one part in much less than $10^{(10^{60})}$.[37]

One does not need to posit a whole solar system (with associated people) "popping" into being. One can posit (with much higher probability) the freak appearance of a single person—a "Boltzmann brain," if you will—within an otherwise chaotic universe.[38] (It does not matter that it would be short-lived.)

Consider a typical multiverse candidate, the string landscape (a generalization of the inflationary theory). Multiverse theory makes a prediction (in accord with the Copernican principle) that we should find our situation to be typical for conscious observers. This applies both to our environment and to ourselves. Now most atheists argue that the mind *is* the brain. So the nonzero probability that brains can form as a thermal fluctuation is a serious problem. But "ordinary observers" (i.e., those formed through the expensive and time-consuming process of cosmic evolution) are far less numerous within the multiverse than Boltzmann brains. Thus, if the landscape were true, we should have found ourselves to be Boltzmann brains. We don't; hence the landscape is strongly likely to be false.[39]

[36] J. Barrow and F. Tipler, *The Anthropic Cosmological Principle* (Oxford: Oxford University Press, 1986), 177.

[37] Penrose, *Emperor's New Mind*, 354 (emphasis added).

[38] D. Page, "Is Our Universe Likely to Decay within 20 Billion Years?" (2006), http://arxiv.org/abs/hep-th/0610079 (accessed October 7, 2008).

[39] It might be easier to grasp the need for typicality if you realize that these thermal fluctuations represent a legitimate competitor to Darwinian evolution as an explanation for the origin of

One can also argue that these "Boltzmann brains" pop into being complete with false memories of a universe like ours. This is also far more likely than the formation of people (with legitimately earned memories), planets, stars, galaxies, etc., via cosmic evolution. Thus the world is actually an illusion (similar to the situation in the movie *The Matrix*). This latter option demonstrates that multiverse theory can lead to pure "brain-in-a-vat" solipsism.[40] The multiverse undercuts warrant for belief in the past and present world. This is a remarkable endgame for the supposed "unfettered Reason" of Enlightenment thinking.

Problem 4. Tiebreaker B: Observers Plus an Observation Platform

Jay Richards and Guillermo Gonzales, a philosopher and a scientist who have ties to the intelligent design movement, have demonstrated another tiebreaker in their book *The Privileged Planet: How Our Place in the Cosmos Is Designed for Discovery*.[41] While the Strong Anthropic Principle can explain, perhaps, the aspects of a life site with respect to *survivability*, it cannot explain why Earth's place in the universe is an extremely rare site where *observability* (of the universe) is possible. The intersection of two totally independent and rare phenomena— *survivability of observers* + *a nice observatory*—is fishy. Richards and Gonzales argue that this intersection represents *specified complexity*, which is the information signal of a designer.

Problem 5. Possible Worlds and the Ontological Argument

Jay Richards asks us to consider another refutation of an atheist Many Worlds: Christian Alvin Plantinga's modal version of the onto-logical argument. In the strong form of the SAP, all possible worlds are considered actual. But if this is so, then if it is even remotely possible

---

the species. Given that both are accepted theories, the atheist seems committed to arguing that we should believe in Darwin because Darwinian worlds are far more likely.

[40] Philosopher Nick Bostrom has argued that if artificial intelligence is actually possible, then it is far more likely that we are simulations living within someone's digital computer program as opposed to a real world. This situation implies that the apparent laws of physics are arbitrary. The warrant for scientific practice is thus undercut, eliminating the supposed ground for postulating a multiverse in the first place.

[41] G. Gonzalez and J. Richards, *The Privileged Planet: How Our Place in the Cosmos Is Designed for Discovery* (Washington: Regnery Publishing, 2004).

that God (the necessary being) has reality (i.e., He is in one possible world), then this necessity implies He must be present in *all* possible worlds. In essence, an atheistic attempt to produce a necessary universe produces God-as-computer-virus which propagates to "infect" every world! As Richards states, "Such can be the penalty for toying with notions such as possibility, necessity, and infinite sets."[42]

Problem 6. Proof of a Transcendent Creator

I have argued elsewhere[43] that extant cosmological models, should they be compatible with a dynamic (common sense) view of time, seem to have a beginning according to the following matrix:

Model Average Expansion History	Condition Requiring a Beginning
1. Expanding	singularity theorems
2. Asymptotically static	metastability
3. Cyclic	Second Law of Thermodynamics
4. Contracting	acausal fine-tuning

For example, a recently proven theorem[44] (Borde and others 2003) has demonstrated the following: any universe (including appeal to higher dimensional cosmology, other pre-big bang cosmology, inflationary or noninflationary, quantum, etc.) that, on average, expands has to connect in a finite time to a "past boundary." Considering the following argument, then, the second premise seems true:

1. That which begins to exist must have a cause.
2. The universe began to exist.
3. Therefore, the universe has a cause.

[42] J. Richards, "Many Worlds Hypotheses: A Naturalistic Alternative to Design," *Perspectives on Science and the Christian Faith* 49 (December 1997): 218–27, http://www.asa3.org/ASA/PSCF/1997/PSCF12–97Richards.html.

[43] W. L. Craig and J. Sinclair, "The Kalam Cosmological Argument," in the *Blackwell Companion to Natural Theology*, eds. W. L. Craig and J. P. Moreland (Oxford: Blackwell, 2009), forthcoming.

[44] A. A. Borde, A. Guth, and A. Vilenkin, "Inflationary Spacetimes Are Not Past-Complete," *Physical Review Letters* 90 (2003): 151301, http://arxiv.org/abs/gr-qc/0110012 (accessed Oct. 7 2008).

Thus, if the first premise is true, the universe (i.e. *nature*) has a cause which is *super to nature* (thus transcendent or supernatural). And it may well be that a cause of this type can only create a lower ontology "creature" as a product of free choice.[45]

Now proof of a transcendent Creator does not get you all the way to the Christian God, but an atheist should prefer a model without one. Multiverse options, except the extreme Wheeler-DeWitt models (which are atemporal by nature, and others that deconstruct the notion of time thus denying that anything "begins to exist") seem vulnerable to the above argument.

Conclusion

There are more things in Heaven and Earth, Horatio, than are dreamt of in your philosophy.[46]

—*Shakespeare*

We have seen that an atheist multiverse is a plausible candidate if:

1. There is hard proof, or at least good inference as a natural extrapolation, of an observationally tested theory.
2. Contrary positive evidence for a singular universe is weaker than said proof.
3. There aren't additional tiebreakers (between Design & SAP) over and above observer survivability.
4. It avoids "strong" multiverse theory, which makes all possible worlds actual, because this appears to entail God's presence in all possible worlds.
5. It embraces strong multiverse theory as a form of MWI quantum mechanics and a means to avoid a transcendent Creator (by deconstructing time).

Atheist multiverse theory meets none of the possible conditions, and 4 and 5 are inherently incompatible.

We pay a high price for a philosophy of science that, as a matter of convention, rules out the simplest and most viable solution to the

---

[45] W. L. Craig, "The Ultimate Question of Origins: God and the Beginning of the Universe," *Astrophysics and Space Science* 269–70 (1999): 723–40, http://www.leaderu.com/offices/billcraig/docs/ultimatequestion.html (accessed Oct. 7, 2008).
[46] Shakespeare: *Hamlet*, Act I, scene V.

problem of origin and "apparent" design. Unfortunately science is not a search for truth when it comes to the question of God.

The current system *does* provide a compensatory advantage. The best minds in the world work around the clock in an explicit effort to produce materialist solutions to the origins problem. Failure in this enterprise, and sometimes direct contrary/positive evidence for creation gives the Christian the best available witness, the "hostile" expert.

We are in the midst of round four of a five-round debate with respect to the Anthropic Principle. In round one Brandon Carter brought to light the inadequacy of the Copernican Principle but attempted to obey the philosophy of science by resorting to the WAP. In round two theist philosopher Richard Swinburne exposed weakness in the WAP by such devices as the firing squad example and produced a demonstration of the Anthropic "coincidences" by appeal to a personal explanation (design). In round three atheist philosophers and orthodox scientists evolved to the SAP. In round four thinkers have exposed inadequacy in the SAP.

The fifth round could easily devolve into an embrace of pure skepticism whereby the concept of "universe" as an objective observer-independent construct disappears.[47] Also possible is a demonstration of the multiverse's better compatibility with theism than with atheism. What seems unlikely, though, is that the multiverse concept will ultimately undermine the support that theism enjoys from modern cosmology.

> *There is a theory which states that if ever anyone discovers exactly what the Universe is for and why it is here, it will instantly disappear and be replaced by something even more bizarre and inexplicable.*
>
> *There is another theory which states that this has already happened.*[48]
>
> —*Douglas Adams*

---

[47] Such as the "Decoherent Histories" account of cosmologist Jim Hartle.
[48] Adams, *Hitchhiker's Guide.*

Chapter 3

CONFRONTING NATURALISM: THE ARGUMENT FROM REASON

Victor Reppert

Naturalism and the New Atheism

A recent phenomenon known as the New Atheism has arisen in the past couple of years. In one sense nothing is new about the doctrine of atheism itself. It has been around for centuries. Atheism is the doctrine that there is no God, and the atheism of Richard Dawkins is in this respect no different from the atheism of Baron d'Holbach. But there is a difference in the way the New Atheists advocate for atheism. Aggressive advocates of atheism, they maintain that religious belief is not only false but also held in an irrational way by adherents and is morally pernicious. They feel no obligation to respect the religious beliefs of others; rather, their stated goal is to usher in the end of religious belief, especially belief in the existence of God.

One of the central claims they make is there is no evidence whatsoever for belief in the existence of God. All of the evidence lies firmly on the side of unbelief, not on the side of belief. Persons who believe in God do so for irrational motives, not because there are any good reasons to believe in God. To be rational is to form beliefs in accordance with the methods of natural science; natural science leads us in the direction of atheism; therefore all reasonable people should be atheists and not theists.

The work of many atheists, such as Dawkins or Dennett, is not merely to defend atheism, the view that there are no gods, but to uphold and support their positive philosophy, a doctrine that could best be described as metaphysical naturalism. A metaphysical naturalist maintains that the natural order is all there is. As Carl Sagan put it, the cosmos is all that was, is, or ever will be. This belief in philosophical naturalism is supposed to be what we should believe instead of Christian theism.

Is naturalism the inevitable, logical result of scientific thinking? It seems hard to deny the legitimacy of science as a way of knowing. Even young-Earth scientific creationists do not say that the Christian faith is true and that science is just wrong. Rather, they say that if science had been done right, it would have upheld the traditional teaching drawn from a literal (I would say hyperliteral) reading of the book of Genesis.

In my view there is a profound problem with naturalism. In order for natural science to be possible, a natural world must be analyzable in scientific terms. However, scientists must also use scientific methods to discover the truth about the natural world. The contention of the argument from reason is that if the world were truly what naturalism says it is, there would be matter, but there would be no scientists to discover the properties of matter.

Defining the Debate: The Great Divide

The argument from reason begins by defining two worldview types: mentalistic worldviews, according to which mental states are basic causes, and nonmentalistic worldviews, according to which no mental states are basic causes. To understand the idea of basic causes, the following account from Keith Parsons is helpful:

> Hence, for Swinburne, to say that a law of nature is unexplained is to say that there is no explanation of why a certain material body possesses the particular powers and liabilities that it has. Of course, the powers and liabilities of one body may be explained in terms of the powers and liabilities of the constituent bodies and those in turn by even more fundamental entities. Presumably, though, rock bottom is eventually

reached. At present, rock bottom would be the powers and liabilities of such entities as quarks and electrons. . . . To say that there is no explanation of why a quark, given that it is a fundamental particle, has the powers and liabilities that it has, seems tantamount to saying that there is no explanation for why a quark is a quark. Surely anything with different powers and liabilities would not be a quark.[1]

Basic causes are causes at rock bottom, in the sense that no underlying explanation is to be found. Christian theism is a worldview according to which basic causes are mental. If God chooses to create the world, there is no underlying nonmental explanation for this creation. God, it is supposed, creates the world because doing so is good, and there is no underlying explanation in terms of blind causes.

Let us take a different case—that of rocks falling down a mountain in an avalanche. When the rocks fall, they do not miss my head because they don't think it would be nice to hit me or hit me because they think I have it coming to me. Rather, the rocks blindly fall with no regard to the interests of the people who may or may not be hit. On nonmentalistic worldviews the world is at bottom as blind as a bunch of rocks falling down the mountain. However, through the pressures of natural selection, perhaps we find things in the world that imitate what we would ordinarily ascribe to a designer. If we hold to a non-mentalistic worldview, we might say that "the purpose of your eye is to see" but what we mean is that features of the eye were selected because of their visual advantage. A mentalistic explanation is on the surface, but dig deeper, and "mind" is analyzed out. By contrast, on a theistic worldview, even if the falling of the rocks in the avalanche was not specifically preordained by God, at least the physical laws and physical objects are the product of intelligent design.

The Marks of the Mental

Someone denying the ultimacy of mind maintains that four features of the mental must not be found on the rock-bottom level of the

---

[1] K. Parsons, *God and the Burden of Proof* (Amherst: Prometheus, 1989), 91–92.

universe. The first mark of the mental is purpose. If there is purpose in the world, it betokens the existence of a mind that has that purpose. So for anyone who denies the ultimacy of the mind, an explanation in terms of purposes requires a further nonpurposive explanation to account for the purpose explanation. The second mark of the mental is intentionality or aboutness. Genuinely nonmental states are not about anything at all. The third mark of the mental is normativity. If there is normativity, there has to be a mind for which something is normative. A normative explanation must be explained further in terms of the nonnormative. Finally, the fourth mark of the mental is subjectivity. If there is a perspective from which something is viewed, that means, once again, that a mind is present. A genuinely nonmental account of a state of affairs will leave out of account anything that indicates what it is like to be in that state.

If the mind is not ultimate, then any explanation that is given in terms of any of these four marks must be given a further explanation in which these marks are washed out of the equation.

Minimal Materialism

A worldview which affirms that the mind is not ultimate has three minimal characteristics.[2] First, the "basic level" must be mechanistic, and by that I mean that it is free of purpose, free of intentionality, free of normativity, and free of subjectivity. It is not implied here that a naturalistic world must be deterministic. However, whatever is not deterministic in such a world is brute chance and nothing more.

Second, the "basic level" must be causally closed. Nothing that exists independently from the physical world can cause anything to occur in the physical world. That is, if a physical event has a cause at time t, then it has a physical cause at time t. Even if it is merely a necessary condition or contributing cause, that cause is not a determining cause; there cannot be something nonphysical that plays a role in producing a physical event. If, before an event occurred, you knew everything about the physical level (the laws and the facts), you could

[2] V. Reppert, *C. S. Lewis's Dangerous Idea* (Downer's Grove, IL: InterVarsity Press, 2003), 52–53; see also W. Hasker, *The Emergent Self* (Ithaca: Cornell University Press, 1999), 59–64.

add nothing to your ability to predict where the particles will be in the future by knowing anything about anything outside of basic physics.

Third, whatever is not physical, at least if it is in space and time, must supervene on the physical. Given the physical, everything else is a necessary consequence. In short, what the world is at bottom is a mindless system of events at the level of fundamental particles, and everything else that exists must exist in virtue of what is going on at that basic level. This understanding of a broadly materialist worldview is not a tendentiously defined form of reductionism; it is what most people who would regard themselves as being in the broadly materialist camp would agree with, a sort of "minimal materialism." Not only that, but any worldview that could reasonably be called "naturalistic" is going to have these features, and the difficulties I will be advancing against a "broadly materialist" worldview thus defined will be a difficulty that will exist for any kind of naturalism.

At the same time we must be careful. No *planets* are mentioned in basic physics, yet planets can and do exist as conglomerations of entities at the basic level. In the case of planets, however, given enough information about the basic particles, and knowing what a planet is, the question is closed as to whether a planet is there. I have not ruled out by definition the possibility that, for example, intentionality might exist at a nonbasic level even though it is missing at the basic level. I will instead argue that a naturalistic world would not contain such elements.

The Epistemological Commitments
of Philosophical Naturalists

I have delineated the metaphysical commitments of those who deny that the mental is basic to the universe. At the same time atheists like Richard Dawkins are not philosophical skeptics. They hold that there is genuine knowledge, discovered by science. They are scientific realists who believe that science discovers the truth about the way reality is. That is why they object, for example, to religious believers who hold to theism as true and thus broadly informative about the nature of reality, including the natural world. They think science has discovered that evolution is true and creationism is false. They think physicists discover the truth, which means they believe that physicists make correct mathematical inferences. They think we literally add, subtract, multiply, divide, square, and take square roots of numbers.

In a recent paper William Hasker has recommended that the Argument from Reason be presented as a transcendental argument which identifies the necessary presuppositions of the fact of scientific inference and goes from there to draw the implications of these. He writes:

> The objection is not merely that naturalism has not yet produced an explanation of rational inference and the like, as though this were a deficiency that could be remedied by another decade or so of scientific research. The problem is that the naturalist is committed to certain assumptions that preclude in principle any explanation of the sort required. The key assumptions are three in number: mechanism (the view that fundamental physical explanations are nonteleological), the causal closure of the physical domain, and the supervenience of the mental on the physical. So long as these assumptions remain, no amount of ingenious computer modeling can possibly fill the explanatory gap. In order to bring out this feature of the situation, I propose that the first two stages of the Argument from Reason are best viewed as a transcendental argument in roughly the Kantian sense: They specify the conditions which are required for experience of a certain sort to be possible—in this case the kind of experience found in the performance of rational inference.[3]

Consider the following list of presuppositions of reason. These presuppositions have transcendental justifications. The justification goes from the fact that at least one person has made a rational inference (such as a mathematical calculation) and establishes that these conditions must obtain if that rational inference has taken place.

---

[3] W. Hasker, "What About a Sensible Naturalism?: A Response to Victor Reppert," *Philosophia Christi* 5 (2003): 61.

1. States of mind have a relation to the world we call intentionality, or aboutness. The intentionality I am referring to is propositional in nature. Our possessing this kind of intentionality means that we are capable of having, entertaining, believing, and desiring states of affairs propositionally described. We recognize the propositional contents of our thoughts.

2. Thoughts and beliefs can be either true or false.

3. Human beings can be in the condition of accepting, rejecting, or suspending belief about propositions.

4. Logical laws exist.

5. Human beings are capable of apprehending logical laws.

6. The state of accepting the truth of a proposition plays a crucial causal role in the production of other beliefs, and the propositional content of mental states is relevant to the playing of this causal role.

7. The apprehension of logical laws plays a causal role in the acceptance of the conclusion of the argument as true.

8. The same individual entertains thoughts of the premises and then draws the conclusion.

9. Our processes of reasoning provide us with a systematically reliable way of understanding the world around us.[4]

Unless all of these statements are true, it is incoherent to argue that one should accept naturalism based on evidence of any kind. Nor would it be possible to accept the claim that one should accept evolution as opposed to creationism because there is so much evidence for evolution. Nor could one argue that one should be supremely confident that use of the scientific method will result in an accurate understanding of reality. Unless all these statements are true, there are no scientists, and no one is using the scientific method.

To see how the transcendental justification works, consider the possibility that reality consists of nothing but a turnip with whipped cream on top. Of course this flies in the face of all the empirical evidence, but we can argue further that if this were so, no one would be able to reason to that conclusion. Given the way this argument is structured, one could not use the Paradigm Case argument to argue

[4] Reppert, *Dangerous Idea*, 73.

that since there has to be a contrast between valid and invalid inference, inference would also have to be possible in the turnip world. No, the fact that we can make such a distinction provides a transcendental basis for believing that we do not live in the turnip world.

The Irreducibility of Propositional Content

In my previous book on the argument from reason, I generated six versions of the argument from reason. I am going to talk about one of them, what I called in my book the argument from propositional content—the argument that if science is true, then we as human beings are in states with determinate propositional content; but if naturalism is true, we should never be in such propositional states. In order to satisfy the epistemological commitments of philosophical naturalism, naturalists must affirm that we are in determinate propositional states. In order to satisfy their metaphysical commitments, naturalists must deny that we are ever in determinate propositional states.

James Ross, in his essay "Immaterial Aspects of Thought," presents an argument against a physicalist account of propositional content which I will call the Argument from Determinate Content. He writes:

> Some thinking (judgment) is determinate in the way no physical process can be. Consequently, such thinking cannot be a (wholly) physical process. If all thinking, all judgment, is determinate in that way, no physical process can be (the whole of) any judgment at all. Furthermore, "functions" among physical states cannot be determinate enough to be such judgments, either. Hence some judgments can be neither wholly physical processes nor wholly functions among physical processes.[5]

Yet, he maintains, we cannot deny that we perform determinate mental operations. He writes:

> I propose now, with some simple cases, to reinforce the perhaps already obvious point that pure function has to be wholly realized in the single case, and cannot consist in the array of "inputs and outputs" for a certain kind of thinking. Does

[5] J. Ross, "Immaterial Aspects of Thought," *The Journal of Philosophy* 89 (1992): 136–50.

anyone deny that we can actually square numbers? "4 times 4 is sixteen"; a definite form ($N \times N = N^2$) is "squaring" for all relevant cases, whether or not we are able to process the digits, or talk long enough to give the answer. To be squaring, I have to be doing some thing that works for all the cases, something for which any relevant case can be substituted without change in what I am doing, but only in which thing is done.[6]

I should add that if we don't literally add, subtract, divide, multiply, square numbers, and take their square roots, not to mention perform all the complicated mathematical operations involved in, say, Einstein's theory of relativity, then physicalism, which not only says that reality is physical but that physics, at least approximately, gets it right, is up the creek without a paddle.

Ross's argument can be formalized as follows.

1. Some mental states have determinate content. In particular, the states involved in adding, subtracting, multiplying, dividing, in squaring numbers and taking their square roots, are determinate with respect to their intentional content.

2. Physical states are indeterminate with respect to intentional content. Any physical state is logically compatible with the existence of a multiplicity of propositionally defined intentional states, or even with the absence of propositionally defined intentional states entirely.

3. Therefore, the mental states involved in mathematical operations are not and cannot be identical to physical states.

Some naturalistic theories have been developed to provide a physicalist account of intentionality. Feser delineates four types of theories of this nature: conceptual role theories, causal theories, biological theories, and instrumentalist theories.

Conceptual role theories explicate intentional states in terms of their conceptual roles, that is, in relation to other intentional states. Of course, this does not explain why there is a network of intentional states in the first place.[7]

---

[6] Ibid.

[7] E. Feser, *Philosophy of Mind: A Short Introduction* (Oxford: Oneworld Press, 2005), 136.

A more popular approach to coming up with a naturalistic account of intentionality is causal theories of intentionality. These appeal to the causal relations that intentional states stand to items in the external world. Thus if I believe that there is a computer monitor in front of me as I type these words, there is a causal connection between the monitor and my visual cortex, which causes states of my brain to be affected by it.

Causal theories of reference have certainly been advanced, but many of these do not suggest that causal relationships alone are sufficient to fix reference. On a Kripkean view of the causal theory of reference, a name's referent is fixed by an original act of naming (also called a "dubbing" or, by Kripke, an "initial baptism"), whereupon the name becomes a rigid designator of that object. Later uses of the name succeed in referring to the referent by being linked to that original act via a causal chain. In other words, what causation explains, according to this theory, is how references are transmitted once an initial act of naming, an intentional state (both in the sense of being intended and in the sense of possessing "aboutness"), is performed. How such actions could be performed in the first place is not accounted for in causal terms. To do the work the naturalist requires, we need to explain even the initial act of naming in causal terms.

When we start talking about propositional states, we have to ask how any specification of causal relations can possibly entail the existence of meaning at all. Let us say a bird is hardwired to let out a certain squawk when something approximately the shape of a hawk is nearby. There is a regular causal relation between the appearance of a hawk and the occurrence of the squawk. In one sense we can say that the squawk is about the hawk. Something could, of course, touch off the "hawk" signal and the subsequent evasive action without being a hawk. It does not mean that the bird has the ability to distinguish a hawk from any and all nonhawks. A properly constituted doppelgänger could fool it. Expecting fire when one sees smoke is not the same as inferring fire from smoke. We say that "smoke means fire," but what this amounts to is that smoke and fire are often conjoined in experience. We often experience smoke before we experience fire, but it turns out upon examination of the causal relations that fire causes smoke and not vice versa. We say that "smoke means fire," but that means smoke and fire are conjoined in our experience. The "meaning" is imposed by human understanding, not in the world as it is in itself.

As Feser writes:

> Any account of such theories could give the relevant causal relations holding between a particular mental state and a particular object in the external world will require picking out a particular object in the beginning point of the causal series (call it A) and a particular end point (B) as the mental state doing the representing. . . . Nothing in the flux objectively either the determinate starting point or a particular sequence or the determinate ending point. It is we who pick certain events and count them as beginnings and endings; their status as beginnings and endings is relative to certain purposes and interests of ours.[8]

In short, there is a difference between causing action appropriate to something being the case (causing the bees to go where the nectar is) and declaring it to be the case that the nectar is in such and such a place. Science is inherently declarative, and requires understanding. It is tempting but erroneous to attribute a declarative character to bee dances and birdsongs. Casual connections are invariably insufficient to provide determinacy of propositional content. Without determinacy of propositional content, the type of rational inference in science cannot occur.

Another theory looks to biological role or function as a basis of determining content. However, Dennett has successfully argued that biological function also leaves propositional content indeterminate. Evolutionary function is essentially fluid in nature, and to get something as determinate as propositional content out of biological function is asking too much of it. (What is *the* biological function of feathers on a bird?)

John Searle writes:

> So far no attempt at naturalizing content has produced an explanation (analysis, reduction) of intentional content that

---

[8] Ibid., 145.

is even remotely plausible. A symptom that something is radically wrong with the project is that intentional notions are inherently normative. They set standards of truth, rationality, consistency, etc., and there is no way that these standards can be intrinsic to a system consisting entirely of *brute, blind, nonintentional causal relations.* There is no mean [middle] component to billiard ball causation. Darwinian biological attempts at naturalizing content try to avoid this problem by appealing to what they suppose is the inherently teleological [i.e., purposeful], normative character of biological evolution. But this is a very deep mistake. There is nothing normative or teleological about Darwinian evolution. Indeed, Darwin's major contribution was precisely to remove purpose, and teleology from evolution, and substitute for it purely natural forms of selection.[9]

Or as Feser puts it:

Talk of purposes and functions, if taken literally, seems to presuppose intentionality; in particular it seems to presuppose the agency of an intelligence of one who designs something for a particular purpose. But the aim of Darwinian evolutionary theory is to explain biological phenomena in a manner that involves no appeal to intelligent design. . . . Just as modern physics has tended to explain phenomena by carving off the subjective qualitative appearances of things and relocating them into the mind, so too did the Darwinian revolution in biology push purpose and function out of the biological realm, making them out to be mind-dependent and devoid of objective reality.[10]

In point of fact, the ruthless naturalist W. V. Quine has argued that the reference of our terms is indeterminate and that there is no fact of the matter as to what our words refer to.[11] However, this has disastrous consequence for the practice of science. Only if our terms

[9] J. Searle, *The Re-Discovery of the Mind* (Cambridge: Cambridge University Press, 1992), 50–51 (his emphasis).
[10] Feser, *Philosophy of Mind*, 149.
[11] W. V. Quine, *Word and Object* (Cambridge: MIT Press, 1960), chaps. 1 and 2.

have determinate reference can we reason to conclusions. Consider the following argument about the unsharpened pencil.

1. Going to class is pointless.
2. An unsharpened pencil is pointless.
3. Therefore, going to class is an unsharpened pencil.

The argument's confusion about meaning makes an apparently valid argument invalid.

Our ability to reason logically can exist only if we are able to identify sameness of meaning. Dennett's view of the mind essentially affirms the Quinian thesis of indeterminacy, and indeed Dennett thinks this kind of indeterminacy is a consequence of philosophical naturalism.

> And why not? Here, I think, we find as powerful and direct an expression as could be of the intuition that lies behind the belief in original intentionality. This is the doctrine Ruth Millikan calls *meaning rationalism*, and it is one of the central burdens of her important book, *Language, Thought, and Other Biological Categories*, to topple it from its traditional pedestal. . . . Something has to give. Either you must abandon meaning rationalism—the idea that you are unlike the fledgling cuckoo not only in having access, but in having privileged access to your meanings—or you must abandon the naturalism that insists that you are, after all, just a product of natural selection, whose intentionality is thus derivative and hence potentially indeterminate.[12]

If meanings are indeterminate, then it's indeterminate what Dennett means by anything he says. No one can possibly determine whether any argument is valid because if, say, it's a categorical syllogism, there's no way to determine whether we've got three terms, four terms, five terms, or six terms. So let's have a look at Dennett's argument.

1. If naturalism is true, then meaning is indeterminate.
2. Naturalism is true.
3. Therefore, meaning is indeterminate.

---

[12] D. C. Dennett, "Evolution, Error and Intentionality" in *The Intentional Stance* (Cambridge: MIT Press, 1987), 313. The book mentioned is R. G. Millikan's *Language, Thought, and Other Biological Categories: New Foundations for Realism* (Cambridge: MIT Press, 1987).

And here's mine.

1. If naturalism is true, then meaning is indeterminate.
2. Meaning is determinate (a presupposition of reason and science).
3. Therefore, naturalism is false.

Perhaps the indeterminacy of meaning is benign and not such that it undermines science in the radical way in which I have described. Consider Kripke's distinction between addition and what he calls "quaddition," where addition has the form x + y but quaddition has the form x + y if x and y are less than 57, 5 otherwise.[13] If mathematics is indeterminate between addition and quaddition, science is in trouble.

Another approach to intentionality, attributed to Dennett, regards propositional states in instrumental terms. That essentially makes all intentionality derived intentionality. But derived from what? If we have intentionality because we take ourselves to have intentionality, then how do we account for the intentional state of taking ourselves to have intentionality?

A number of arguments have been presented against the possibility of reducing determinate beliefs and desires to physical states. Quine's argument for the indeterminacy of translation, Kripke's adapted Wittgenstein argument, Davidson's argument against psychophysical laws,[14] and Nagel's discussions in *The Last Word*[15] have this implication. However, different philosophers have drawn different conclusions from the arguments for irreducibility. Since reason cannot be reduced to physical relations, materialists have to use other strategies to fit reason into a physicalist world.

Propositional Attitudes and the Supervenience Strategy

Another popular view, which has even been accepted by some Christians, is a nonreductive materialist position. On this view intentional states are not eliminated; they are not reducible to physical

---

[13] S. Kripke, *Wittgenstein on Rules and Private Language* (Cambridge: Harvard University Press, 1982).

[14] D. Davidson, "Mental Events," in *Experience and Theory*, L. Foster and J. W. Swanson, eds. (London: Duckworth, 1970).

[15] T. Nagel, *The Last Word* (Oxford: Oxford University Press, 1997).

states. They are, however, supervenient upon physical states. Mental
states are not identical to physical states, but given the state of the
physical, there is only one way the mental can be.

Of course, earlier I indicated that supervenience of all nonphysical
states on physical states is part of what is required for a worldview to
be naturalistic. However, if mental states can be reductively analyzed
in terms of physical states, then the supervenience is simply obvious. A
difference in B requires a difference in A because, in the final analysis,
Bs just *are* As. Again, if the B states are eliminated from the ontology,
then we don't have to worry about a difference in B that is not guaranteed by a difference in A. However, for many, perhaps most, philosophers who believe in a broadly materialist worldview, the reductionist
and eliminativist positions are both implausible. For these philosophers the supervenience relation has a job to do: it explains how it is
possible for everything to be in the final analysis physical while at the
same time maintaining the irreducibility and the autonomy of the
mental realm.

Philosophers often distinguish between weak supervenience and
strong supervenience. According to weak supervenience, B properties weakly supervene on A properties if and only if things that are
alike in their A properties are always alike in their B properties. What
this establishes is a constant conjunction between A properties and
B properties. It does not really show that there is anything about the
A properties that guarantees that the B properties will always be the
same. Nevertheless, we must remember what caused problems for
reductionist accounts of mental states. The physical is incurably indeterminate with respect to propositional states. Whatever story we
tell at the physical level is compatible with a multiplicity of stories at
the mental level. This kind of constant conjunction claim, however,
explains little. There is, for example, a constant conjunction between
increases in the homicide rate in New York City and increases in the
rate of ice cream consumption. We could say that the homicide rate
supervenes on the rate of ice cream consumption, but we will have
explained nothing. We will not have shown that ice cream consumption is responsible for homicides, or vice versa, or whether these are

just two unrelated effects of a common cause (an increase in the city's temperatures).[16]

A good deal of confusion in the discussion of neuroscientific discoveries and their relation to the philosophy of mind often occurs at this point. What neuroscience is often able to do is provide *correlations* between certain mental states and activity in certain parts of the brain. These are often taken as proof of materialism, but there is no good reason dualists should not expect these correlations to exist. Further, correlation between mental states and physical states is not the same as identification of mental states with physical states.

Strong supervenience is the claim that B properties strongly supervene on A properties just in case things that are alike in A properties must be alike in B properties. On this view the supervenience isn't just a brute conjunction; it is necessarily so. However, as an attempt to explain anything, this seems inadequate as well. Religious explanations are often taken to task as being God-of-the-gaps explanations; this just seems to be a necessity-of-the-gaps explanation. "Why, if Jones's beliefs could be five or six different ways given the physical, or perhaps, given the mental, Jones could be a zombie with no beliefs at all, does Jones have the beliefs he has?" If the answer is "Well, there's this strong supervenience relationship that exists between the physical and the mental, so it's necessary," it looks as if we are taken no closer to an explanation as to why Jones has the beliefs he has.

Why does the supervenience relation exist, if it does? Is it pure dumb luck? Is it a Leibnizian preestablished harmony set up before the foundation of the world by God? (This might not be naturalistically acceptable.) Presumably, it is not a physical relation, so why does it exist? Unless something about the physical guarantees that the mental be only one way, the supervenience relation needs to be explained. There is what James Stump calls a "classic reflexivity problem" for the supervenience theorist. For supervenience theory everything is either physical or supervenes on the physical.[17] So the supervenience relation is going to have to be either physical or supervene on the physical, if

---

[16] J. B. Stump, "Non-Reductive Materialism: A Dissenting Voice," *Christian Scholar's Review* 36/1 (2006): 67.
[17] Ibid., 70.

supervenient physicalism is true. But does it? Stump summarizes an argument originally presented by Lynch and Glasgow to contend that the supervenience relation itself cannot be admitted into the supervenient materialism's ontology, which I have altered slightly for the sake of congruence with previous discussion:

1. For physicalists, all facts must be materialistically acceptable. That is, they are facts about physical things, or about things which are ontologically distinct from the physical, but strongly supervene on the physical.

2. There must be some fact—the explanation—in virtue of which B-properties supervene on A-properties; called the S-facts. What kind of facts are S-facts? There are two options for materialistically respectable facts:

   a. They themselves could supervene on A-properties. But then there is an infinite regress problem, for now we have to explain this new supervenience relation, which in turn needs to be explained, and so on *ad infinitum*. So this is no good.

   b. Or, the S-facts could not just be further A-properties, that is, facts about the physical entity. But then these facts do not bridge the explanatory gap between the B-facts and the A-facts.[18]

Perhaps the supervenience theorist can simply accept the supervenience relation as an unexplained brute fact. However, as J. P. Moreland argues, this is also deeply problematic for the supervenience theorist: First, he highlights the claim made by supervenience theorist Terence Horgan that in a broadly materialist universe the truths of supervenience must be explainable rather than *sui generis*. As Horgan points out, if there are going to be any brute unexplainable givens in a materialist universe, it must be the physical facts themselves, not some fact concerning interlevel supervenience.[19] Second, the truth of supervenience does not look like something science could possibly have discovered,

---

[18] Ibid.
[19] T. Horgan, "Non-Reductive Materialism and the Explanatory Autonomy of Psychology" in *Naturalism: A Critical Appraisal*, ed. S. J. Wagner and R. Warner (Notre Dame: University of Notre Dame Press, 1994), 295–320.

and so to accept supervenience as a brute fact would be to accept the idea that truths about the world can be figured out by philosophical rather than scientific means, and this is anathema to most contemporary naturalists.[20] Also, this position begs the question against people like Swinburne and Robert Adams, who maintain that the supervenience of the mind stands in need of a theistic explanation.[21]

Second, debate about just what kind of supervenience holds between physical and mental states is not a scientific question and cannot be settled by scientific theorizing. Further, supervenience theory involves terms and concepts that are not the terms and concepts of natural science. As Moreland puts it:

> Naturalists criticize Cartesian dualism and its problem of interaction between radically different sorts of entities. In my view, the dualist has the resources to answer this problem because of her commitment to entities, relations, and causation that go beyond those in the physical sciences. But the same cannot be said for naturalism, and what is sauce for the goose is sauce for the gander. Naturalists have the very same kind of problem that they claim as a difficulty for the Cartesian. And given the philosophical constraints that follow from accepting the naturalist epistemology, etiology, and ontology, it is more difficult to see how a naturalist could accept mental/physical supervenience than it is to understand how a Cartesian without those constraints could accept mental/ physical interaction.[22]

Intentionality is more than just a puzzle for naturalism; it is a deep and profound problem distinct from, and as serious as, the "hard problem" of consciousness. Reduction of understood intentional states and propositional intentional states seems to be inherently impossible. Elimination of those states eliminates states essential to the operation of the natural sciences on which the credibility of naturalism is founded. Nonpropositional successors to propositional

---

[20] J. P. Moreland, "Should a Naturalist Be a Supervenient Physicalist?" *Metaphilosophy* 29/1 and 2 (1988): 35–57.
[21] Ibid.
[22] Ibid.

attitudes cannot do the job assigned to them. Supervenient materialism commits the materialist to a materialistically unacceptable relation
between the physical and the mental and, as we shall see, presents serious problems in accounting for mental causation.

Theories of the universe that make the mental a basic fact of reality, such as theism, pantheism, or idealism, do not have the problem
of unacceptably terminating explanatory chains with mental states. If
the mental is part of the basic furniture of the universe, then it seems
a good deal easier to see how it could end up being instantiated in
human beings.

God of the Gaps

Another argument frequently advanced against virtually any piece
of natural theology is the God-of-the-gaps charge. In fact, this is one
of the most popular items in the atheist playbook. We know from
the history of science that many things that were thought in the past
to require an explanation in terms of divine agency are now known
to have naturalistic explanations. Rainbows, for example, were once
thought to have been put in the sky as a sign; we now know that they
can be naturalistically explained in terms of light refraction. Various
biological systems show a harmony between means and ends which
in the past were cannon fodder for the design argument but are now
explicable in terms of random variation and natural selection. So if
we think something cannot be explained in physical terms, just give
scientists some time, and they'll figure it out sooner or later.

An instance where the God-of-the-gaps objection appears strong is
in the case of Newton's account of the orbits of the planets. His theory
would have expected the orbits to go somewhat differently from the
way they go, and so he postulated God as the one who keeps the
planets in line. Laplace later developed a theory that didn't require
this kind of divine tinkering, and when asked about Newton's theistic
theory, he said, "I have no need of that hypothesis."

However, I am not sure that every argument that points to an explanatory difficulty for the naturalist can be effectively answered with
a God-of-the-gaps charge. Consider, for example, being at a dinner

party with someone who is given a large amount of water and creates from it an equal volume of wine. (It tastes like really good wine, not that cheap stuff.) Can we reasonably say that we just have a gap in our understanding? As Robert Larmer points out, our understanding of how wine is made is precisely what makes it so difficult to explain naturalistically:

> What should be at issue in assessing "God of the gaps" arguments is whether they have met these conditions. Claims regarding events traditionally described as miracles and claims regarding the origin and development of life are where "God of the gaps" arguments are most commonly met. In the case of events traditionally described as miracles, it seems very evident that our increased knowledge of how natural causes operate has not made it easier, but more difficult, to explain such events naturalistically. The science underlying wine-making is considerably more advanced today than it was in first century Palestine, but our advances have made it even more difficult to explain in terms of natural causes how Jesus, without any technological aids, could, in a matter of minutes, turn water into high quality wine. Indeed, it is the difficulty of providing a naturalistic account of such events that leads many critics to deny that they ever occurred; though this looks suspiciously like begging the question in favour of naturalism. It is clear that if such events have occurred, the advance of science has made them more, rather than less, difficult to explain in terms of natural causes. Employing a "God of the gaps" argument that the occurrence of such events would constitute good evidence for supernatural intervention within the natural order seems entirely legitimate.[23]

I maintain that there are gaps and there are gaps. It's not just pointing to an unsolved engineering problem in nature. First, the categories of the mental and the physical are logically incompatible categories. You start attributing mental properties to physics and you might end up being told that you are no longer describing the physical at all.

---

[23] R. Larmer, "Is There Anything Wrong with 'God of the Gaps' Reasoning?" *International Journal for Philosophy of Religion* 52 (2002): 129–42.

Purpose, normativity, intentionality, or aboutness—all of these things are not supposed to be brought in to the physical descriptions of things, at least at the most basic level of analysis.

Let's consider the gap between the propositional content of thought and the physical description of the brain. My claim is that no matter in how much detail you describe the physical state of the brain (and the environment), the propositional content of thought will invariably be undetermined. This isn't my claim or C. S. Lewis's; this argument was made by the archnaturalist W. V. Quine. It's not a matter of getting a physical description that will work. The logico-conceptual gap is always going to be there regardless of how extensively you describe the physical. Bridging the chasm isn't going to be a matter of simply exploring the territory on one side of the chasm.

I conclude, therefore, that God-of-the-gaps or even a soul-of-the-gaps response to the argument from reason does not work. I am not saying that we just cannot figure out right now why the mental states involved in rational inference are really physical; I am suggesting on principled grounds that a careful reflection on the nature of mind and matter will invariably reveal that there is a logical gap between them that in principle can't be bridged without fudging categories.

Conclusion

The New Atheists are wrong, therefore, to suppose that there is no good reason to reject their naturalistic atheism in favor of theism. There are profound philosophical questions, not ones that will automatically be dispelled by the forward march of science. In fact, I believe that the forward march of science will make the problems worse instead of better for the naturalist. The onward march of science will discover extensive *correlations* between physical and mental states but will leave the logico-conceptual distinction between these two categories unchanged.

Chapter 4

BELIEF IN GOD: A TRICK OF OUR BRAIN?

Michael J. Murray

Math, Physics, and Babies

Anyone who has read even a little bit of psychology knows that the human mind is a strange thing. For example, we show marked and consistent psychological tendencies to think that, say, people with dilated pupils are more attractive, that people who smile a lot are untrustworthy, and that anything that has touched animal waste is disgusting. Where do we get these psychological dispositions? For hundreds of years, the prevailing view in psychology was that these beliefs resulted either from cultural influences that shaped our reasoning and information processing or simply from outright instruction ("Don't touch the dog poop, Johnny! You'll get sick!").

But the prevailing view was wrong. We now have conclusive evidence that human minds come into the world with all sorts of "software" both preinstalled and booted up. Some of this software manifests itself right from birth, while other bits of it become operative at specifiable times in human development. For example, it has been shown that, from birth, human beings have certain beliefs about both mathematics and physics. Babies know, for example, that one plus one is not three, and they know that solid objects fall to the floor unless something or someone holds them up.

How do we know this? Like us, babies have certain ways of signaling their state of mind through their behavior. When you give babies the same sensory stimulus over and over, they (like us) tend to get bored with it and subsequently start to ignore it. When, on the other hand, you give them a series of novel, different, and unexpected sensory stimuli, they show their surprise by keeping their attention fixed on the unexpected event. Show them a picture of a red ball, and they will look. Flash it again, and they look again. Flash it a third, fourth, and fifth time, and in most cases their attention will start to drift, and they will start to attend to other things. This fact gives us a signal about babies' states of mind. When their attention remains fixed, it is obvious that what they are looking at is surprising or new to them. When their attention wanes, we can guess that what they are experiencing is old hat. Psychologists can thus infer some aspects of baby belief by measuring how long they fix their attention on certain things (that is, by measuring their "gaze time").

How does this help us figure out babies' beliefs about math and physics? In one experiment researchers put babies on a table that had a screen that could be raised and lowered. When the screen is first put in place, the babies could see that there was nothing behind it. Experimenters would bring one object behind the screen from the left, and another from the right. Anyone who can think mathematically should then expect to find two objects behind the screen. And in fact, when the screen is dropped and there are two objects there, babies tend to look away quickly since that is just what they expected. That's boring! But when the screen drops and there is one object, or three objects, babies tend to gaze for a much longer time. In cases where one plus one does not seem to equal two, they are surprised. This shows us that babies know that one plus one equals two, not one or three.[1]

Another way we can look for beliefs that arise from built-in "software" is to look for beliefs that are *pervasive across times and cultures*. Widespread beliefs like that might sometimes be explainable simply in terms of experience. If we found that people across the globe uniformly believe that, say, all human beings have two feet, we could chalk that up as something learned through common human experience. But

---

[1] P. Bloom, *Descartes' Baby* (New York: Basic Books, 2004).

other pervasive beliefs seem to arise despite an absence of sufficient sensory evidence. Such beliefs are said to arise despite a "poverty of the stimulus," and when such beliefs occur, we have reason to look for built-in, onboard processing mechanisms that provide what our experiences do not. A good example of this is the belief that rotting food, corpses, and animal waste are dangerous. This set of beliefs and the accompanying desires, known in psychology as "contagion avoidance," is found across cultures, even in cases where people have little or no direct evidence for its truth. We are, it seems, just "wired" to believe it.[2]

Human Hardwiring and Morality

As scientists noted that such similarity of belief can often best be explained by the human brain's hardwiring, these scientists were naturally led to look for other areas of common belief in babies as well as across human times and cultures. While there are many such areas, I will discuss just two: human beliefs in and about morality and religion. Morality and religion, like the beliefs mentioned above, are pervasive across times and cultures. The details differ in important and sometimes striking ways. But it is just as striking that every culture indeed has both moral codes and religious beliefs and practices. And this fact led some scientists to suppose that human brains are hardwired to form beliefs about morality and religion as well.

There is indeed a good deal of evidence that lots of human behavior we would describe as "moral" arises from innate or hardwired dispositions. Like beliefs and desires associated with contagion avoidance, moral beliefs and desires appear to be part of our built-in "operating system." One quick example will suffice to give us a glimpse of this. Across times and cultures human beings display firm beliefs and feel strong desires pulling them in the direction of punishing those who do wrong. When we learn that someone has abused a child, or even when we see someone run a red light (perhaps right in front of the police

---

[2] P. Boyer, "Religious Thought and Behaviour as By-products of Brain Function," *Trends in Cognitive Science* 7/3 (2003): 119–24.

cruiser!), we feel strongly that the wrongdoer deserves to be penalized (the severity of the suffering depending on the severity of the crime).

One might think that this disposition toward punishment is just a reasoned reaction to fundamental principles of morality and justice. But there is good evidence that something more is going on. In fact, there is reason to think that our tendency to want to punish is wired into our thought processes in a way that runs far ahead of any carefully reasoned thought process. This has been made evident by a variety of experiments, perhaps the most telling of which is one carried out by the Swiss scientist and economist Ernst Fehr. In Fehr's study subjects would play a game with a series of groups of three other individuals. Each person starts the game with $20. In the game each player can contribute as much as they choose, $0–$20, to a central pool of funds. After the contributions are made, the total pot is revealed and tallied, and each player receives back 40 percent of the total amount contributed. Thus, if everyone donated all his money, the total pot would be $80, and each player would receive 40 percent of that total ($32), thus generating a $12 profit (as should be clear, the game includes a *bank* to supply additional funds to the pot if necessary). However, if one player contributes *nothing* and the rest contribute all of theirs, the total pot would be $60, and each player—including the noncontributor—would receive $24 dollars. The cheapskate would now have his original $20 *plus* the $24 earned from other contributions to the pot, for a total of $44, while his fellow players had earned a mere $4 profit. This, as you might guess, would make the other players angry. As the experiment is set up, players would play with (or against!) their fellow players only *one time* (something they are told before the game starts). So, if you were the cheapskate, you could move on to the next round of the game, with all new players, and no one would know of your past cheapskate behavior. In other words, your cheating behavior need never "come back to haunt you" in future rounds.

However, Fehr's game had one further twist. After the funds were contributed, tallied, and redistributed, players had a chance to do one more thing. Each player could contribute up to $10 to punish another player of their choosing (for any reason). For every dollar spent on punishing, the victim of the punishment would be charged $3. The funds received from all of the punishing activity went back into the bank.

A player who wants to maximize her earnings (if reasoning carefully) should (a) contribute nothing and (b) never punish. Let's think just about (b) here. Punishing in this game really serves no point for the punisher. For the punisher, it simply costs him money that will never be recouped in future rounds (since even if the punisher is deterred, that will only help the punished players' *future* fellow players). And yet, despite this, players in the game show a marked tendency to spend a lot of their resources on this pointless punishing activity.

What does this show? The reasonable conclusion is this: we are hardwired to seek to punish wrongdoers even when there is no possible future benefit to doing so. This aspect of our moral beliefs and desires is an innate disposition that we can escape only by expending great effort to resist our innate tendencies.

Human Hardwiring and Religion

In recent years some psychologists have gone even further, arguing that in addition to many of our fundamental moral beliefs and desires, many of our natural dispositions toward religion are also hardwired into our brains. In fact a wide range of evidence from psychology, neuroscience, and evolutionary theory has been mustered as a way of showing that, like the aspects of morality described above, God is hardwired into our brain. And some scientists have argued that this fact leads to devastating conclusions for religious believers.

Does recent psychology and neuroscience show us that belief in God is the result of a hardwired natural psychological process? The answer to that question is "probably." Evolutionary and cognitive psychologists have recently developed a number of different naturalistic explanations of religion. These explanations aim to show that human beings are naturally disposed toward religious belief and ritual because of certain innate or native "mental tools." Some theorists go on to argue that we have these mental tools because they, or the religion that they spawn, are and/or were adaptive for our ancestors and were thus passed down to us.

What sort of evidence is there for such a claim? The answer to that question depends on which of the six major models of explanation one adopts. The most popular model (which we can call the "Cognitive Model") argues that human beings have specific and identifiable mental tools that make religious belief easy and natural. For example, we have a mental tool that makes us think there are agents around when we detect certain sounds (bumps in the night), motions (rustling in the bushes), or configurations (crop circles) in nature. This "Hyperactive Agency Detection Device" (or "HADD") leads us to hypothesize invisible agents that, for example, control the forces of nature. And this disposes us to belief in the supernatural.

In addition, our minds are naturally disposed to remember and transmit ideas that violate certain *innate expectations* we have about the workings of the world. For example, we are born (it is claimed) thinking that agents are *physical things*. When we (through HADD) are led to hypothesize agents causing the lightning or the wind, we assume that these are invisible, supernatural agents. But invisible supernatural agents are, given our innate categories, counterintuitive and strange. And because of their distinctive strangeness, we easily remember them and talk about them, and this makes these religious concepts spread rapidly from mind to mind (thus explaining the tendency of religious concepts to spread quickly).[3]

In addition, there is strong evidence that we are naturally disposed from an early age to see *goal-directedness* in everything, including the natural world. Cognitive theorists call this tendency "intuitive theism" or "natural teleology" since it is a tendency to see purposiveness as a pervasive feature of our world. This naturally disposes us to believe in a purpose-giving force in the universe, that is, to believe in gods or a God.[4]

Some advocates of the Cognitive Model further argue that religious beliefs and behavior carry useful benefits for religious individuals and religious groups. For example, it is argued that religious individuals and groups are much more inclined to abide by moral rules and engage in cooperative behavior, traits that are useful in large interacting

---

[3] P. Boyer, *Religion Explained* (New York: Basic Books, 2001).
[4] D. Kelemen, "Are Children 'Intuitive Theists'?" *Psychological Science* 15 (2004): 295–301.

groups where individuals specialize and are forced to rely on one another for survival.[5] This claim is based not only on commonsense beliefs or anecdotal observation but on systematic empirical study. For example, Jesse Bering[6] has shown that, even from an early age, children tend to follow rules more consistently when they are primed to believe that a supernatural agent is watching them. In one experiment subjects were brought into a room and shown a box under two conditions. In one condition the child is told that there is an invisible princess in the room named Alice, who is carefully watching the whole experiment. In the control condition, children are not told any story about Alice. The children were then told that inside the box was a special prize and that they could have the prize only if they could guess what it was without looking. After giving the child the instructions, the experimenter tells the child that he needs to step out of the room for the moment. Children who had received the Alice prime cheated significantly less than those who did not, and even among cheaters it took much longer for primed subjects to cheat than subjects who were not primed.

Evidence indicates similar effects in adults. Norenzayan and Sharif had pairs of students play the dictator game. In this game one subject is given a sum of money which he can share with his partner. The game is played only one time, and the giver can choose to give the receiver all of the money, only some of it, or none of it. The giver then keeps the rest. Prior to playing the game, students are required to read scrambled sentences. In one condition the scrambled sentences contained one or more of the following words: *spirit, divine, God, sacred,* and *prophet.* In the other condition the sentences contained no words with religious connotations. Givers were provided with $10 to distribute. The results showed the student primed with the religious words before the start of the game gave, on average, $2 more to the receiver than those without the prime ($4.56 vs. $2.56). This is at least some indication that

[5] J. Haidt, "Moral Psychology and the Misunderstanding of Religion," in *The Spiritual Primate: Scientific, Philosophical, and Theological Reflections on the Origin of Religious Belief,* ed. M. Murray and J. Schloss (Oxford: Oxford University Press, 2008).

[6] J. M. Bering, "The Evolutionary History of an Illusion: Religious Causal Beliefs in Children and Adults," in *Origins of the Social Mind: Evolutionary Psychology and Child Development,* ed. B. Ellis and D. Bjorklund (New York: Guilford Press, 2004) 411–37.

distinctively religious concepts dispose us toward greater cooperative behavior and thus enhance the "usefulness" of religion.[7]

Is Religion an Artifact of the Brain?

A great deal of additional evidence of this sort makes it seem that religion is a natural product of the mental tools of a properly functioning human mind. But doesn't this show that religion is just a trick our minds play on us? Some scientists and philosophers have answered with a resounding yes! Michael Persinger, professor of behavioral neuroscience at Laurentian University, argues that this work shows us that "God is an artifact of the brain." Archatheist Richard Dawkins concludes that "the irrationality of religion is a by-product of the built in irrationality mechanism in the brain." Matthew Alpers, author of *The God Part of the Brain*, argues as follows:

> If belief in God is produced by a genetically inherited trait, if the human species is "hardwired" to believe in a spirit world, this could suggest that God doesn't exist as something "out there," beyond and independent of us, but rather as the product of an inherited perception, the manifestation of an evolutionary adaptation that exists exclusively within the human brain. If true, this would imply that there is no actual spiritual reality, no God or gods, no soul, or afterlife. Consequently, humankind can no longer be viewed as a product of God but rather God must be viewed as a product of human cognition.[8]

Even less subtle is Jesse Bering, who is quoted as saying that with such research "we've got God by the throat and I'm not going to stop until one of us is dead." For Bering the deliverances of the psychology of religion are "not going to remain in the privileged chapels of scientists and other scholars. It is going to dry up even the most verdant

[7] A. Sharif and A. Norenzayan, "God Is Watching You: Supernatural Agent Concepts Increase Prosocial Behavior in an Anonymous Economic Game," *Psychological Science* 18 (2007): 803–9.

[8] M. Alper, *The God Part of the Brain—a Scientific Interpretation of Human Spirituality and God* (New York: Rogue Press, 2000), 79.

suburban landscapes, and leave spiritual leaders with their tongues out, dying for a drop of faith."[9]

Are these scientists right? Has science showed belief in God to be a delusion? Not exactly. It looks as if those drawing this radical conclusion must be arguing as follows:

1. The development of the human mind through natural history has provided those minds with a number of special properties.
2. When considering the natural and social world, these properties encourage humans to believe in *gods*.
3. Therefore, the development of human minds has produced belief in *gods* (i.e., *God* is an "accident" of evolution.)
4. Therefore, belief in *gods* is false.

However, this argument commits a well-known logical fallacy called the "genetic fallacy." Genetically fallacious reasoning aims to argue for the truth or falsity of a belief simply from considerations of the origin of belief. But, of course, perfectly true beliefs can emerge even from crazy sources. I might think there are 449 people in the library because my watch reads 4:49. Can we conclude that this belief is *false* as a result of my strange reasoning? Of course not. It may be true, despite the strange origin.

Still we can modify the above argument in such a way that it does not commit the fallacy but still seems to raise trouble for religious belief, as follows:

1. The development of the human mind through natural history has provided those minds with a number of special properties.
2. When considering the natural and social world, these properties encourage humans to believe in *gods*.
3. Therefore, the development of human minds has produced belief in *gods* (i.e., *God* is an "accident" of evolution.)
4. Therefore, belief in *gods* is unwarranted.

Just as my belief that there are 449 people in the library on the basis of reading my watch would be *unwarranted*, perhaps believing in the

---

[9] J. Reischel, "The God Fossil," *Broward-Palm Beach New Times*, March 9, 2006.

existence of God based on the workings of the identified mental tools would be unwarranted.

But would it be? Let's look at the argument again, taking out the italicized word *gods* and replacing it with any of the following: *human minds, rocks, rainbows, the past, that science can discover the truth,* etc. Surely scientists would accept that each of the sentences including the replacement words is true. But those scientists would be equally convinced that the conclusion of those arguments is, in each case, false. Human minds naturally form beliefs in those things, and in doing so, we think, they get things right. So why not conclude that we get things right when it comes to belief in God? What makes this case different? One could say: "Well, because religious belief is false." But that is not much of an argument; it just assumes what the critic was trying to prove.

Perhaps the problem raised by these accounts is something different altogether. We might put the worry this way: in the case of our natural disposition to believe in rocks or human minds, the beliefs we form are caused by rocks and human minds acting directly on our minds (through our senses, for example). But in the case of religious belief, belief in God arises from our "agency detector" firing off in the presence of the wind and the waves. That makes these religious beliefs very different. Rock beliefs are caused by rocks while God beliefs are caused by . . . the wind. So, one might say, we would believe in God *even if there were no God.* And that is a problem.

This critic is right—if this is the way things are, that would be a problem. If our belief in God has no causal connection with the actual existence of God, that would seem to undermine the justification of our belief. But it is not clear that things are that way, even if these scientific accounts are right. For these scientific accounts to generate a real problem, (5) would have to be true:

5. Human minds would exist and believe in God, even if there were no God.

Is it true? I don't think so. I don't think there would be a *universe* if there were no God. I don't think the universe would be *fine-tuned for life* if there were no God. And I don't think there would be *any actual life, believers, human beings,* or *religion* either if there were no God. Am I wrong? If I am, nothing about evolutionary or cognitive psychology leads me to conclude that I am. So, contrary to our initial conclusion, these psychological accounts of religious belief do not teach us that we would have religious beliefs whether or not they are true. And so they do not undermine the justification for religious belief. As a result, this argument fails.

Perhaps there are other reasons to think that these psychological accounts raise problems for religious belief, but it is not at all clear what those reasons would be. For the moment it seems perfectly acceptable for the Christian to hold that God created the world, human beings, and human minds in such a way that when they are functioning properly, they form beliefs in the existence of rocks, rainbows, human minds, and God.

For now, what we should conclude is that contemporary psychology has shown us (rather unsurprisingly) that, in the words of Oxford psychologist Justin Barrett, "Belief in gods and God particularly arises through the natural, ordinary operation of human minds in natural ordinary environments."[10] This discovery echoes the claim made four hundred plus years earlier by John Calvin that "there is within the human mind, and indeed by natural instinct, an awareness of divinity."[11]

[10] J. Barrett, *Why Would Anyone Believe in God?* (Lanham, MD: Alta Mira Press, 2004).
[11] J. Calvin, *Institutes of the Christian Religion,* ed. John T. McNeill (Philadelphia: Westminster/John Knox Press, 1960), 1.3.1.

Chapter 5

THE MORAL POVERTY OF EVOLUTIONARY NATURALISM

Mark D. Linville

Darwin's account of the origins of human morality is at once elegant, ingenious, and woefully inadequate. In particular, that account, on its standard interpretation, does not *explain* morality but, rather, explains it *away*. We learn from Darwin not how there could *be* objective moral facts but how we could have come to *believe*, perhaps erroneously, that there are.

Further, the naturalist, who does not believe that there is such a personal being as God, is in principle committed to Darwinism, including a Darwinian account of the basic contours of human moral psychology. I'll use the term *evolutionary naturalism* to refer to this combination of naturalism and Darwinism. And so the naturalist is saddled with a view that explains morality away. Whatever reason we have for believing in moral facts is also a reason for thinking naturalism is false. I conclude the essay with a brief account of a theistic conception of morality and argue that the theist is in a better position to affirm the objectivity of morality.

A Darwinian Genealogy of Morals

According to the Darwinian account, given the contingencies of the evolutionary landscape—i.e., the circumstances of survival—certain behaviors are adaptive; and so, any *propensity* for such behaviors will also be adaptive. Such explains the flight instinct in the pronghorn, the spawning instinct in the cutthroat salmon, and my instinctual aversion to insulting Harley riders in biker bars. Insofar as such propensities are genetic (at least the first two examples would seem to qualify here), they are heritable and thus likely to be passed down to offspring.

Imagine, for example, a time in the early history of hominids when the circumstances of survival prompted an early patriot (and kite-flying inventor perhaps) to advise, "We must all hang together, or assuredly we shall all be torn apart by ravenous wolves." Insofar as such cooperation depends on heritable dispositions of group members, those dispositions will confer fitness.

Darwin speaks of "social instincts" that are at the root of our moral behavior. These include a desire for the approbation of our fellow humans and a fear of censure. They also include a general sympathy for others. He explains:

> In however complex a manner this feeling may have originated, as it is one of high importance to all those animals which aid and defend one another, it will have been increased through natural selection; for those communities which included the greatest number of the most sympathetic members, would flourish best, and rear the greatest number of offspring.[1]

A favored "complex manner" of the origin of such feelings involves an appeal to two varieties of altruism: *kin altruism* is directed at family members, chiefly one's offspring; and *reciprocal altruism* is directed at nonfamily members and even to strangers. The former is an other-regarding attitude and behavior, particularly concerning one's own children but extending in descending degrees to other family members, that does not seek any returns. The advantage, of course, is in the reproductive success. The sense of parental duty that is possessed by, say, a female sea turtle ensures only that she lay her eggs somewhere above the high tide mark. From there her relatively self-sufficient offspring are on their own against daunting odds—something like a 1 in 10,000 chance of reaching maturity. Those odds are offset by the

---

[1] C. Darwin, *The Descent of Man and Selection in Relation to Sex* (New York: Barnes and Noble Publishing, 2004), 88.

sheer numbers of hatchlings so that a fraction manage to survive the elements and elude myriads of predators.

Such a numbers strategy would hardly work for the human species, given the utter helplessness of the human infant. Babies tend to suffer an inelegant fate if left untended. The probability that a human infant will die if left to his own resources at, say, just above the high tide mark, is a perfect 1. And those same odds would prevail for each of 10,000 similarly abandoned babies. (Word would spread quickly in the wild: "Hey, free babies!") Human parents possessed of no more parental instinct than sea turtles would find that their line came to an abrupt end. Thus, a strong sense of love and concern is adaptive and heritable and has the same function, a means to reproductive success, among humans that hatchling self-sufficiency and sheer numbers have among turtles.

Reciprocal altruism, on the other hand, is rooted in a tit-for-tat arrangement that ultimately confers greater reproductive fitness on all parties involved. Consider, for instance, the symbiotic relationship that exists between grouper and cleaner shrimp. Though the shrimp would certainly make a nice snack for a hungry grouper when it is busily flossing the fish's teeth *from the inside*, the benefit of long-term hygiene (Whiter teeth! Fresher breath!) outweighs that of short-term nourishment, and so the fish is programmed to pass on the prawn. The shrimp, of course, benefits from a delectable meal of the gunk otherwise responsible for halitosis in grouper.

Similarly, there is benefit to be gained from cooperative and altruistic behavior among humans. For example, Darwin observes "A tribe including many members who, from possessing in a high degree the spirit of patriotism, fidelity, obedience, courage, and sympathy, were always ready to aid one another, and to sacrifice themselves for the common good, would be victorious over most other tribes; and this would be natural selection."[2] And membership in such a victorious tribe has its advantages. To attempt a metaphor, when a baseball team functions like a well-oiled machine, say, with a Tinker, Evers, and Chance infield, the likelihood that *all* of the members will sport World Series rings is increased.

Thus, the human moral sense, conscience, is rooted in a set of social instincts that were adaptive given the contingencies of the evolutionary

[2] Ibid., 112.

landscape. Of course, there is more to the moral sense than the instincts Darwin had in mind. All social animals are possessed of such instincts, but not all are plausibly thought of as moral agents.[3] According to Darwin, *conscience* emerges out of a sort of "recipe." It is the result of the social instincts being overlaid with a certain degree of rationality. He writes:

> The following proposition seems to me in a high degree probable—namely, that any animal whatever, endowed with well-marked social instincts, the parental and filial affections being here included, would inevitably acquire a moral sense or conscience, as soon as its intellectual powers had become as well, or nearly as well developed, as in man.[4]

Wolves in a pack know their place in the social hierarchy. A lower ranked wolf feels compelled to give way to the alpha male. Were he endowed with the intellectual powers that Darwin had in mind, then, presumably his "moral sense" would tell him that obeisance is his *moral duty*. He would regard it as a moral fact that, like it or not, alpha interests trump beta or omega interests. And our grouper, if graced with rational and moral autonomy, might reason, "It would be *wicked* of me to bite down on my little buddy here after all he has done for me!"

Of course, such a "recipe" is precisely what we find in the human species, according to Darwin. We experience a strong prereflective pull in the direction of certain behaviors such as the care for our children or the returning of kindness for kindness; and, on reflection, we conclude that these are our moral duties.

Evolutionary Naturalism and Moral Knowledge

It is not clear that the resulting account of the origin and nature of human morality does full justice to its subject. For one thing, it is hard to see why anyone who accepts it is warranted in accepting *moral*

---

[3] And, of course, though any two species of social animals have in common the fact that they are prompted by social instincts, the resulting behavior may vary widely. It is not clear, for instance, which of the grazing Guernseys is the "alpha cow." Wiener dogs seem not to come equipped with the obsessive herding instincts of border collies and would likely endure derisive laughter from the sheep if they did.

[4] Darwin, *Descent*, 81.

realism—the view that there are objective, mind-independent moral facts that we sometimes get right in our moral beliefs. For it would appear that the human moral sense and the moral beliefs that arise from it are ultimately the result of natural selection, and their value is thus found in the *adaptive behavior* they encourage. But then it seems that the processes responsible for our having the moral beliefs that we do are ultimately *fitness aimed* rather than *truth aimed.* This is to say that in such a case *the best explanation for our having the moral beliefs we do makes no essential reference to their being true.*

If we have the moral beliefs we do because of the fitness conferred by the resulting behavior, then it appears that we would have had those beliefs whether or not they were true. Some writers have taken this to imply that ethics is "an illusion fobbed off on us by our genes in order to get us to cooperate."[5] This suggests that there are no objective moral facts, though we have been programmed to believe in them. A more modest conclusion might be that we are not in a position to *know* whether there are such facts because our moral beliefs are undercut by the Darwinian story of their genesis. This is because that story makes no essential reference to any such alleged facts. Thus, our moral beliefs are without warrant. But if our moral beliefs are unwarranted, then there can be no such thing as moral knowledge. And this amounts to moral skepticism.

If the argument developed here succeeds, its significance is in its implications for the naturalist, who maintains that reality is exhausted by the kinds of things that may, in principle, be the study of the empirical sciences. For the naturalist's wagon is hitched to the Darwinian star. Richard Dawkins was recently seen sporting a T-shirt that read, "Evolution: The Greatest Show on Earth, the Only Game in Town." Perhaps Dawkins's shirt reflects his more careful comment elsewhere that, "although atheism might have been *logically* tenable before Darwin, Darwin made it possible to be an intellectually fulfilled atheist."[6] Before Darwin the inference to Paley's Watchmaker seemed natural, if not inevitable, given a world filled with things "that give the appearance of having been designed for a purpose."[7] Naturalism

---

[5] M. Ruse and E. O. Wilson, "The Evolution of Ethics," in *Religion and the Natural Sciences,* ed. J. E. Huchingson (Orlando: Harcourt Brace, 1993), 310–11.
[6] R. Dawkins, *The Blind Watchmaker* (New York: Norton & Co., 1986), 6.
[7] Ibid., 1.

without Darwinism is a worldview at a loss for explanation. Further, to appeal to natural selection to explain libidos and incisors but to withhold such an explanation for human moral psychology is an untenable position. Moral behavior is not the sort of thing likely to be overlooked by natural selection because of the important role it plays in survival and reproductive success.[8] But if naturalism is committed to Darwinism, and Darwinism implies moral skepticism, then naturalism is committed to moral skepticism.

Darwinism and Normativity

In *The Descent of Man*, Darwin asks, "Why should a man feel that he ought to obey one instinctive desire rather than another?"[9] His subsequent answer is that the stronger of two conflicting impulses wins out. Thus, the otherwise timid mother will, without hesitation, run the greatest risks to save her child from danger because the maternal instinct trumps the instinct for self-preservation. And the timid man, who stands on the shore wringing his hands while allowing even his own child to drown out of fear for his own life, heeds the instinct for self-preservation.[10]

What Darwin never asks, and thus never answers, is why a man *ought*, in fact, to obey the one rather than the other. The best he offers here is the observation that *if* instinct A is stronger than B, then one *will* obey A. What he does not and, I suggest, *cannot* say is that one *ought* to obey A or that one *ought* to feel the force of A over B. That is, whereas Darwin may be able to answer the *factual* question that he *does* ask—why people believe and behave as they do—this does nothing to answer the *normative* question of how one *ought* to behave or of what sets of instincts and feelings one *ought* to cultivate in order to be virtuous. It is, of course, one thing to explain why people believe and

---

[8] T. Sommers and A. Rosenberg, "Darwin's Nihilistic Idea: Evolution and the Meaninglessness of Life," *Biology and Philosophy* 18/5 (2003): 653–88.

[9] Darwin, *Descent*, 91.

[10] I cannot resist including a personal anecdote here. I once rescued a young man from drowning in the Mississippi River. After I swam out and pulled him to shore, his mother, who had watched helplessly from the beach, explained that she *would* have saved him herself but she could not go into the water because her toe was infected. She produced the sore toe. I had to agree that it did look very sore.

behave as they do; it is another to say whether their beliefs are true (or at least warranted) and their behaviors right. As it stands, Darwin appears to have precious little of moral import to say to the timid man.

One could, I suppose, reply on Darwinian grounds that the father who lacks a strong paternal instinct is *abnormal*, lacking traits that are almost universally distributed throughout the species and are, perhaps, even kind defining.[11] Darwin refers to the man who is utterly bereft of the social instincts as an "unnatural monster." Doesn't this observation lend itself to a normative evaluation of behaviors? Who wants to be a *monster*, after all? But it is not at all clear that this can give us what is needed. After all, departure from a statistical average is not necessarily a bad thing. If the average adult's IQ is around one hundred, Stephen Hawking is something of a freak. And, presumably, the first hominids to use tools (Hawking's direct ancestors perhaps?) or to express themselves in propositions were unique in their day.[12] Indeed, the Gandhis and Mother Theresas of the world are certainly abnormal, enough that one evolutionary naturalist refers to them as "variations," yet we tend to like having them around.

I suppose that the evolutionary naturalist could go on to observe that not only do we notice that the timid father is *different* in that his parental instinct was not sufficient to prompt him to rescue his child, but it is a difference that naturally elicits negative *moral emotions*. We disapprove of him and think him blameworthy. Indeed, perhaps the man later experiences some negative moral emotions himself such as "remorse, repentance, regret, or shame."[13] According to Darwin, the sense of guilt is the natural experience of anyone who spurns the prompting of any of the more enduring social instincts, and it bears some similarity to the physical or mental suffering that results from

---

[11] The Chinese philosopher Mencius seems to have maintained that the possession of at least the rudimentary "seeds" of the virtues (e.g., the feeling of commiseration is the seed of the virtue of *jen,* "human-heartedness") are essential to humanity so that anyone lacking them would not be human.

[12] Consider Gary Larson's cartoon depicting a group of cave men. To the left is a small group huddled around a fire, roasting drumsticks by clenching them in their fists *directly over the flames.* They are all obviously in agony. To the right is another fire with only one cook. He has the meat roasting on a stick and is seated at a comfortable distance. A member of the group to the left has noticed this, and is saying, "Look what Og do!"

[13] Darwin, *Descent,* 94.

the frustration of any instinct of any creature. Darwin considers the suffering of the caged migratory bird that will bloody itself against the wires of the cage when the migratory instinct is at its height. Indeed, he considers that conflict between the migratory and maternal instincts in the swallow, which gives in to the former and abandons her young in the nest. He speculates, "When arrived at the end of her long journey, and the migratory instinct has ceased to act, what an agony of remorse the bird would feel, if, from being endowed with great mental activity, she could not prevent the image constantly passing through her mind, of her young ones perishing in the bleak north from cold and hunger."[14]

Like the moral sense in general, guilt is the yield of a sort of recipe: one part spurned instinct to one part "great mental activity" that permits remembrance and remorse. And so, when our timid man's own personal danger and fear are past so that the strength of his selfish instinct has receded, the scorned paternal instinct will have its revenge. Also, because we are social animals, we are endowed with sympathies that make us yearn for the approbation of our fellows and fear their censure. The cowardly father is thus likely in for a long bout of insomnia. Further, Darwin may explain that the experience of remorse may result in a resolve for the future, with the further result that the paternal instinct is bolstered and stands a greater chance of being the dominant of two conflicting instincts. Thus, "conscience looks backwards, and serves as a guide for the future."[15]

But even if we are assured that a "normal" person will be prompted by the social instincts and that those instincts are typically flanked and reinforced by a set of moral emotions, we still do not have a truly normative account of moral obligation. Nothing in Darwin's own account indicates that the ensuing sense of guilt, a guilty *feeling*, is indicative of *actual* moral guilt resulting from the violation of an objective moral law. The revenge taken by one's own conscience amounts to a sort of *second-order* propensity to feel a certain way given one's past relation to conflicting first-order propensities (e.g., the father's impulse to save his child versus his impulse to save himself). Unless we import normative

[14] Ibid.
[15] Ibid., 95.

considerations from some other source, it seems that, whether it is a first- or second-order inclination,[16] one's being prompted by it is more readily understood as a *descriptive* feature of one's own psychology than material for a normative assessment of one's behavior or character. And, assuming that there is anything to this observation, an ascent into even higher levels of propensities ("I feel guilty for not having felt guilty for not being remorseful over not obeying my social instincts") introduces nothing of normative import. Suppose you encounter a man who neither feels the pull of social, paternal, or familial instincts nor is in the least bit concerned over his apparent lack of conscience. What, from a strictly Darwinian perspective, can one say to him that is of any serious moral import? "You are not moved to action by the impulses that move most of us." Right. So?

The problem afflicts contemporary construals of an evolutionary account of human morality. Consider Michael Shermer's explanation for the evolution of a moral sense, the "science of good and evil." He explains:

> By a moral sense, I mean a moral feeling or emotion generated by actions. For example, positive emotions such as righteousness and pride are experienced as the psychological feeling of doing "good." These moral emotions likely evolved out of behaviors that were reinforced as being good either for the individual or for the group.[17]

Shermer goes on to compare such moral emotions to other emotions and sensations that are universally experienced, such as hunger and the sexual urge. He then addresses the question of moral motivation.

> In this evolutionary theory of morality, asking "Why should we be moral?" is like asking "Why should we be hungry?" or "Why should we be horny?" For that matter, we could ask, "Why should we be jealous?" or "Why should we fall in love?"

---

[16] So if the impulse either to save the child or one's own hide is a first-order inclination, second-order inclinations would include feelings of, say, guilt or pride regarding the first-order propensities and resulting actions.

[17] M. Shermer, *The Science of Good and Evil* (New York: Times Books, 2004), 56.

The answer is that it is as much a part of human nature to be
moral as it is to be hungry, horny, jealous, and in love.[18]

Thus, according to Shermer, given an evolutionary account, such a
question is simply a nonstarter. Moral motivation is a given as it is
wired in as one of our basic drives. Of course, one might point out
that Shermer's "moral emotions" often *do* need encouragement in a
way that, say, horniness, does not. More importantly, Shermer apparently fails to notice that if asking, "Why should I be moral?" is like
asking, "Why should I be horny?" then asserting, "You ought to be
moral" is like asserting, "You ought to be horny." As goes the inter-
rogative, so goes the imperative. But if the latter seems out of place,
then, on Shermer's view, so is the former.

One might thus observe that if morality is anything at all, it is *ir-
reducibly normative* in nature. But the Darwinian account winds up
reducing morality to descriptive features of human psychology. Like
the libido, either the moral sense is present and active or it is not. If it
is, then we might expect one to behave accordingly. If not, why, then,
as a famous blues man once put it, "The boogie woogie just ain't in
me." And so the resulting "morality" is that in name only.

In light of such considerations, it is tempting to conclude with C. S.
Lewis that, if the naturalist remembered his philosophy out of school,
he would recognize that any claim to the effect that "I ought" is on a
par with "I itch," in that it is nothing more than a descriptive piece of
autobiography with no essential reference to any actual obligations.

A Naturalist Rejoinder

A familiar objection to my line of argument is that it assumes what is
almost certainly false: that all significant and widely observed human behavior is genetically determined as the result of natural selection. Daniel
Dennett refers to this assumption as "greedy reductionism." Dennett
observes that all tribesmen everywhere throw their spears pointy-end
first, but we should not suppose that there is a "pointy-end first gene."[19]

---

[18] Ibid., 57.
[19] D. Dennett, *Darwin's Dangerous Idea: Evolution and the Meanings of Life* (New York: Simon
and Schuster, 1996), 486.

The explanation rather resides in the "nonstupidity" of the tribesmen. And when C. S. Lewis's character, Ransom, was at first surprised to discover that boats on Malacandra (Mars) were similar to earthly boats, he caught himself with the question, "What else could a boat be like?'" (The astute Lewis reader might also have noticed that Malacandran hunters throw *their* spears pointy-end first, despite being genetically unrelated to humans, just as Dennett might have predicted.) Some ideas are just better than others and, assuming a minimal degree of intelligence, perhaps we have been equipped to discover and implement them.

One might thus insist that perhaps all that evolution has done for us is to equip us with the basic *capacities* for intelligent decision-making and problem-solving, and the enterprise that is human morality is the product of human rationality, not the mere outworking of some genetic program. If the process that has led to our having the moral beliefs we do has involved conscious rational reflection, then we have reason for optimism regarding our facility for tracking truth. We have no more cause for moral skepticism than we do, say, mathematical skepticism.

The same greedy reductionism might be thought to plague my argument that Darwinian accounts of human morality are merely descriptive. I have said above that, "unless we import normative considerations from some other source," we are left with a merely descriptive rather than a normative account. My critic may insist here that we *do* bring in normative considerations from elsewhere, namely, from moral theory. If there are true moral principles that yield moral directives and values, then, regardless of how one *does* feel and behave, it will remain the case that he *ought* to behave in a certain way. For example, should it prove true that humans have a natural propensity for xenophobia as a part of their evolutionary heritage, we might nevertheless conclude that, say, a respect-for-persons principle requires that they overcome such fear and potential mistreatment of strangers. The mere fact that people have a propensity for a behavior does not entail that it is justified.

I plead not guilty to the charge of greedy reductionism. The argument in no way supposes that well-formed moral beliefs are somehow programmed by our DNA. Richard Joyce considers the belief, "I ought to reciprocate by picking up Mary at the airport."[20] He then

---

[20] R. Joyce, *The Evolution of Morality* (Cambridge: MIT Press, 2006), 180.

asks, "What does natural selection know of *Mary* or *airports*?" Or consider a mother's belief, "I ought to ensure that my child gets plenty of fruits and vegetables." There is, of course, no imperative regarding the dietary needs of toddlers that may be read off the DNA. One might as well suppose that there is a genetically programmed human tendency directed specifically at popping bubble wrap.

But Darwin's account certainly *does* imply that the *basic predisposition* for repaying kindness with kindness or for caring for one's offspring *is* programmed and that such programs run as they do because of the reproductive fitness that is, or *was* for our remote ancestors, achieved by the resulting behaviors.

Philosopher Mary Midgley speaks of instincts as "programs with a gap."[21] Consider, for instance, the migratory instinct of the sandhill crane. The basic drive to follow the sun south every winter is genetically programmed. But a "gap" allows for variations in the itinerary. Midgley notes that the more intelligent the species is the wider is the gap, so that room is available for deliberation and rational reflection. Less psychologically complex creatures may be strictly determined in their behavior by their genetic hardwiring. As P. G. Wodehouse's newtloving character, Gussie Fink-Nottle explains to Bertie Wooster, "Do you know how a male newt proposes, Bertie? He just stands in front of the female newt vibrating his tail and bending his body in a semicircle."[22] Assuming Gussie's description is accurate, we may also safely assume that newt courting behavior, unlike that observed in aristocratic British bachelors, is genetically choreographed. In humans, the "gap" allows for countless ideas and beliefs that clearly are the products of *culture* rather than biology.

Still, the *basic programming* itself is, on Darwin's scheme, determined by our genetic makeup, and, therefore, so is the range of rational options in that "gap" of deliberation. Given the perennial problem of tribal warfare, early tribesmen *reasoned* that thrown spears are far more effective than thrown bananas. But had humans evolved to be nonaggressive herbivores, spears might have been, well, pointless. Had the course of human evolution been such that human infants, like baby

---

[21] See M. Midgley, *Beast and Man* (London: Routledge Press, 1979).
[22] Taken from P. G. Wodehouse, *Right Ho, Jeeves* (New York: Penguin, 2000), chap. 2.

sea turtles, were self-reliant, the human maternal instinct might never have evolved as a means to the end of reproductive fitness. Indeed, Darwin thought that, had the circumstances for reproductive fitness been different, then the deliverances of conscience might have been *radically* different. "If . . . men were reared under precisely the same conditions as hive-bees, there can hardly be a doubt that our unmarried females would, like the worker-bees, think it a sacred duty to kill their brothers, and mothers would strive to kill their fertile daughters, and no one would think of interfering."[23] As it happens, we *weren't* "reared" after the manner of hive bees, and so we have widespread and strong beliefs about the sanctity of human life and its implications for how we should treat our siblings and our offspring.

But this strongly suggests that we *would* have had *whatever* beliefs were ultimately fitness producing given the circumstances of survival. Given the background belief of naturalism, there appears to be no plausible Darwinian reason for thinking that the fitness-producing predispositions that set the parameters for moral reflection have anything whatsoever to do with the truth of the resulting moral beliefs. One *might* be able to make a case for thinking that having true beliefs about, say, the predatory behaviors of tigers would, when combined with the understandable desire not to be eaten, be fitness producing. But the account would be far from straightforward in the case of moral beliefs.[24] And so the Darwinian explanation undercuts whatever reason the naturalist might have had for thinking that any of our moral beliefs is true. The result is moral skepticism.

If our *pretheoretical* moral convictions are largely the product of natural selection, as Darwin's theory implies, then the moral theories we find plausible are an *indirect* result of that same evolutionary process. How, after all, do we come to settle upon a proposed moral theory and its principles as being true? What methodology is available to us?

---

[23] Darwin, *Descent*, 82.

[24] Here's why. This would imply, for instance, that human mothers are possessed of a powerful maternal instinct for the prior reason that they have a moral duty to care for their children. But, given naturalism, the simpler explanation for the maternal instinct is just that it confers reproductive fitness. Why think that moral facts have any role to play, particularly when we observe similar instinctual behavior in animals that are not plausibly thought of as moral agents? Further, to what mechanism could the naturalist plausibly appeal to explain how reproductive fitness "tracks" moral truth? For more on this, see S. Street's excellent paper, "A Darwinian Dilemma for Realist Theories of Value," *Philosophical Studies* 127 (2006): 109–66.

By way of answer, consider the following "chicken and egg" question. Which do we know more certainly: the belief, *It is wrong to stomp on babies just to hear them squeak*, or some true moral principle that entails the wrongness of baby-stomping? In moral reflection, do we begin with the principle and only then, principle in hand, come to *discover* the wrongness of recreational baby-stomping as an inference from that principle? Or do we begin with the belief that baby-stomping is wrong and then arrive at the principle that seems implicated by such a belief? Pretty clearly, it is the latter. We just find ourselves with certain beliefs of a moral nature and actually appeal to them as touchstones when we engage in conscious moral reflection. Indeed, if we were to conclude that some philosopher's proposed moral principle would, if true, imply the moral correctness of recreational baby-stomping, then we might say, "So much the worse for that proposed principle." As philosopher Mary Midgley has put it, "An ethical theory which, when consistently followed through, has iniquitous consequences is a bad theory and must be changed."[25] This methodology, which begins with deep-seated, prereflective moral beliefs and then moves to moral principles that are implicated by them, is sometimes called *reflective equilibrium.*[26]

Presumably, reflective equilibrium, employed by bee-like philosophers in those worlds envisioned by Darwin, would settle on moral principles that implied the rightness of such things as siblicide and infanticide. Thus, the deliverances of the moral theories endorsed in such worlds are but the by-products of the evolved psychologies in such worlds. But, again, this suggests that *our* pretheoretical convictions are largely due to whatever selection pressures happened to be in place in *our* world. If this is so, then the deliverances of those moral theories that *we* endorse, to which we might appeal in order to introduce normative considerations, are, in the final analysis, by-products

---

[25] M. Midgley, "Duties Concerning Islands," in C. Pierce and D. VanDeVeer, eds., *People, Penguins and Plastic Trees* (Belmont, CA: Wadsworth Publishing, 1986), 157.

[26] Reflective equilibrium involves more than this one-way move from particular beliefs to general principles. In actual practice, it begins with those prereflective beliefs, moves from there to systemizing principles and then back to other particular beliefs that are entailed by the principles. There is always a standing possibility that an entailed belief is incompatible with one or another of the beliefs with which one began. In that case, adjustment and revision is called for. The goal is to arrive at a set or system of principled beliefs that is internally consistent and plausible.

of *our* evolved psychology. The account, as it stands, thus never takes us beyond merely descriptive human psychology.

A Theistic Alternative

The worry, then, is that our efforts at moral reflection are compromised by features of our constitution that are in place for purposes other than the acquisition of truth. As philosopher Sharon Street puts it, "If the fund of evaluative judgments with which human reflection began was thoroughly contaminated with illegitimate influence . . . then the tools of rational reflection were equally contaminated, for the latter are always just a subset of the former."[27]

In order to inspire confidence in those initial evaluative judgments of which Street speaks, the moral realist owes us some account of their origin that would lead us to suppose that they are reliable indicators of truth. What we need is some assurance that our original fund is *not* contaminated. And so our question is, What reason have we for supposing that the mechanisms responsible for those judgments are *truth aimed?* What we seek is what Norman Daniels calls "a little story that gets told about why we should pay homage ultimately to those [considered] judgments and indirectly to the principles that systematize them."[28]

The theist may here oblige us in a way that the naturalist may not. Robert Adams, for example, has suggested that things bear the moral properties that they do, good or bad, insofar as they resemble or fail to resemble God. He goes on to offer the makings of a theistic "genealogy of morals."

> If we suppose that God directly or indirectly causes human beings to regard as excellent approximately those things that are Godlike in the relevant way, it follows that there is a causal and explanatory connection between facts of excellence and beliefs that we may regard as justified about excellence, and

[27] S. Street, "A Darwinian Dilemma for Realist Theories of Value," *Philosophical Studies* 127 (2006): 125.
[28] N. Daniels, "Wide Reflective Equilibrium and Theory Acceptance in Ethics," *Journal of Philosophy* 76/5 (1979): 265.

hence it is in general no accident that such beliefs are correct when they are.[29]

The theist is thus in a position to offer Daniels's "little story" to explain the general reliability of those evaluative judgments from which reflective equilibrium takes its cue. Certain of our moral beliefs—in particular, those that are presupposed in all moral reflection—are truth aimed because human moral faculties are designed to guide human conduct in light of moral truth.[30] The moral law is "written upon the heart" (Rom 2:15), the apostle Paul wrote to the church in Rome.

Conclusion

A century ago, the philosopher Hastings Rashdall observed:

> So long as he is content to assume the reality and authority of the moral consciousness, the Moral Philosopher can ignore Metaphysic; but if the reality of Morals or the validity of ethical truth be once brought into question, the attack can only be met by a thorough-going enquiry into the nature of Knowledge and of Reality.[31]

We have seen that both the evolutionary naturalist and the theist may be found saying that certain of our moral beliefs are by-products of the human constitution: we think as we do largely as a result of our programming. Whether such beliefs are warranted would seem to depend on who or what is responsible for the program. And this calls for some account of the metaphysical underpinnings of those beliefs and the mechanisms responsible for them. Are those mechanisms truth aimed? Are they in good working order? The sort of account available to the evolutionary naturalist ends in moral skepticism. The theist has a more promising story to tell.[32]

---

[29] R. M. Adams, *Finite and Infinite Goods* (Oxford: Oxford University Press, 1999), 70.

[30] For the purposes of this argument, the appeal to "design" leaves open the question of whether the process responsible for the appearance of moral agents was evolutionary in nature. Daniels's "little story" requirement is satisfied whether the tale involves special creation or directed evolution.

[31] H. Rashdall, *The Theory of Good and Evil* (Oxford: The Clarendon Press, 1907), 192.

[32] As always, I wish to thank David Werther for his many helpful comments on and criticisms of earlier versions of this essay.

Chapter 6

DAWKINS'S BEST ARGUMENT AGAINST GOD'S EXISTENCE[1]

Gregory E. Ganssle

As is evident from the essays in this book, the New Atheists put forward many arguments against the existence of God. In this essay I will look at what I think is the strongest argument against the existence of God that any of these authors has put forward. This argument is one offered by Dawkins.

Dawkins's best argument is built on the claim that a universe made by God would be different than one that is a product only of natural processes. That is, God's existence ought to make some difference to the world that is detectable. He claims: "A universe with a creative superintendent would be a very different kind of universe from one without."[2] If God's existence made no difference at all to what we observe about the universe, we would wonder why belief in God mattered.

Given that a theistic universe should be different from an atheistic one,[3] which is reflected in our universe? Dawkins claims that our universe fits well with an atheistic worldview. It is different, he insists, from what

---

[1] This chapter is a revised version of my essay, "Dawkins's Best Argument: The Case Against God in *The God Delusion,*" which appeared in *Philosophia Christi,* Series 2, 10/1 (2008): 39–56; and chapter 7 of my book, *Reasonable God: Engaging the Face of Atheism* (Waco, TX: Baylor University Press, 2009).

[2] R. Dawkins, *The God Delusion* (Boston: Houghton Mifflin, 2006), 55.

[3] For simplicity, I equate a naturalistic universe with an atheistic universe (one in which God does not exist.) For the purposes of this essay, I take as the most viable alternatives the atheistic universe and the theistic universe. I do not consider the possibility of views such as Buddhism or polytheism.

fits with the view that God exists. Our observations about the world show us that it has the marks of an atheistic universe rather than the marks of a theistic one. We can sketch Dawkins's argument as follows:

1. A universe made by God would be different from one made by only natural occurrences.
2. Our universe fits better with a naturalistic universe than with a theistic universe.
3. Therefore our universe is more likely to be a naturalistic universe than a theistic universe.

Preliminary Observations

Before I interact with this argument, I want to make some preliminary observations. First, this argument is the best because it supports the conclusion to a degree. Aspects of the universe as we know it fit better with a naturalistic worldview than with a theistic worldview, and these aspects raise the likelihood that atheism is true. The second observation is that this argument does not aim to *prove* that God does not exist. Rather it aims to show that it is more likely that God does not exist than that He does. It is an *evidential* argument. Dawkins is right when he insists, in many places throughout his book, that he is not providing a watertight proof that God does not exist. One cannot prove God's existence or nonexistence. The reason watertight proof is not to be found is not because claims about God have some special status. Arguments for the claim that God exists (or does not exist) are philosophical arguments, and philosophical arguments are almost never watertight proofs. Watertight proofs are found largely in mathematics and logic. Nearly every philosophical claim and every philosophical argument are evidential. There are always premises that are not established beyond the possibility of doubt.

Not only are philosophical disputes evidential in nature; they are cumulative as well. In investigating the case for some philosophical claim such as the existence of God, we take all of the evidential arguments together and try to determine in which direction the total case points. Some arguments or lines of evidence point in one direction, while others point in the opposite direction. The cumulative nature of arguments is common throughout the disciplines as well. One line of argument by itself rarely establishes some significant claim with a high degree of confirmation. Dawkins is right to develop this argument along evidential lines in this way.

Third, this argument is about *fittingness*. The argument claims that ours is the sort of universe that fits better with the view that there is no God. It also claims that the universe as we find it does not fit as well with the existence of God. In this way we can test our two worldviews. We can figure out what sort of universe best fits with each, and we can see through empirical and other means whether the nature of the universe fits better with one theory or the other.

It is important to clarify the notion of fittingness that is at work. The issue of whether some observation fits or does not fit with a claim or a theory can be called an *issue of connectedness*. Connectedness comes in degrees. An observation connects more or less well with the theory or claim in question. There is little precision here, but we can recognize different general levels of connectedness and, consequently, different strengths of connectedness claims. For example, to say that some theory *requires* some claim be true or that some fact requires a certain theory be true is a tight level of connectedness. We can find such a tight level positively or negatively. For example, some philosophers have argued that the existence of God *requires* that the universe have no evil in it at all. This claim means, of course, that the existence of evil is *incompatible* with theism.[4] This kind of requirement is the highest level of connectedness that can be proposed.

A moderate level of connectedness involves *expectations*. Any theory leads us to expect certain things to hold and other things not to hold. These things may not be required (such that their not holding is incompatible with the theory), but the expectation can be strong. One rule of thumb that may indicate some feature is to be expected if a theory is true is if the lack of that feature would be at all surprising given the truth of the theory.

---

[4] For the standard example, see J. L. Mackie, "Evil and Omnipotence," *Mind* 64 (1955): 200–12. Few philosophers today defend the claim that theism requires a universe without evil.

There is a level of connectedness that is even less tight than expectation. Dawkins's argument trades on this level. It is the level of *fittingness*. Certain observations fit better with one theory than with another, even if the theory would not lead us to expect the details of the observation. Human interaction often appeals to this sort of connectedness. You may have no reason to *expect* to see me in Starbucks, but it certainly fits with what you know about me (if you know anything about me at all!).

The advantage of taking Dawkins's argument as one concerning fittingness rather than expectation is that the argument is for a weaker claim. If he is putting forward a weaker claim, challenging it is more difficult. Raising objections to strong claims (such as that evil is incompatible with theism) is not difficult. One has only to undermine the strong connection. A weaker claim, however, is more difficult to challenge. Dawkins's argument, because it is based on claims about fittingness, is a stronger argument.

Dawkins's Argument

Having explained some important background observations, I want to turn to the argument itself. Each of the two premises must be investigated. If both are true, then the argument works, and the conclusion is established. The first premise is the claim that a universe made by God would be different from one made by natural occurrences. Again, we must do a little clarifying work. If the argument is to progress, the difference between the theistic universe and the atheistic universe must be a *detectable* difference. What is it, then, that makes something detectable? Dawkins is disposed to think of detectability in terms of sense experience and the methods of the natural sciences. Something that is in principle subject to scientific investigation is detectable. We ought to wonder if other sorts of observations can show us that there is a detectable difference between theories.

For example, ethical theories can differ from one another in detectable ways. If one theory prohibits lying in every circumstance while a second theory allows lying under specified conditions, there is a detectable difference between them. This is not the sort of detectable difference that decisively falsifies one of the theories. We would have to have a sense already that lying is permitted in some circumstances (or that it is never permitted) in order to use this difference to choose between theories. The difference between the theories is also not due to some empirical observations. The difference is due to the sort of moral assessment that each theory supports.

Given that there ought to be detectable differences between the claim that the universe is theistic and the claim that it is not theistic, even if these differences do not have to be empirically detectable, we can grant that the first premise of the argument is true. It remains to investigate the second premise. Does the universe as we observe it fit better with the theistic story than it does with the atheistic story? We must make careful observations to see whether there are good reasons to think that the second premise is true.

Although Dawkins does not spell out the way our universe fits with atheism precisely, he does point in the direction of what he has in mind. His view is that any naturalistic universe with complex life would include a long period of biological development through a process something like natural selection. This notion is built into his articulation of the naturalistic worldview that is an alternative to the God Hypothesis. He states that position: "Any creative intelligence, of sufficient complexity to design anything, comes into existence only as the end product of an extended process of gradual evolution."[5] Furthermore, I think he holds that a theistic universe would most likely *not* include a long process of biological development. He does not make this claim explicitly in connection with this argument, but it seems to lie behind his approach. In this case his argument is that natural selection does not fit well in a theistic universe, but it fits neatly in a naturalistic universe. Since the evidence for natural selection is overwhelming, the probability that the universe is naturalistic is very high.

To what degree does biological development through natural selection fail to fit neatly with a theistic universe? I do think there is a degree to which it *does* run counter to theism. In a theistic universe the origin of various life forms is not restricted to gradual processes. God could use any process He wants to create living things. It is perfectly possible, if God exists, that He just brings living things into existence in all their va-

---

[5] Dawkins, *God Delusion*, 31.

riety at one moment. He is not restricted to processes that run over long periods of time. In this way our expectations about the development of biological life in a theistic universe ought to be wide open. Theism does not *rule out* a long process of biological development, but theists are not restricted to such theories by their theistic commitments.

An atheistic universe, in contrast, lacks the resources for instantaneous creation of all life forms. It would be completely baffling if complex life emerges instantly in a universe without God. Complex life would require some kind of long developmental process. This process would not need to be through genetic variation and natural selection, but it would need to be gradual. It would need to be, it turns out, something like the way we find it.

Since the theistic universe is compatible with a variety of mechanisms for the development of complex biological life, the fact of gradual development through natural selection does not provide specific evidence for theism. Since the naturalistic universe *seems to require* some kind of long-term biological process for complex biological life, the fact of natural selection does support the claim that the universe is naturalistic. This aspect of the universe we find, then, supports the claim that there is no God. Natural selection provides evidence for atheism even though it is not incompatible with theism.

A Response to Dawkins's Argument

That natural selection lends evidence to the claim that the universe is naturalistic is part of what makes this argument the best one Dawkins offers. If all we look at is the development of complex biological life, his case would appear to be strong. Other aspects of the universe as we find it, however, point in the opposite direction. At least four major elements of our universe fit significantly better with a universe in which God exists than in the atheistic universe. These elements are: (1) the universe is ordered and susceptible to rational investigation; (2) it is a world with consciousness; (3) it is a world with significant free agency; and (4) it is a world with objective moral obligations. Each of these aspects fits neatly into a theistic world but is not at home in a naturalistic world. It is not that they are incompatible with naturalism, but they do not fit neatly into the naturalistic world.

I want to be clear about the structure of the argument I am developing here. I do not mean to argue directly from these four features of the world to the claim that God exists. I am trying to put forward an argument structured in a way that is strongly analogous to Dawkins's argument. Gradual development of complex life through natural selection is something that fits better with naturalism than with theism. This fact, as a result, supports the claim that God does not exist. Features of the world that fit better with theism than with naturalism will support the claim that God does exist. If the arguments are strongly analogous, and I am right about how these features fit with theism, then either Dawkins's argument is not very strong after all, or the universe as we find it points more clearly in the direction of theism than it does atheism. I am not going to commit myself to the latter claim here.

1. A world that is ordered and susceptible to rational investigation fits better in a theistic universe. If God exists, the universe is the product of purposeful action. It is made by an intelligent mind for reasons. The fact that the universe is made by a mind for reasons leads us to expect that it can be grasped rationally. It makes sense that stable laws would allow predictions to be made and inferences to be drawn. It is not merely the case that an ordered universe fits better with theism; the level of connectedness is stronger than that. An ordered universe is what we would expect if God exists. If God exists and made the universe for reasons, it would be surprising if that universe exhibited none of the order that would make it susceptible to rational investigation. If it would be surprising that it would not be ordered, then its being ordered is something we would expect on the view that God exists.

A naturalistic universe, however, would not have to be susceptible to rational investigation. It fits perfectly well with a naturalistic universe that it be wildly chaotic. Of course, being susceptible to rational investigation is not incompatible with a universe without God, but the theory that God does not exist allows the universe to exhibit any one of a wide variety of descriptions as far as order is concerned. The fact that our universe is in fact ordered and susceptible to investigation fits better with the claim that God does exist.

2. A world with consciousness fits better in a theistic universe. Human consciousness involves several features that are difficult to fit with naturalism. Two of these features are the first-person experience and the intentionality of some of our mental states.[6] The first-person experience is illustrated by the fact that we have a special kind of access to our own mental states. I know that I am thinking about coffee at a particular time. I may not know what you are thinking. My access to your thoughts is indirect. You can tell me you are thinking about coffee, or I can deduce it from your behavior or your habits, but I can know my own thoughts directly.[7] I have ownership of my own first-person perspective.

The intentionality of mental states involves the feature that our thoughts represent or are about things in the world. Right now we can think about Niagara Falls, even though it may be hundreds of miles from where we are. How is it that something inside me, my mental states, can be about something outside of me? This is the puzzle of intentionality. Intentionality sometimes does not seem mysterious to us because we are language users. Noises articulated by a person or marks on a paper also can be about things in the world. That a string of marks such as, "There is a hot cup of coffee in the kitchen" can express (truly or falsely) a fact about the world is due, however, to the prior activity of conscious minds. We assign meaning to language. Its meaning is, then, derivative. Both the first-person perspective and the intentionality of mental states are some of the challenges for contemporary philosophy of mind.

If God exists, then the primary thing that exists is itself a conscious mind of unlimited power and intellect. This mind has its own first-person perspective, and it can think about things. The notion that such a mind, if it creates anything, would create other conscious minds that have their own first-person perspectives and can think about things is not a great mystery. Is the existence of created conscious beings something we ought to *expect* if theism is true? I want to be cautious

---

[6] R. Van Gulick lists seven features of consciousness including the qualitative character of conscious experience, the phenomenal structure, the intrinsic subjectivity of consciousness, the self-perspectival organization, and the unity of conscious experience. See R. Van Gulick, "Consciousness," in *The Stanford Encyclopedia of Philosophy*, ed. Edward N. Zalt, http://plato.stanford.edu/entries/consciousness/#4.

[7] To be sure, we do not know directly all of our mental states. We do have privileged access to some of them.

here.[8] We could develop an argument that consciousness is good and a God who is good would have reason to create other conscious beings. If this line of thought is strong, then we would have reason to expect other conscious beings to exist if God does. I do not want to press this line because I do not need to pursue it. All I need is to argue that the existence of conscious minds *fits better* with theism than with the view that the universe is naturalistic.

The view that there is no God, especially on Dawkins's version, includes the claim that any complicated living things that exist are the product of a long natural process of development from simpler living things. Any species of animals that have conscious minds originates ultimately from species that have no conscious minds by processes that are not executed by any conscious mind. If atheism is true, it is somewhat unusual that there would be any conscious minds.

I am not arguing that any naturalistic theory of consciousness will be less than plausible.[9] Rather, I am arguing that the phenomena itself is not something that fits easily into a naturalistic world. The attempt to explain consciousness within the parameters of naturalism has been designated the *hard problem* of consciousness.[10] The difficulty is indicative of, among other things, the lack of fit between atheism and the existence of conscious beings. The existence of conscious beings, like the order of the universe, is a detectable feature of the universe that confirms theism as contrasted with atheism.

3. A world with significant free agency fits better in a theistic universe. Many philosophers believe two things about human freedom. They believe that if an act is determined in any way it cannot be free, and they believe that human beings have a significant degree of freedom. They are incompatibilists and libertarians. Freedom is not compatible with determinism, and we do have some significant freedom. Other philosophers are incompatibilists but not libertarians. They believe

---

[8] The following discussion owes much to cautions and suggestions put forward in conversation by Bill Alston.

[9] Some argue in this way. For example, J. P. Moreland, "The Argument from Consciousness," in *The Rationality of Theism*, ed. P. Copan and P. K. Moser (London: Routledge, 2003), 204–20, and C. Taliaferro, "Naturalism and the Mind," in *Naturalism: A Critical Analysis*, ed. W. L. Craig and J. P. Moreland (London: Routledge, 2000), 133–55.

[10] D. J. Chalmers, "Facing Up to the Problem of Consciousness," *Journal of Consciousness Studies* 2 (3) (1995): 200–19, http://www.imprint.co.uk, and *The Conscious Mind* (New York: Oxford University Press, 1996).

that freedom and determinism are not compatible but that we are not free in the relevant sense. Such philosophers are often called hard determinists.[11] Still others are compatibilists of one sort or another. They believe that an action can be both determined and free. Determinism, on their view, does not preclude the kind of freedom necessary to ground moral responsibility.[12] If the libertarians are right, then not everything about human beings is causally determined. Thus the world of people is not a causally closed world.

If human beings are free in the sense that I am describing, then this fact is another feature of the universe that fits much better with theism than with atheism. In a naturalistic universe that is ordered enough to have complex life, we would expect events to proceed from previous events. Whether this universe would be determined, we would not expect the sort of beings that can purposely initiate actions that result in new chains of events. Yet this is the sort of agency we may have. That there are persons with libertarian agency does not seem to fit if the universe is naturalistic.[13]

If God exists, however, He acts for reasons. He chooses, among other things, to create the universe, the stars and planets, and to create other minds, plants, and animals. He creates these things because He wants to do so. He did not have to do so. He causes them to come into existence. He is not constrained to do so by factors outside Himself. God Himself is free in a libertarian sense. It is not mysterious that God would create beings that are free in the same sense. In a way similar to our discussion of consciousness, we see that the primary thing that exists in the theistic universe is a being with libertarian agency. That we find ourselves with this sort of freedom, then, is something that fits well into the theistic story. The connection between a theistic universe and the existence of other agents who are free in a libertarian sense may even be stronger. If God's reasons to create human beings include

---

[11] An example is D. Pereboom. See his *Living Without Free Will* (Cambridge: Cambridge University Press, 2001).

[12] For examples of the compatibilists, see the many essays in *The Oxford Companion to Free Will*, ed. R. Kane (Oxford: Oxford University Press, 2001). D. Dennett's work on human freedom is *Elbow Room: The Varieties of Free Will Worth Wanting* (Cambridge: MIT Press, 1984).

[13] Others who make similar arguments include P. Unger, "Free Will and Scientificalism," *Philosophy and Phenomenological Research* 65 (2002): 1–25; and S. Goetz, "Naturalism and Libertarian Agency," in *Naturalism: A Critical Analysis*, ed. Craig and Moreland, 156–86.

His purposes for their moral and spiritual development, the existence of libertarian freedom is even more to be expected. To be sure, many do not think we have this sort of freedom. They may be right, but the case for libertarian freedom is strong enough that it lends support to the sort of argument I am presenting.

4. *A world with objective moral obligations fits better with a theistic universe.* Moral obligations are objective in the sense that they hold whether one wants them to hold or one wants to fulfill them. A claim such as "It is wrong to torture a person to death just for fun" seems to be true, and the obligation it prescribes seems to be binding on all human beings. It is hard, after all, to imagine that such an obligation is binding only because of the desires or goals of some individual person or of some society. To think that objective moral obligations exist is reasonable.[14]

If there are such obligations, they make up another detectable feature of the universe that does not fit well within a naturalistic worldview. Philosopher John Mackie, in his rigorous defense of atheism, admits that such values would ground a strong argument for God:

> [Objective moral values] constitute so odd a cluster of qualities and relations that they are most unlikely to have arisen in the ordinary course of events, without an all-powerful god to create them. If, then, there are such intrinsically prescriptive objective values, they make the existence of a god more probable than it would have been without them.[15]

Philosophers who might be concerned about the theistic implications of objective moral obligations can go in one of two directions. The first direction is to argue that there are no moral obligations that are objective in the way described. This view is held by Mackie and others.[16] Attempts to develop such arguments have to overcome a significant

[14] Of course a full defense of the reality of objective obligations would have to engage all of the alternative theories. Such a defense is far outside the scope of this essay. It is enough to note that many people think there are such obligations.

[15] J. L. Mackie, *The Miracle of Theism* (Oxford: Oxford University Press, 1982), 115–16.

[16] Besides *The Miracle of Theism*, chap. 6, see his *Ethics: Inventing Right and Wrong* (New York: Penguin, 1977). For a variety of views that seem to deny the objectivity of obligations, see S. Blackburn, *Spreading the Word* (New York: Oxford University Press, 1984); and his *Ruling Passions* (Oxford: Clarendon Press, 1998). Also see A. Gibbard, *Wise Choices, Apt Feelings* (Cambridge: Harvard University Press, 1990) and M. Timmons, *Morality Without Foundations* (New York: Oxford University Press, 1999).

challenge. It is difficult to make plausible that our fundamental moral claims are either simply mistaken or just a matter of preferences.

The second direction is to try to ground the objectivity of morality apart from God.[17] This direction might be fruitful. The important point here is that even if objective moral obligations are not incompatible with a naturalistic worldview, they can be shown to be more fitting with a theistic position.

If God created human beings, He did so for a reason or reasons. Some of these reasons may ground moral obligations. For example, if God made us with moral ends in mind—if He made us so that we would embody certain virtues, for example—His setting up moral reality the way He did makes a good deal of sense. If God has spiritual purposes for us—that we would find a relationship with Him and experience Him as our highest good—He may set up moral rules as guidelines for how best to do that. Whatever God's purposes are, He would make us the kinds of beings that are subject to moral truths and that can understand and act on them.

Paul Draper is an agnostic philosopher who made a similar point to me in the context of another paper I published. He wrote, "A moral world is, however, very probable on theism."[18] In other words, if theism is true, we ought to expect a moral world, that is, a world with objective moral obligations. In contrast, such obligations do not fit as well in an atheistic world.

Sizing Up My Response to Dawkins's Argument

Dawkins's best argument against the existence of God goes as follows:

1. A universe made by God would be different from one made by natural occurrences.

2. Our universe fits better with a naturalistic universe than with a theistic universe.

---

[17] Some examples include Richard Boyd, "How to Be a Moral Realist," in *Essays on Moral Realism*, ed. G. S. McCord (Ithaca: Cornell University Press, 1988), 181–228; D. Brink, *Moral Realism and the Foundations of Ethics* (Cambridge: Cambridge University Press, 1989); and P. Railton, "Moral Realism," *Philosophical Review* 95 (1986): 163–207. Theistic philosopher R. Swinburne also wants to ground moral obligations apart from God. See *The Existence of God* (Oxford: Clarendon Press, 1979), chap. 9.

[18] P. Draper, e-mail correspondence, October 28, 1999, cited in G. E. Ganssle, "Necessary Moral Truths and the Need for Explanation," *Philosophia Christi* Series 2, vol. 2, no. 1 (2000): 105–12.

3. Therefore our universe is more likely to be a naturalistic universe than it is to be a theistic universe.

The main work in this argument is done by the second premise, that our universe fits better with a naturalistic universe than it does with a theistic universe. The detectable feature Dawkins points to that is an indication of this better fit is complex life developed over a long period of time through natural selection. In a universe with no God but with complex life, we would expect there to have been a long process of development. The fact that life did develop in this way, then, lends confirmation to the atheistic hypothesis. One virtue of Dawkins's best argument, then, is that it identifies one way in which the universe we observe points to the conclusion that no God exists. I have identified, however, four other detectable features of our universe that may be relevant to premise 2 of the argument. Each of these four features fits better with a theistic universe than with an atheistic universe.

Many philosophers have developed theories to show that these features of the universe are compatible with a naturalistic worldview. Some of these strategies are pretty good. Even if these attempts are successful, they would not undermine the strength of my criticisms of Dawkins's argument. My criticisms are not some version of a "God of the gaps" strategy. It is not the lack of a good naturalistic explanation that supports my criticism. Regardless of the availability of naturalistic explanations, these features still fit better with the view that God exists. The four features I identify show that there is good reason to reject the second premise of Dawkins's argument. Either this premise is not true or, at the very least, Dawkins has not given us strong reasons to think that it is true. Therefore, the argument he presents turns out to be not well supported. Dawkins's best argument in the end does not deliver.

Conclusion

The New Atheists present and allude to a variety of arguments either that God does not exist or that belief in God is rationally suspect. Despite the eloquent writings of the New Atheists, the reader is left with the conclusion that the case against God, as presented, is not sufficient to worry someone who already believes in God. Nor should this argument challenge one who considers belief in God for the first time.

Part 2

THE JESUS OF
HISTORY

Chapter 7

CRITERIA FOR
THE GOSPELS' AUTHENTICITY

Robert H. Stein

During the middle of the twentieth century, the leading voice
in New Testament (NT) studies was Rudolf Bultmann. This
was due not only to his writings but also because many of the students he trained went on to occupy prestigious chairs in NT both in
Germany and in other countries. Along with other scholars such as
K. L. Schmidt (*Der Rahmen der Geschichte Jesus*, 1919) and Martin
Dibelius (*Die Formgeschichte des Evangeliums*, 1919), Bultmann (*Die
Geschichte der Synoptischen Evangelien*, 1921) pioneered the work of
form criticism in the NT and with his disciples presented a negative
picture of the historical value of the NT Gospels. In America this view
was represented well by Norman Perrin who stated: "Clearly, we have
to ask ourselves the question as to whether [a] saying [in the Gospels]
should now be attributed to the early Church or to the historical Jesus,
and *the nature of the synoptic tradition is such that the burden of proof
will be upon the claim to authenticity*" (his italics).[1]

Against this radical approach moderate and conservative scholars
directed two lines of argument. One sought to demonstrate the general reliability of the gospel traditions and the NT Gospels. The other
sought to demonstrate the authenticity of the individual traditions.
The former involved several approaches. These included attacking the

---

[1] N. Perrin, *Rediscovering the Teaching of Jesus* (New York: Harper & Row, 1967), 39. Such an
approach was dominant for the most part in the work of the Jesus Seminar.

radical presuppositions of much form criticism and arguing instead that during the period between the death and resurrection of Jesus and the writing of the canonical Gospels the tradition was supervised carefully by the "eyewitnesses and servants of the word,"[2] which is exactly what the earliest historical account referring to the transmission of the gospel traditions states:

> Since many have undertaken to set down an orderly account of the events that have been fulfilled among us, just as they were handed on to us by those who from the beginning were eyewitnesses and servants of the word, I too decided, after investigating everything carefully from the very first, to write an orderly account for you, most excellent Theophilus, so that you may know the truth concerning the things about which you have been instructed. (Luke 1:1–4)[3]

One cannot simply ignore or dismiss the role of the eyewitnesses in the transmission process of the Gospel traditions as easily as the radical form critics do. Their role in this process was already established during the ministry of Jesus when they were sent out to proclaim His words and deeds (cf. Mark 6:7–13,30). A second argument in favor of the general reliability of the NT Gospels involves the traditional claim that they were authored by eyewitnesses (Matthew with the first Gospel and John with the fourth) and by companions of eyewitnesses (Mark with Peter, Luke with Paul).[4] Conservative scholars tend to argue for such "apostolic" authorship and radical scholars against this. The apologetic concern that lies behind such views is evident. The former seek to defend the early claims of such ties found in the tradition because this would mean that eyewitnesses are responsible for

---

[2] See R. H. Stein, *Studying the Synoptic Gospels: Origin and Interpretation*, rev. ed (Grand Rapids: Baker, 2001), 195–221.

[3] Scriptures quotations are from the New Revised Standard Version (NRSV).

[4] Orthodox Christianity through the centuries has always maintained that the Bible was written by those "moved by the Holy Spirit" (2 Pet 1:21) and as a result that the Bible is "inspired by God" (2 Tim 3:16). Those who believe this are thus predisposed to accept the authenticity of what is found in the Gospels and the rest of the Bible. The present essay does not deal with this, however, for it surveys the use of various criteria to establish the authenticity of various gospel traditions on the basis of arguments acceptable to both conservative and critical scholars.

the Gospel accounts and it is difficult to claim that all the miracles
they reported were either misunderstood natural events or completely
fabricated by them.[5] On the other hand, radical scholars *must* reject
any real tie between the Gospel writers and the miracle stories they reported because they are working with the presupposition that miracles
do not and cannot occur. Thus, of necessity, they must attribute the
origin and transmission of such accounts to those who were not eyewitnesses and had no association with the eyewitnesses (i.e., to the
"anonymous church").

The second line of argument developed against the views of radical form critics involves the attempt to establish the authenticity of
individual accounts found in the Gospels. These efforts sought to determine the probability of such accounts being "authentic"[6] by means
of certain "criteria."

Positive Criteria for Authenticity

The following is a listing of the major criteria used for establishing
the authenticity of various Gospel traditions.[7] In a number of instances several similar criteria are combined below into one:

1. The Criterion of Multiple Attestation

This criterion investigates the teachings and actions of Jesus to see
if they are found in independent sources of the Gospel tradition. A
common use of this criterion is to see if different sources of the Gospel

---

[5] The idea that the Gospel writers were simply "accommodating" spiritual truths into the
mythical mind-set of their readers by making up fictional miracles is almost universally rejected today. Even radical NT scholars generally agree that the Gospel writers believed that
what they were reporting was true.

[6] By "authentic" is meant that a saying or act of Jesus described in the Gospels goes back to
the historical Jesus. With respect to sayings of Jesus, some scholars have sought to demonstrate
that they are translations of Jesus' actual words, i.e., Jesus' *ipsissima verba* (the exact/very words
of Jesus) or His *ipsissima vox* (not actually a direct translation of the Aramaic sayings but a
close paraphrase of Jesus' very voice). With respect to a Gospel account involving an action
or miracle of Jesus, "authentic" means that the Gospel account reflects accurately what really
took place, i.e., a leper was miraculously healed, a blind man came to see, a dead person was
actually restored to life, etc.

[7] For a helpful bibliography, see the notes of J. P. Meier, *A Marginal Jew: Rethinking the Historical Jesus*, vol. 1 (New York: Doubleday, 1991), 185–95, esp. note 7.

tradition witness to a similar teaching of Jesus. An example of this involves Jesus' teaching that the kingdom of God had arrived in His ministry; i.e., Jesus taught a "realized" eschatology. Building on the fact that the Gospels of Matthew, Mark, and Luke look alike and the generally accepted belief that this was due to Matthew's and Luke's having used Mark and a common non-Markan source/s ("Q"), along with their own special sources not found in the other Synoptic Gospels ("M" for Matthew and "L" for Luke), these different sources (Mark, "Q," "M," and "L") were seen as independent witnesses to Jesus having taught that the kingdom of God had arrived in His ministry. Along with these witnesses found in the Synoptic Gospels,[8] John provides still another witness; and at times the quotation of a Gospel tradition by Paul, James, or another NT writer can also serve as witnesses. Used with care, the Gospel of Thomas (GT) can also serve at times as a witness. When we do this, we find the following sources indicating that Jesus claimed that the kingdom of God had arrived in His ministry: Mark (2:21–22); "Q" (Luke 11:20); "M" (Matt 5:17); "L" (Luke 17:20–21); John (4:23); Paul (1 Cor 10:11; Col 1:13; 1 Thess 2:12); GT (113). Although not an absolute proof, such evidence certainly puts the burden of proof on anyone who would deny that Jesus taught a "realized eschatology."

Another example of a teaching of Jesus that is multiply attested involves His teaching concerning God as "Father." We find this in: Mark (11:25); "Q" (Matt 7:11); "M" (Matt 6:18); "L" (Luke 12:32); John (5:36–47); Paul (Rom 8:15–16; Gal 4:6); GT (40, 44). We find multiple attestation also with respect to Jesus' using the title "Son of Man" for Himself (Mark [8:38]; "Q" [Matt 24:27]; "M" [Matt 10:23]; "L" [Luke 17:22]; John [12:23]); His pronouncement of the coming destruction of the temple (cf. Mark [13:2; 14:57–58; 15:29]; "Q" [Luke 13:34–35]; "L" [Luke 19:41–44; cf. Acts 6:14]; John [2:18–22]); His teaching on divorce (Mark [10:11–12]; "Q" [Luke 16:18]; and Paul [1 Cor 7:10–11]); and the great reversal in which the outcasts are

---

[8] If one accepts the far-less-accepted theory that Luke used Matthew and that Mark used both Matthew and Luke, the multiple sources would be: Matthew, "L," John, Paul, and GT. Since almost all of Mark (97 percent) is found in Matthew, there is essentially no "Mark" source in this view. There are, of course, other even less accepted explanations of how Matthew, Mark, and Luke are related.

entering the kingdom of God and the religious elite are being excluded (Mark [2:15–17; 10:31]; "Q" [Matt 11:16–19]; "L" [Luke 15:1–32; 19:1–10]; "M" [Matt 20:16]; and John [4:1–42]).

Related to multiple attestations by various sources is multiple attestations by various literary forms. We find for example Jesus' teaching concerning the arrival of the kingdom of God in: pronouncement stories (Mark 2:18–20; 10:13–16); miracle stories (Luke 7:11–17; 11:20–21); sayings of Jesus (Mark 1:14–15; Luke 4:42–43); parables (Mark 2:21–22; Luke 14:15–24); etc. Although the expression "kingdom of God/heaven" is not explicitly mentioned in some of these examples, they all teach that the new age, i.e., the kingdom of God, has arrived. These two criteria are most useful in demonstrating the presence of a particular theme in Jesus' teaching rather than that a specific saying is authentic.

Along with establishing the probability of various teachings of Jesus being authentic, this criterion is also helpful in demonstrating Jesus' predilection for certain literary forms. For example, the most famous form of Jesus' teaching, the parable, is found in Mark (4:2–20; 12:1–11; 13:28–29); "Q" (Luke 14:16–24; Matt 25:14–30); "M" (Matt 25:1–13,31–46); "L" (10:29–37; 15:11–32; 16:1–9); and GT (20, 57, 63). With respect to Jesus' use of antithetical parallelism (poetic parallelism in which the second line is the opposite of the first), we find examples in Mark (2:19–20; 7:15; 8:35); "Q" (Matt 6:24; 10:32–33; 12:35); "M" (Matt 5:19; 7:17; 22:14); "L" (6:21a, 25a; 16:10); and GT (41, 119). His use of circumlocution (substituting "heaven," "power," "the Great King," etc.) and the divine passive in which the passive tense is used in order to avoid using the sacred name of God (Exod 20:7) is witnessed to in various sources. Jeremias gives for the latter 21 examples in Mark, 23 in "Q," 27 in "M," and 25 in "L."[9]

2. The Criterion of Embarrassment

This criterion for authenticity seeks out examples of Jesus' teaching and actions that created difficulties for the early church. Such embarrassing material would unlikely have been created by the early church,

---

[9] J. Jeremias, *New Testament Theology: The Proclamation of Jesus*, trans. John Bowden (New York: Scribner's, 1971), 9–14.

for it would have only provided material useful for her opponents. On the contrary, the tendency of the church was to explain and ameliorate such traditions. A number of examples of this criterion come to mind. One involves the baptism of Jesus by John the Baptist. The embarrassment created by Jesus' having experienced John's "baptism of repentance for the forgiveness of sins" (Mark 1:4) early created problems for the church (cf. Matt 3:13–15, Luke's omission of who baptized Jesus [3:21–22], and John's omission of Jesus' baptism altogether [1:19–37]), even as it continues to do so today. Its presence in the Gospel tradition is not due to someone's creating this out of nothing but rather that despite its embarrassment the church "was 'stuck with'"[10] this event in Jesus' life.

The saying of Jesus in Mark 13:32 ("But about that day or hour no one knows, neither the angels in heaven, nor the Son, but only the Father") similarly reveals its authenticity by the difficulty it creates. Who in the early church would have created a saying of Jesus in which He acknowledged His ignorance of the time of the *parousia?* One need only note Luke's omission of this saying from his Gospel and the omission of "nor the Son" from numerous manuscripts of the Matt 24:36 parallel to recognize the difficulty it caused. If one compares the apocryphal gospels of the second, third, and fourth centuries, we find that the attribution of ignorance to the Son of God in Mark 13:32 is diametrically opposed to their tendency to create examples of His divine qualities and miracles and read them back into His infancy.[11] The embarrassment this verse causes is a strong argument for its authenticity.[12]

Other examples of Gospel traditions that have a strong case for being considered authentic due to the embarrassment they cause include: the tradition that Jesus was betrayed by one of His own disciples, Judas Iscariot; Jesus' saying addressed to the rich, young, ruler: "Why do you call me good? No one is good but God alone" (Mark 10:18); the

---

[10] Meier, *A Marginal Jew*, 169.

[11] Compare the Protevangelium of James!

[12] It is interesting to note the exegetical gymnastics that some scholars go through in order to deny that the Son of God was ignorant of the time of the *parousia* because they believe that as God He had to be omniscient. Such scholars would never have created Mark 13:32 and attributed this to Jesus!

threefold denial of Peter, a highly esteemed leader in the early church; Jesus' crucifixion by the Romans; Jesus' saying about being "eunuchs for the sake of kingdom of heaven" (Matt 19:12);[13] and the saying of Jesus in which He quotes His opponents as calling Him "a glutton and a drunkard, a friend of tax collectors and sinners" (Matt 11:19);[14] etc.

3. The Criterion of Dissimilarity

Of all the various criteria this criterion, also called "The Criterion of Discontinuity," was seen as the most valuable new tool for Jesus research in the middle of the twentieth-century. Ernst Käsemann, a disciple of Bultmann, brought this to the forefront of the discussion by stating, "In only one case do we have more or less safe ground under our feet [in seeking authentic material]; when there are no grounds either for deriving a tradition from Judaism or for ascribing it to primitive Christianity."[15]

In actuality this criterion has limited usage, for although the passages that fit this criterion have a strong probability of being authentic, it is applicable to only a small number of examples in the Gospel traditions. Furthermore, if we were to accept as authentic only the Jesus traditions that are dissimilar to the teachings of first-century Judaism and the early church, we might find some material whose authenticity is highly probable, but this would be atypical of Jesus as a whole. To emphasize these unique teachings of Jesus would of necessity lose sight of what is characteristic of Him. It would by definition result in an unjewish and unchristian Jesus! If we were to apply such a standard to the pursuit of the "authentic teachings of Martin Luther," the result would be a Luther who has nothing in common with sixteenth-century Lutheranism and Roman Catholicism. While individual pieces of authentic tradition might be attained, the general portrait of Luther would be grossly misleading.

---

[13] Meier, *A Marginal Jew*, 344, points out that this saying also satisfies the following criterion of dissimilarity.

[14] See J. Breech, *The Silence of Jesus: The Authentic Voice of the Historical Man* (Philadelphia: Fortress, 1983), 22–26.

[15] "The Problem of the Historical Jesus," in *Essays on New Testament Themes*, trans. W. J. Montague (Naperville, IL: Alec. R. Allenson, 1964), 37.

While helpful in identifying individual pieces of authentic tradition, this criterion is limited in providing us with a general understanding of the teachings and acts of Jesus. As for the negative use of the criterion (whenever a Gospel tradition possesses a parallel with first-century Judaism and early Christianity, it must be considered inauthentic), this is completely invalid. Having said this, there are several instances in which this criterion is useful in establishing authenticity: Jesus' rejection of fasting (Mark 2:18–20), which conflicts with the practice of Judaism in His day (Matt 9:14; Luke 18:11–12) and the early church (Matt 6:16–18; Acts 14:23); Jesus' frequent use of *Abba* in prayer, which is unique when compared to first-century Judaism, although it is found frequently in the early church (Rom 8:15–16; Gal 4:6; "Our Father, who . . ."); "there is nothing outside a person that by going in can defile, but the things that come out are what defile" (Mark 7:15) clearly conflicted with contemporary Jewish practice and the concern for not eating "unclean" food as well as the struggle of the early church with this issue (Acts 10–11) make it unlikely that Mark 7:15 is a creation of the early church![16] The fact that parables are found in the four Gospels and not the rest of the NT likewise argues in favor of the parables' being authentic.

A most valuable use of this tool involves the use of the title "Son of Man" by Jesus in the Gospels. The only clear instance of this title in contemporary Judaism in the sense in which Jesus used it is found in Dan 7:13.[17] Although this title is found 69 times in the Synoptic Gospels and 13 times in John, it is found only four times in Acts-Revelation (Acts 7:56; Heb 2:6; Rev 1:13; 14:14), and only in the first instance is it used as a title for Jesus. Thus it appears highly unlikely that the use of this title for describing the Messiah or Jesus could have arisen out of first-century Judaism or the early church.[18]

---

[16] Compare how the struggle over the question of whether Gentile converts had to be circumcised (Acts 15:1) did not lead the early church to create a teaching of Jesus concerning this and place it upon His lips.

[17] The appearance of this title in 2 Esdras/4 Ezra 13 is not an exception, for this work is generally dated ca. AD 90, and the appearance of the title in Enoch 35–71 is most probably due to a later Christian editor.

[18] It should be noted that the favorite titles of Acts-Revelation to describe Jesus are "Christ" and "Lord," whereas Jesus' favorite self-designation in the Gospels was "Son of Man." This suggests that the early church did not tend to insert its favorite Christological titles upon the

4. The Criterion of Aramaic Linguistic and Palestinian Environmental Phenomena

Although often treated as two separate criteria, it is best to treat them together as a single one[19] because they both seek to demonstrate that various Jesus traditions with these characteristics belong to the earliest stages of the Christian tradition and "the closer the approximation of a passage in the Gospels to the style and idiom of contemporary Aramaic, the greater the presumption of authenticity."[20] Although such sayings could have originated in the Palestinian, Aramaic-speaking church, the probability of this material's being authentic is considerably greater than if it betrayed Greek and non-Palestinian characteristics. This is especially true when other considerations also come into play. The presence of the following Aramaic expressions and words on the lips of Jesus in the Greek Gospel of Mark almost certainly go back to Jesus: 3:17 (*Boanerges*);[21] 5:14 (*Talitha cum*); 7:34 (*Ephphatha*); 8:12; 9:1 (*Amēn* translated as "Truly"); 14:36 (*Abba*); 15:34 (*eloi eloi lama sabachthani!*).

From the teachings of Jesus found in the Gospels, it is evident that He made great use of a variety of literary forms, such as antithetical parallelism (more than 138 examples), puns, parables, proverbs, etc. When we realize that a saying such as, "You blind guides! You strain out a gnat but swallow a camel!" (Matt 23:24), results in a pun when translated back into Aramaic (gnat, *galma*; camel, *gamla*), it is highly likely that this goes back to the historical Jesus (cf. other puns found in Mark 1:17; 4:9; 8:35; 10:31; Matt 16:18; Luke 9:59–60; John 3:8; etc.). The presence of a Palestinian context in Jesus' most famous form of teaching, the parables, also supports the authenticity of various parables. The sower in the parable of the four soils (Mark 4:2–20) sowing his seed before plowing appears to portray a uniquely Palestinian custom, and the separation of the good (kosher) fish from the bad (unkosher) fish in the parable of the great net (Matt 13:47–

---

lips of Jesus in the Gospels and that the title "Son of Man" was faithfully retained in the Jesus tradition because it stemmed from Jesus Himself.

[19] C. A. Evans, "Authenticity Criteria in Life of Jesus Research," *Christian Scholar's Review* 19 (1989): 11–12.

[20] H. E. W. Turner, *History and the Gospels: A Sketch of Historical Method and Its Application to the Gospels* (London: A. R. Mowbray, 1963), 77–78.

[21] Cf. *Bariōna* (translated as "Son of Jonah") in Matt 16:17.

50) portrays the practice of Jewish fisherman on a "sea" (probably the Sea of Galilee). Similarly, the hiring of workmen in the parable of the gracious employer (Matt 20:1–16) betrays a Palestinian environment, for elsewhere such work was generally performed by slaves. This, along with the theme of the great reversal brought about by the arrival of the kingdom of God in Matt 20:16 (cf. Mark 10:31,43–44; Matt 19:30; Luke 13:30), argues forcefully for the parable's stemming from Jesus. Whereas the presence of Aramaic linguistic and Palestinian environmental characteristics in the sayings of Jesus does not "prove" that these sayings are authentic, they lend support (sometimes "strong" support) to the probability that they are.

5. The Criterion of Tradition Contrary to Editorial Tendency

This is essentially an aspect of the criterion of dissimilarity applied specifically to the inscripturation of the Jesus traditions in the four Gospels. If we find material in the Gospels that could not have arisen out of the evangelists' own interests but is included despite those interests, this suggests that the tradition was so familiar and well-known that the evangelist did not feel free to omit it: "The inclusion of material which does especially serve his [the evangelist's] purpose may very well be taken as a testimony to the authenticity of that material, or at least to the inclusion of it in the tradition of the Church in such a clear and consistent way that the evangelist was loath to omit it."[22] In such instances the evangelists witness to the antiquity and often the authenticity of the material "in spite of themselves."[23]

Some examples of this are: Jesus' words, "For all the prophets and the law prophesied until John came" (Matt 11:13), which at first glance seems to conflict with Matthew's emphasis elsewhere of the Law's still being binding on Christians (cf. Matt 5:17–20; 7:12; 23:1–3; etc.); the reference to a Roman cohort and tribune (*chiliarchos* [John 18:12]) at the arrest of Jesus seems to conflict with John's tendency to minimize the Roman involvement in the arrest and trial of Jesus; and the portrait of the disciples in Mark, which on the one hand

---

[22] D. G. A. Calvert, "An Examination of the Criteria for Distinguishing the Authentic Words of Jesus," *New Testament Studies* 18 (1972): 219.

[23] M. Bloch, *The Historian's Craft*, trans. J. R. Strayer (New York: Alfred A. Knopf, 1953), 61.

points out their dullness and lack of faith (4:35–41; 6:35–37,52; 8:4, 14–21; etc.) and on the other to their unique calling and leadership position in the church (1:16–20; 2:14; 6:7–13,30; 16:7), argues for both of these portrayals as being historical.

6. The Criterion of Frequency

This criterion is like the criterion of multiple attestation, but instead of seeking to ascertain the breadth of a teaching or literary form in the various sources, it considers the number of times that it is found within the Gospel tradition. It assumes that a teaching of Jesus that appears frequently in the Gospel tradition is more likely to have its origin with the historical Jesus than one that is found seldom. Consequently, just as the multiple witness of various sources to a tradition increases the probability of its being authentic, so the frequency of examples of the tradition also increases its probability. This is especially true if the examples are found in different literary sources. The fact that there are 76 separate sayings of Jesus concerning the kingdom of God found in the Gospels (103 if parallels are included) argues in favor of this being an emphasis in the teachings of the historical Jesus. Likewise, the fact that parables make up 16 percent of Mark, 29 percent of "Q," 43 percent of "M," and 52 percent of "L," and that about one-third of Jesus' teachings in the Gospels is in the form of parables[24] argues for the authenticity of Jesus' use of this literary form. Similarly, the presence of 138 examples of antithetical parallelism in the Gospels[25] and 96 examples of the divine passive (21 in Mark, 23 in "Q," 27 in "M," and 25 in "L")[26] also argues for their origin in the historical Jesus. Whereas the amount of this material in the Gospels does not prove that each individual example is authentic, it shifts the burden of proof from the one who argues in favor of its historicity to the one who argues against it.[27]

---

[24] K. R. Snodgrass, "Parable" in *Dictionary of Jesus and the Gospels*, ed. J. B Green, S. McKnight (Downers Grove, IL: InterVarsity, 1992), 594.

[25] Jeremias, *New Testament Theology*, 14–20.

[26] Ibid., 9–14.

[27] Some other criteria of authenticity that have been suggested are the Criterion of Double Similarity and the Criterion of Modification by Jewish Christianity. With regard to the former, N. T. Wright argues that "when something can be seen to be credible (though perhaps deeply subversive) within first-century Judaism, *and* credible as the implied starting-point (though

7. The Criterion of Coherence

This criterion is built on the results of the six listed above. It maintains that once a critical mass of Jesus' authentic teachings and actions has been established by these criteria, we can then assume that this critically assured minimum can serve as a template to determine other probably authentic material in the Gospels.[28] Although the material fitting the criterion of coherence does not possess the degree of certainty of the first six, it enables scholars to build on the base established by the first six and construct an overall portrayal of the life and teachings of Jesus. Thus we can assume that material fitting: Jesus' teaching on the arrival of the kingdom of God, God as His Father and the Father of those who followed Him, the Son of Man as Jesus' favorite self-designation, His proclamation of the destruction of Jerusalem and the temple in the near future, His baptism by John, His betrayal by one of His disciples, the involvement of the Romans in His arrest and trial, His mother tongue's being Aramaic, His selection of the Twelve to be His disciples despite their many failures, His teaching in parables and antithetical parallelism, etc., should generally be assumed as authentic and that the burden of proof lies with those who deny their authenticity.

Negative Criteria for Authenticity

Along with the positive criteria mentioned above, several criteria have been proposed that would demonstrate the inauthenticity of the material being investigated.

1. The Criteria of Contradiction of Authentic Sayings

This assumes that, if the saying under investigation contradicts a saying that has been demonstrated as authentic, then it must be

---

not the exact replica) of something in later Christianity, there is a strong possibility of our being in touch with the genuine history of Jesus." *Jesus and the Victory of God* (Minneapolis: Fortress, 1996), 132. With regard to the latter criterion, the "Matthean exception clause" ("except on the ground of unchastity" [Matt 5:32]; "except for unchastity" [Matt 19:9])," which were added to the "Q" (Luke 16:18) and Markan versions (Mark 10:11–12; cf. also 1 Cor 7:10–11), is often given as evidence for the originality of the "Q" and Markan version of the saying.

[28] Cf. Perrin, *Rediscovering*, 43, who defines this criterion "material from the earliest strata of the tradition may be accepted as authentic if it can be shown to cohere with material established as authentic by means of the criteria of dissimilarity."

inauthentic. It also assumes that Jesus was consistent and did not con-
tradict Himself. Thus, if we find two sayings of Jesus that conflict with
each other and one has been demonstrated as authentic, the other one
must be inauthentic. It requires, however, that we make sure we interpret the meaning of a saying that is a proverb, which teaches a *general*
truth, according to the rules governing this literary form. If, for example, we do not recognize Jesus' use of hyperbole in the proverb "Do not
judge, so that you may not be judged" (Matt 7:1), we might wrongly
interpret this as contradicting "Do not give what is holy to dogs; and
do not throw your pearls before swine" (Matt 7:6). Matthew, however, clearly did not think they contradicted each other, as the close
proximity of the two sayings in his Gospel indicates. Similarly, Jesus'
saying on hating father and mother (Luke 14:26), whose authenticity is demonstrated by the embarrassment it causes (cf. the parallel in
Matt 10:37), should not be interpreted as standing in contradiction
with Mark 7:9–10 (Jesus' condemnation of the Pharisees for dishon-
oring father and mother by their tradition) because it is an example
of hyperbole. Jesus' frequent use of exaggerated language in His use
of overstatement, hyperbole, proverbs, parables, and poetry[29] should
warn us against seeing contradictions in Jesus' teachings due to a mis-
interpretation of the genre Jesus was using.

2. The Criterion of Environmental Contradiction

There can be little doubt about the validity of this criterion. If a
saying could not have been said by Jesus in the environment of first-
century Palestinian Judaism, it cannot be authentic. A hypothetical
example of this would be a saying such as "No man can ride two
motorcycles." Since motorcycles did not exist in Jesus' day, this cannot be authentic. On the other hand, the saying "It is impossible for a
man to ride two horses (and) to stretch two bows" found in GT 47 is
possible, but it does not satisfy any of the positive criteria mentioned
above. An example sometimes given as fitting this criterion is Mark
10:12, which speaks of a woman divorcing her husband. In general a
Jewish woman could not divorce her husband, but there were excep-

---

[29] See R. H. Stein, *The Method and Message of Jesus' Teachings*, rev. ed. (Louisville: Westminster
John Knox, 1994), 8ff.

tions (Sirach 23:22–27). Furthermore, in Galilee in Jesus' day a most famous example of this involved Herod Antipas, the ruler of Galilee. John the Baptist's criticism of Herod's marrying Herodias, who had divorced Herod's brother, ultimately resulted in John's losing his life (Mark 6:17–29). Thus Mark 10:12 is not an example of such an environmental contradiction. While this criterion is essentially a tautology (i.e., a saying that Jesus could not teach in first-century Palestine, He did not teach!), its usefulness is limited, for it is extremely difficult to determine which sayings of Jesus in the Gospels He could not have said.

3. The Criterion of the Tendencies of the Developing Tradition

This criterion is based on the presupposition that the passing on of the oral traditions of Jesus' words and deeds proceeded according to certain "laws." These laws can then be discovered and applied to the Gospel materials in order to strip away later accretions to the original traditions. These laws were derived by observing how the later Gospels (Matthew and Luke) used their Markan source and by observing the rules of how folktales, songs, and anecdotes were passed down orally. The optimism of discovering these "laws" and the application of them to the Gospel materials, however, was dealt a devastating blow by E. P. Sanders,[30] who argued that such "laws" did not exist and that tendencies toward traditions becoming longer and more detailed (Mark 14:47, "ear" and "slave" with Luke 22:50, "right ear" and John 18:10, "right ear" and "Malchus"; Mark 9:17 and Matt 17:15, "son" with Luke 9:38, "only son"; Mark 3:1 and Matt 12:10, "withered hand" with Luke 6:6, "right hand was withered") are paralleled by examples of traditions becoming shorter and less detailed (Mark 2:3, "four of them" with Matt 9:2, "some people [lit. 'they']" and Luke 5:18, "men"; Mark 5:22 and Luke 8:4, "Jairus, a leader of the synagogue" with Matt 9:18, "a leader of the synagogue"; Mark 6:39, "green grass" with Matt 14:19, "grass" [in Luke 9:14, "grass" is not mentioned]). How does one then apply a "law" that later traditions at times tend to become longer and more detailed and at times tend to become shorter and less

---

[30] E. P. Sanders, *The Tendencies of the Synoptic Tradition* (Cambridge: University Press, 1969).

detailed?[31] It is furthermore uncertain as to the extent that tendencies observed in the passing down of *written* traditions can be transferred to the passing down of *oral* traditions. It should also be pointed out that the tendencies observed in the passing down of folk traditions often involve a period of centuries, whereas the period in which the Gospel traditions were passed down orally before the written Gospels appeared lasted only three to four decades while the eyewitnesses were still alive!

Conclusion

Although in our investigation of the criteria for authenticity we have not discovered any that can prove beyond a shadow of a doubt that a certain teaching or action of Jesus is authentic (the criterion of dissimilarity, however, comes close to this), all the positive criteria, when satisfied, help increase the probability that the passage being investigated is authentic. In the instances when the passage being investigated satisfies several criteria, the probability of its being authentic increased dramatically, and each individual criterion acts as a strand to form a braided cord of positive arguments witnessing to its authenticity. While absolute certainty is not possible,[32] those passages in the Gospels that fulfill these criteria do change the burden of proof. The burden of proof now clearly shifts from the need to prove a passage's authenticity to the need to prove its inauthenticity. Furthermore, if sufficient examples of the Gospel traditions can be shown to be authentic and the Gospel portrayal of Jesus in general can in numerous places be demonstrated as reliable, then the Gospel material as a whole should be assumed to be "innocent (authentic) unless proven guilty (inauthentic)."

---

[31] Cf. Sanders (ibid., 272) who states *"dogmatic statements that a certain characteristic proves a certain passage to be earlier than another are never justified"* (his italics).

[32] This is clear in the classical confessions of the Christian Church. "The Bible evidences itself to be God's Word by the heavenliness of its doctrine, the unity of its parts, its power to convert sinners and to edify saints; but the Spirit of God only, bearing witness by and with the Scriptures in our hearts, is able fully to persuade us that the Bible is the Word of God" (*The Baptist Catechism*, answer to question 5). Similarly, only the Spirit of God, working through various arguments such as the criteria for authenticity can move a person from believing in the probability of the authenticity of a Gospel tradition to being convinced of its certainty.

A major presupposition that dominates the thinking of radical Gospel scholars and is seldom acknowledged, however, predetermines the conclusion of any investigation of a Gospel tradition dealing with certain acts of Jesus. As a result these actions, even if they were to satisfy all the positive criteria for authenticity, are assumed inauthentic. This presupposition has furthermore nothing to do with the investigation of the Gospel material. For many biblical scholars, careful historical research, i.e., "the historical critical method," assumes a closed universe, in which miracles cannot happen. Consequently, before any miracle story is investigated, the conclusion as to its historicity has already been made. The stories are inauthentic; they are myths. Miracles do not happen! It is evident that for followers of this understanding of the historical critical method, the criteria for authenticity, while useful with respect to the teachings of Jesus, are useless for investigating any of the traditions of Jesus' miracles in the Gospels. The criteria are worthless because of a predetermined presupposition that precludes the possibility of miracles. All such accounts must be "myths," and criteria for investigating what happened in history cannot be used with respect to fictional accounts.

For those who maintain that the universe is open to the God who created it and therefore that miracles are possible, the criteria for authenticity are useful in establishing continuity between the Jesus of history and the Christ of faith found in the Gospels. By use of the various criteria, the probability of numerous sayings and nonmiraculous actions of Jesus being authentic can be demonstrated. Similarly, by various criteria, especially the criteria of multiple attestation and Aramaic and Palestinian environmental phenomena (Mark 1:40–45 [esp. v. 44]; 5:35–43 [esp. v. 41]), the authenticity of the miracles stories is strongly attested. Together they give strong support to the overall reliability of the portrayal of Jesus found in the Gospels.

Chapter 8

JESUS THE SEER

Ben Witherington III

All scholars agree on few things when it comes to the historical Jesus. One of those, however, is that Jesus used two key phrases in His public discourse: "Son of Man" and "kingdom of God." What is seldom asked about this usage is: "Is there an Old Testament [OT] text where we find both these phrases or essential concepts together?" The answer surprisingly is yes.

Daniel 7

Daniel 7:13–14 reads as follows:

> "In my vision at night I looked, and there before me was one *like a son of man* [*bar enasha*], coming with the clouds of heaven. He approached the Ancient of Days and was led into his presence. He was given authority, glory and sovereign power; all peoples, nations and men of every language worshiped him. His dominion is an everlasting dominion that will not pass away, and his kingdom is one that will never be destroyed" (my emphasis).[1]

This text should be compared to Dan 7:25–27 where we are told this everlasting kingdom is handed over to the saints and is taken away from the beastly ruler and empire which had existed before. The whole

[1] Scripture quotations are from the New International Version (NIV).

pattern of inhumane empires (four of them) followed by a human and humane one is the big picture. This should be compared to 2 Sam 7:12: "When your days are over . . . , I will raise up your offspring to succeed you, . . . and I will establish his kingdom."

Notice the difference between these two texts which were read messianically in Jesus' day. The one refers to a normal succession of a royal family—from David to his offspring. The other refers to an everlasting kingdom ruled by "the one like a son of man" who can be so closely identified with the saints that they can be said to rule in Him or through Him. Daniel 7:13–14 is remarkable in another regard as well. The figure in question comes down (not up) from heaven for the judgment scene upon the earth and is handed authority, power, etc., to rule by the Ancient of Days. Of course in the OT the *yom Yahweh* was normally envisioned as the Day that Yahweh came down in theophanic fashion and judged.

The Son of Man

Even on a minimalist approach to the evidence about the historical Jesus, while we do not much find Jesus calling Himself Son of David, nor does He ever cite 2 Samuel 7, scholars are clear about Jesus referring to Himself as Son of Man, and His speaking of an everlasting kingdom which He is inaugurating. The question that begs to be asked is, "What kind of person thinks he can personally reign forever—not him and his offspring but just him?" Or again, what sort of person thinks he can bring the eschatological saving reign of God upon the earth, the one that eclipses and replaces all previous human attempts at dominion?

My answer is, "A person who thought he was both human and divine." And here is the interesting bit. The title "Son of Man," not the title "Messiah" or some other more familiar ones, has the potential to convey the notion of both humanness and more than humanness. And interestingly, the title Son of Man was not all that much used in early Jewish messianic speculation, and so Jesus was free to fill it with the content He had in mind without being pigeonholed by other people's preconceived notion of what a Savior or Messiah must be, and do. In short, Jesus, in His prevalent use of these two concepts conveyed an exalted image of who He is and what He came to do and be, and this and a few other things Jesus said likely led to exclusive claims being made about Him by His first followers, claims such as Jesus being the way, the truth, and the life and no one comes to God except through Jesus. While that claim is found in John 14, in essence the same sort of claim is made by Jesus in Matthew 11 where Jesus says that no one knows the Father except the Son and those to whom the Son reveals God. Notice the language of special revelation. Jesus claims to have special revelation from God that others do not have. This saying, if authentic, places Jesus in the category of a remarkable seer. Do we have other evidence that suggests this as well? In fact we do.

The earliest form of the story of Jesus' baptism is in Mark's Gospel, a story which all stripes of scholars believe contains historical substance, not least because you don't make up a story about your messianic figure being baptized by another remarkable prophetic figure if you want people to think Jesus is more important than John the Baptizer. In order to understand the account fully in Mark 1, we need to say something about the history of prophecy.

Prophecy in the ancient Near East (ANE), including in the biblical tradition, was a complex phenomenon. One of the features which rose to prominence in biblical prophecy during the exile was apocalyptic prophecy, which is to say prophecy based on visions. Sometimes these were day visions; sometimes they came in the form of night visions or dreams, but in either case they were different from the earlier oracular forms of prophecy which were a matter of the prophet's listening and then repeating verbatim what he believed the deity was saying. With visionary prophecy a whole new element was added to the picture—namely, what the prophet had seen in a vision. I need to be clear at this juncture that visions, whether waking or in dreams, were not seen as purely subjective phenomena in antiquity—not something generated, for example, by an overactive imagination or wish projection. No, these were seen as one form of revelation from God; and increasingly during and after the Babylonian exile (sixth century BC), they were seen as the main form of revelation from God.

Scholars have often remarked on the fact that Jesus does not use the oracular formula "thus says Yahweh," nor does He quote God, so to speak. On this basis some scholars have concluded that Jesus was not a prophet in the Old Testamental sense. This, however, is incorrect as it involves mistaking the part for the whole. Jesus clearly was not an *oracular* prophet like Isaiah or Amos. Rather, He was a *visionary* prophet like Daniel or Zechariah. It is no accident that Jesus was indebted to these two sources for His sense of calling and self-understanding. He, too, was a visionary prophet like those earlier Jewish figures.

In the Markan account of the baptism, we find several major features of a visionary account. The sky is said to split open (cf. Rev 1:4); the Spirit of God descends, which is described in typical apocalyptic diction ("it was like . . ."); and then and only then, Jesus hears the divine voice speaking directly to Him, saying, "You are my beloved Son." Mark's account differs clearly enough from Matthew's in that it recounts a public occasion but a private vision that happened on that public occasion. The voice from above did not speak to everyone but only to Jesus. The Matthean account makes it a more public affair. We need to stick with the earlier account.

What we can say about what happened on this occasion, besides Jesus' being baptized by John, is that Jesus received identity confirmation, an indirect commissioning, and indeed an empowering for ministry. Only after this event the ministry is said to begin. We are told in Mark 1:15 that Jesus begins with a proclamation John himself could have made: "Repent for the Dominion of God is at hand."

Less often noticed than some of these features of the story is the connection it has with the sequel. Mark 1:12 is emphatic: the Spirit cast Jesus out into the Judean wilderness, and He spent 40 days there being tempted by Satan. He is with the wild animals, and angels attend him. What is less seldom noticed is that having just been called God's Son, He is now tested as a royal figure in a fashion like the king was tested in Daniel when he was out in the fields with the animals or as Solomon was tested in *Wisdom* of *Solomon* (one of the apocryphal books included in the Septuagint). But here again we are still in the realm of vision, visions that Jesus saw while in the wilderness.

The Son of God

Mark, of course, only mentions the visionary experience in passing, but Matthew and Luke give us a detailed account. The Matthean account seems to be closer to the original form of the story, and we will follow it. Notice immediately that Jesus is tested in regard to the same title that had been revealed to Him at the baptism: "Son of God" (in the form "if you are the Son of God, then . . ."). Of course, some scholars have scoffed at treating this story as historical, completely forgetting it is possible to take this as the relating of a visionary experience Jesus had while full of the Spirit, and we might add in a limenal state (i.e., when consciousness hovers between the visionary and the nonvisionary). Matthew is explicit that Jesus had these visions from the nefarious one *after* having fasted for 40 days and 40 nights, which makes the first temptation, to turn stones into bread, a natural one. Now one of the most remarkable features about this visionary encounter with the adversary, Satan, is that Satan is tempting Jesus to do things mere mortals cannot do. I have known some people who can turn bread into stones but not any that have been tempted to do the opposite. The point here is that Jesus is being tempted to act in a fashion that only a divine Son of God was capable of doing. This story then undergirds the theology that Jesus was no ordinary or mundane messianic figure, and as with the title "Son of Man," the story suggests a more than mundane character for Jesus.

Now a temptation is hardly a temptation if you know perfectly well you can't carry it off. The point here is that Jesus is being tempted to act in ways that would obliterate His true humanity and His identification with us. The essence of Jesus' being truly human and acting in accord with that is being put to the test. To be human means to have certain limitations of time, space, knowledge, and power. Yet Jesus believed He could transcend these limitations in some fashion, and here He was being tempted to go ahead and do so. What kind of person believes such things about himself? Notice then that Jesus responds to Satan by quoting Scripture, a resource any human being could use to combat evil. Jesus throughout these Gospels acts by the power of the Spirit and by using the Word of God, the same two resources these Gospels say Jesus bequeathed to His followers. This is interesting.

Returning to the vision itself, we see the second temptation is to cast Himself off the pinnacle of the temple. Here Satan becomes the exegete and cites Ps 91:11–12 to encourage Jesus to do it. The text refers to ministering angels who would bear Him up if He leaped off the pinnacle and not allow Him to harm Himself. This is interesting since Mark had mentioned that Jesus was ministered to by angels in the wilderness. But again, Jesus resists the temptation. Notice that here Jesus responds, in a battle of Bible quotes, "Do not put the Lord your God to the test" (Matt 4:7). Scholars have resisted seeing this as evidence that Jesus placed Himself in the category of the Lord God, but surely that is the most natural implication here, and it is interesting that Jesus' brother James is later to say emphatically that God cannot be tempted and He tempts no one (Jas 1:13). Perhaps he knew of the story of Jesus' vision quest and battles with the powers of darkness.

The third and final test is indeed the climactic one where Jesus is offered the kingdoms of the world if He will just bow down and worship Satan. Jesus refuses to do so and like a good monotheist says only the one God should be worshiped. Notice and compare the reply to test 2 and the reply to test 3. In test 2 Jesus identifies Himself with the Lord God; in test 3 His reply distinguishes Himself from Yahweh. What sort of person sees both identity with and distinction from God as categories he could freely use to describe himself?

Lest we think that we have exhausted the evidence for Jesus as a Seer, it is not so. There are interesting logia, like Luke 10:18 where Jesus, upon the report of His disciples performing exorcisms successfully like their Master, says, "I saw Satan fall like lightning from heaven." This should be compared to a text like Mark 3 where Jesus' exorcisms are recognized by His antagonists, but they attribute them to His being in league with the Devil. Jesus counters by saying that to the contrary He had first to bind that strong man Satan before He could loose his captives. Far from being in league with Satan, the work of Jesus has been to destroy his strongholds and liberate his captives. This is what Luke 10:18 suggests as well. The most frequent sort of miracle predicated of Jesus in Mark is exorcism. Furthermore, it is the sort of activity which led to later rabbinic charges that Jesus was a magician, dabbling in the dark arts. There must indeed be a historical foundation for this aspect of Jesus' ministry, whatever one may personally believe about demons.

Whether one personally believes in the powers of darkness is irrelevant to the historical quest for understanding Jesus, as many early Jews, probably most of them, did believe in such beings, and there is no good reason to doubt Jesus did as well. We cannot eliminate evidence from our quest for the historical Jesus just because we don't share such a belief system or particular belief. Jesus was without doubt different from many moderns in what He believed, and if the goal is to understand Him and understand His self-understanding and presentation, then it is a mistake to evaluate the evidence with certain antisupernatural prejudices or biases in place. This may tell us much about ourselves, but such biases skew a fair and accurate assessment of Jesus' self-understanding and self-presentation.

Our next port of call is Matt 11:27, the so-called Johannine thunderbolt. This text presents Jesus as claiming that no one knows the Father but Jesus and those to whom Jesus reveals Him. It speaks to Jesus' apocalyptic mentality and frame of reference. The basic assumption of apocalyptic is that heavenly and spiritual things are now hidden from fallen mortal gaze and can only be known if they are revealed through a revelator, one who sees into the other realm. Jesus is presented as one such person who does so. Indeed, Jesus presents Himself as one who plays out the apocalyptic script of Daniel and Zechariah not only by proclaiming the kingdom and calling Himself Son of Man but even by performing prophetic sign acts like riding into Jerusalem on a donkey, as Zechariah spoke of, or cleansing the temple. The closer we look at the drama of Jesus' life, the more He seems to be dancing to an apocalyptic tune not entirely of His own making.

And this brings us to the trial narrative in Mark 14. After offering a whole chapter of prophetic pronouncements about the near and more distant future, in Mark 13 (notice that the cosmic signs are only associated with the Second Coming account, whereas the signs upon the earth are associated with preliminary mundane events which lead to the destruction of the temple), we have the trial narratives seriatim.

While Jesus predicted the demise of the Herodian temple within a biblical generation (40 years)—a prediction which was "spot on," as the British would say, since the temple fell in AD 70 and Jesus made the prediction in AD 30 not long before His own demise—what is more important for our purposes is that the predictions about the return of the Son of Man in Mark 13:32 prepare for the prediction at the trial narrative in Mark 14:62 where Jesus partially quotes Dan 7:13. Here to the high priest who assumed he was judging Jesus and would have the last word about Him, Jesus in effect turns the tables and says to the high priest, "Yes, I am Messiah, Son of God, but what you really need to know is that you will see the Son of Man coming on the clouds to a theater near you, judging you." What kind of person thinks his own life will have an earthly sequel?

I have stuck carefully to our earliest witness Mark and the Synoptics in this essay without bringing the later fourth Gospel into the discussion. This was intentional, but the Christological portrait of Jesus in Mark is hardly any less exalted than the one in John; it's just differently focused. John famously does not give us exorcism stories, nor does he mention Jesus' being an exorcist. But just as the first canonical Gospel raises the question, "What sort of person can get in a championship cage match with Satan and live to tell the tale?" so the last Gospel raises the question, "What sort of person thinks he came from God, and is 'of God'?" The claims are presented differently, but the end result is much the same. The canonical Gospels present this in a clearly heavenly light, all the while emphasizing His true humanity as well. In other words, there is no nonmessianic Jesus to be found at the bottom of the well of historical inquiry. Jesus made some remarkable claims for Himself and His ministry; the historian's job is not to explain the claims away but rather to explain them.

Concluding Remarks

As I draw this essay to a close, I would like to remind us all that who a person is, who a person claims to be, and who others say a person is can be different. The age-old question "Who do you say that I am?" is actually preceded by the historical question, "Who did Jesus think He was, and whom did He claim to be?" There is continuity between Jesus' self-understanding, His self-presentation, and the later theologizing that was done about Jesus. They are not identical, but a historical continuum binds these things together.

The earliest disciples after Easter had been Jesus' disciples before Easter; and Easter, whatever it entailed, did not have the effect of creating massive amnesia on the part of these persons. A historian has to explain how the high Christology of the church could have arisen after the unexpected and precipitous demise of Jesus through crucifixion. This conundrum becomes more puzzling, not less, for those who don't believe in Jesus' rising from the dead than for those who do.

Martin Dibelius, the old German form critic, said that one must posit a large enough X to explain how Easter faith could have arisen after the shaming and crucifixion of Jesus. On any showing the crucifixion should have put an end to the Jesus movement once and for all in an honor and shame culture like early Judaism. The disciples on the road to Emmaus in Luke 24 were not heading for a spiritual retreat experience; they were leaving town with their tails between their legs mumbling "we had hoped [past tense] that he was the one who was going to redeem Israel" (v. 21). Their actions spoke as loudly as their words: they had abandoned such hope until fate, in the form of an appearance of a stranger, intervened. The X which Dibelius spoke of, which bridges the life of Jesus and the rise of Christianity, must include the fact that Jesus made some exalted claims about Himself directly and indirectly long before His disciples responded in kind. He is, as Eduard Schweizer once said, "the man who fits no formula."[2] In this regard He was as much of an enigma as the visions He related to His followers. It still takes divine intervention from above to decode the man and His mysterious self-revelation, for "no one knows the Son except the Father"—or so I'm told.[3]

---

[2] See chapter 2, "The Man Who Fits No Formula," in E. Schweizer, *Jesus*, trans. D. E. Greene (London: SCM, 1971).
[3] For further discussion on the themes in this essay, see B. Witherington III, *Jesus the Seer: The Progress of Prophecy* (Peabody, MA: Hendrickson, 1999).

Chapter 9

THE RESURRECTION OF JESUS TIME LINE
THE CONVERGENCE OF EYEWITNESSES
AND EARLY PROCLAMATION

Gary R. Habermas

P erhaps the majority of defenses of Jesus' resurrection concentrate on three different aspects: the failure of naturalistic theories to explain this event, historical evidences for Jesus' appearances, as well as the empty tomb. In this essay I will take a different tack. I will begin with the late first century and work my way back to the death of Jesus in about AD 30.[1] My purpose will be to establish a different approach to the proclamation of the resurrection. I contend that current critical scholarship even agrees to the exceptionally early date of this proclamation as well as the eyewitness nature of those who made the claims.

Before beginning, we need to set a couple of key parameters regarding the study of historiography. Certainly in the recent writing of history, perhaps the two major components of any study are, wherever possible, to secure testimony that is both eyewitness and as close as possible to the events in question, especially when there are also enough data to answer alternative scenarios. Eyewitness testimony plus early observation are certainly crucial. They were also valued in ancient times as well.[2]

---

[1] I am using "about AD 30" as the crucifixion date, but if it were 33, as some scholars say, then the dates would simply move forward. While the earlier dates would change, the distances in between would remain the same, up until 1 Corinthians (about 55).

[2] For example, second-century historian Lucian of Samosata wrote arguably the only ancient

AD 60–100: The Composition of the Gospels

When speaking of the death and resurrection of Jesus, most evangelical apologists begin with the reliability of the four Gospels. A popular approach often argues that these books were written either by apostles (as with Matthew and John) or their close associates (as with Mark and Luke) and that these volumes were written between AD 60 and 100. The point is that since these books were written 30 to 70 years after Jesus' death, they provide excellent material for reconstructing the earliest years of the Christian faith. As such we can learn credible information regarding Jesus' crucifixion as well as His resurrection appearances.

On the other hand, however, nonevangelical scholars generally dispute these specific authors although they change only slightly the dates of composition. They usually treat the four Gospels as anonymous documents although there are some notable exceptions.[3] Scholars differ as to how much of the Gospel accounts reflect reliably historical information. Like the dates given by evangelicals, these books are usually dated between AD 60 and 100, although the critical tendency is to date the Synoptic Gospels a little later. Mark is often placed at about AD 70, while Matthew and Luke are dated about AD 80–85. There is widespread agreement regarding John, which is generally placed by all scholars in the last decade of the first century. Even critical scholars tend to differ only slightly from these common dates.[4]

How do these critical conclusions affect the defense of the resurrection mentioned above? Interestingly, in spite of questioning the authorship of the Gospels, critical scholars have also defended the

work on the art of historiography, entitled *How to Write History* (in *Lucian in Eight Volumes*, trans. K. Kilburn, The Loeb Classical Library, vol. 6 [Cambridge: Harvard University Press, 1959]). Lucian addressed the subject of weeding out subjective factors from the historian's work (6:7–15, 72–73, 39–43), as well as the proper use of eyewitness testimony, unlike the unnamed historian who claimed to be an eyewitness but Lucian decided he plainly was not (6:43–47)!

[3] For the best recent example of a critical scholar who defends the use of reliable and even eyewitness traditions behind the Gospels, see R. Bauckham, *Jesus and the Eyewitnesses: The Gospels as Eyewitness Testimony* (Grand Rapids: Eerdmans, 2006).

[4] For example, B. D. Ehrman, *The New Testament: A Historical Introduction to the Early Christian Writings*, 2nd ed. (New York: Oxford University, 2000), 43; R. W. Funk, R. W. Hoover, and the Jesus Seminar, *The Five Gospels: The Search for the Authentic Words of Jesus* (New York: Macmillan and Polebridge Press, 1993), 128.

historicity of the resurrection although they usually emphasize Paul's epistles.[5] Even for those who prefer the Gospel traditions, we are somewhere between three and seven decades after the events in question. Especially since we are dealing with the events of ancient history, this is a relatively short period of time. After all, the well-known biography of Alexander the Great, included by Plutarch in his *Lives*, was composed approximately four centuries after Alexander's death.

AD 50–62: Dating the "Authentic" Pauline Epistles

As just hinted, most critical scholars today rely chiefly on Paul's epistles when speaking of particulars regarding Jesus' death and resurrection. Of the 13 books that bear His name, six to eight are accepted as being authentic. In the latter group the unanimously accepted texts include at least Romans, 1 and 2 Corinthians, Galatians, Philippians, and 1 Thessalonians. Philemon and Colossians are sometimes included, as well. These books are usually dated in the decade between AD 50 and 60. Even critical scholars agree regarding both Paul's authorship and the dates.[6]

These "authentic" Pauline epistles are preferred even over the Gospels because of the critical belief that we know the author and dates of composition for these writings whereas we do not know the authors and are somewhat less specific regarding the dates of the Gospels. Further, Paul spends less time on the life of Jesus in general but provides important specifics regarding Jesus' death and resurrection appearances from a much earlier time.

The key text in this regard is certainly 1 Cor 15:3ff. In the previous two verses, Paul refers to his earlier preaching to this audience. So while the epistle was written approximately 54–55, Paul's original preaching in Corinth would have been dated at least a couple of years earlier, perhaps as early as 50, as noted by Koester.[7]

---

[5] The best example is N. T. Wright, *The Resurrection of the Son of God* (Minneapolis: Fortress, 2003). For Wright's conclusions on the Gospel data, see especially chapter 9; for Paul's testimony, see chapters 5–8.

[6] For example, Ehrman, *New Testament*, 44; Funk and Hoover, *Five Gospels*, 128; H. Koester, *Introduction to the New Testament*, 2 vols., *History and Literature of Early Christianity* (Philadelphia: Fortress, 1982), 2:103–4.

[7] Koester, *Introduction*, 2:103–4.

We have some important reasons for favoring Paul's epistles over the Gospels. Paul wrote this material concerning Jesus' death and resurrection appearances in 1 Cor 15 just 25 years after the crucifixion of Jesus, but he preached this message to the Corinthians several years earlier, about 20 years after the events. This latter figure is only half the time span from Jesus to the Gospel of Mark and less than one-third the distance between Jesus and the Gospel of John. As we will see, Paul's account provides far more reasons than these.

In one of the most important comments in the entire New Testament, Paul tells us that he received the material in 1 Corinthians 15:3ff from someone else. As he states: "For what I received I passed on to you as of first importance" (1 Cor. 15:3).[8]

This comment opens an entirely new window on the question of reliability. Here we must interrupt briefly our current discussion. What if there were some way to know the nature of the earliest apostolic preaching and teaching between the years of AD 30 and 50? What if we knew some of the content of the earliest Christian preaching prior to the writing of the first New Testament book? Some will say that we already have this sort of material in the book of Acts. However, that book is regularly dated between AD 65 and 85, or 35 to 55 years after the crucifixion.[9] Again, this is a respectable time frame for ancient reports. But what if we had material from even prior to the early Pauline epistles?

Actually, several New Testament portions make precisely this claim. We just mentioned one of the texts in 1 Cor 15, where Paul states that he passed on precisely what he had received from others (v. 3). Paul mentions two other examples in the same book, both of which occur in chapter 11. He praises his hearers for holding firmly to the traditions or teachings he passed on to them (v. 2). Later he reported that he had received the tradition regarding the Lord's Supper and passed it along to his readers (11:23).

Many other texts in the New Testament make similar claims. Sometimes a teaching is introduced with the words, "Here is a trust-

---

[8] Scripture references are from the New International Version (NIV).
[9] J. Drane, *Introducing the New Testament* (San Francisco: Harper and Row, 1986), 236–38.

worthy saying."[10] Somewhat reminiscent of 1 Cor 11:2, the early Christians were to continue in the teachings or traditions they had received (2 Thess 3:6).

On other occasions, even though there is no explicit statement from the author that a tradition is being passed on, critical scholars are still in wide agreement with regard to a number of these texts. They are often indicated by the sentence structure, diction, parallelism, and other stylized wording. Sometimes these texts are apparent because the syntax breaks between the citation and the larger text, just like when we try to quote someone today and we sometimes cannot make our syntax fit theirs. On still other occasions texts contain brief theological snippets that appear to be passed down for purposes of memorization. A great example is what is generally agreed by both liberals and conservatives alike to be a Christological hymn in Phil 2:6–11.

One benefit of these early traditions (also called creeds or confessions) is that they reproduce teachings that are sometimes earlier than the book in which they appear. Therefore, if the material is also deemed to be reliable, especially if it appears to be apostolic in nature, then it exhibits both trustworthy comments that are also early, sometimes exceptionally so.[11]

Precisely for this last reason we must ask what is the most likely scenario for Paul's reception of the tradition in 1 Cor 15:3ff? The apostle claims in a straightforward manner that he passed this information on as he received it. Do we have any information regarding when Paul may have received this account? And who passed it on to him? Since it concerns the death and resurrection appearances of Jesus, the center of early Christianity, having some indication of Paul's source is important.

AD 34–36: Paul's First Trip to Jerusalem

Strangely enough the next stage in the process was discovered not by biblical conservatives but by critical scholars. Further, there is near

---

[10] See 1 Tim 1:15; 3:1; 4:9; 2 Tim 2:11; cf. Titus 1:9.

[11] For the best treatment of this subject, see the classic volume by O. Cullmann, *The Earliest Christian Confessions*, trans. J. K. S. Reid (London: Lutterworth, 1949); cf. J. Jeremias, *The Eucharistic Words of Jesus*, trans. N. Perrin (London: SCM, 1966).

unanimity regarding these conclusions from those who address the issues. Paul asserts more than once that he received traditions from others and passed them on to his hearers. Does he give any indications of where and when he obtained these data?

From everything we know, Paul was a careful scholar. He had been trained well in the Old Testament tradition, referring to himself as an individual who was exceptionally zealous for the Law, as a Pharisee and "a Hebrew of Hebrews" (Phil 3:4–6). He had advanced beyond others of his own age and distinguished himself by supporting without question the tradition of Judaism. As such, he violently persecuted early Christians (Gal 1:13–14). Then he testified that he met the risen Jesus, accounting for the total transformation of his life (1 Cor 9:1; 15:8–10; Gal 1:15–16).

Paul attests that immediately after his conversion, he did not consult with anyone. Since he had seen an appearance of Jesus and had been instructed by him to preach to the Gentiles, he did not think it was necessary to check this all out with others. Jesus' authority was greater than that of anyone else. However, three years later he did visit Jerusalem and spent 15 days with Peter and James, the brother of Jesus (Gal 1:15–18).

What happened during this incredible meeting involving these three great Christian leaders? It must have been eventful, to say the least. In the now famous words of Cambridge University New Testament scholar C. H. Dodd, "We may presume that they did not spend all the time talking about the weather."[12]

What did they discuss? It might be said that the first rule of literary criticism is to interpret a text in its context. Applying that rule here, the context both immediately before and immediately after Paul's statement concerns the nature of the gospel message. Therefore, critical scholars have long thought that the context makes clear that this subject would form the center of this historic meeting. Besides, what else would Paul and the other two apostles more likely discuss other than the center of their faith? For these reasons it is widely concluded that the gospel constituted the focus of their conversation.

[12] C. H. Dodd, *The Apostolic Preaching and Its Developments* (Grand Rapids: Baker, 1980, repr.), 16.

Further, the majority of critical scholars who answer the question think that Paul received the early tradition recorded in 1 Cor 15:3ff. during this visit to Jerusalem and that he received it from Peter and James, who, incidentally, are the only other individuals besides Paul whose names appear in the list of Jesus' resurrection appearances. Based on the usual date for Paul's conversion of between one and three years after Jesus' crucifixion, Paul's reception of this material in Jerusalem would be dated from approximately four to six years later, or from AD 34–36. On many occasions I have documented this critical scholarly conclusion as to when and from whom Paul received this material.[13] Bauckham has also recently noted the scholarly consensus on this point.[14]

Besides the subject matter itself and the three individual names in the list of appearances, another hint regarding this process is found in Gal 1:18. When speaking of his time with Peter and James, Paul used the Greek term *historēsai*, which is often defined as gaining knowledge by personal inquiry or investigation.[15] So Paul apparently meant us to understand that he was using this quality time with the other two apostles in order to probe their understanding of the gospel message. But even without his telling us this, it makes the most sense of his taking a trip to Jerusalem to speak with the major apostles there. Moreover, the topic was important to Paul, for he paused afterward to tell his reader: "I assure you before God that what I am writing you is no lie" (Gal 1:20).

We must keep in mind here the vital difference between the formal tradition that Paul passed along to others, which as far as we know was written down for the first time in 1 Cor 15:3ff., and the particular *content* about which that tradition speaks. Virtually nothing depends on Paul's having received this tradition during precisely this meeting in Jerusalem, even though that is when critical scholars tend to place it. By far the more important matter concerns Paul's knowledge of the

[13] For examples, see G. R. Habermas, *The Historical Jesus: Ancient Evidence for the Life of Christ* (Joplin, MO: College Press, 1996), especially 152–57; "The Resurrection Appearances of Jesus," in R. D. Geivett and G. R. Habermas, *In Defense of Miracles: A Comprehensive Case for God's Action in History* (Downers Grove, IL: InterVarsity, 1997), esp. 263–70.

[14] Bauckham, *Jesus*, 265–66.

[15] See W. Farmer, "Peter and Paul, and the Tradition Concerning 'The Lord's Supper' in I Corinthians 11:23–25," *Criswell Theological Review* 2 (1987): 122–30.

gospel content as preached by Peter and James, the brother of Jesus, which comprises the creed. Thus, all we really need to know here is that Paul discussed the gospel particulars with them, and this seems well assured.

In fact, critical scholars are so sure about this last point that Dodd concluded, "The date, therefore, at which Paul received the fundamentals of the gospel cannot well be later than some seven years after the death of Jesus Christ. It may be earlier." Therefore, "Paul's preaching represents a special stream of Christian tradition which was derived from the main stream at a point very near to its source." And lest some say that Paul confused this message, Dodd concludes, "Anyone who should maintain that the primitive Christian gospel was fundamentally different from that which we have found in Paul must bear the burden of proof."[16] But we do not have to take C. H. Dodd's word for all this. I have listed dozens of contemporary critical scholars, including skeptics, who espouse the general scenario we have outlined here.[17]

Thus, the majority of critical scholars think that Paul received his traditional material on the death and resurrection of Jesus from Peter and James the brother of Jesus while he was in Jerusalem, approximately a half dozen years after Jesus' crucifixion. I made the further point that even if one questions the precise time and place of Paul's actual reception of this creedal material, it is exceptionally difficult to avoid the conclusion that these three apostles at least discussed the nature of the gospel content at that time.

AD 45–50: Paul's Later Trip to Jerusalem

Here we must digress a bit in our time line before we can keep moving backward toward Jesus' death. This occasion was better left until after the previous discussion. Immediately after describing his trip to Jerusalem, Paul relates that he visited the city of Jerusalem again, 14 years later (Gal 2:1). During what year did this second meeting occur? Paul dates it from his previous discussion in chapter 1, causing scholars to wonder whether Paul meant the time from his conversion

---

[16] Dodd, *Apostolic*, 16.

[17] For these lists, see G. R. Habermas, *The Risen Jesus and Future Hope* (Lanham, MD: Rowman and Littlefield, 2003), endnotes 75–102, in particular.

or from his first trip to Jerusalem. Also, scholarly opinion varies as to whether the meeting in Gal 2:1–10 is the same as the account in Acts 15:1–31. Regardless, the difference is slight. Koester prefers a date of AD 48.[18]

Once again Paul's topic is clearly that of the gospel. It seems to me that verse 2 is among the most incredible comments in the New Testament. Paul attested that he specifically journeyed to Jerusalem to visit the leading apostles, in order to set before them the gospel message that he had been preaching "for fear that I was running or had run my race in vain" (Gal 2:2).

What an incredible admission! Here we have the apostle to the Gentiles acknowledging that he submitted himself to the apostolic authorities in Jerusalem in order to ascertain if the gospel message he was preaching was on target. Had he been mistaken, there could have been dire circumstances for the Gentile members of the early church, hence Paul's fear.

Besides Peter and James, the brother of Jesus, the apostle John was also present (2:9). It is difficult to miss the stellar makeup of this group. One could hardly imagine a single authority in the early church more influential than these four. We are told that Paul's companions Barnabas and Titus were also present (2:1). To this group Paul presented his gospel message for their inspection. The verdict was that the other three apostolic leaders "added nothing to my message" (2:6). Further, they extended fellowship to Paul and Barnabas, recognizing their mission to the Gentiles (2:9). The other apostles did exhort them also to take care of the poor, which Paul says he was eager to do anyway (2:10).[19]

Paul could not have hoped for a better verdict! We assume that he, Peter, and James were on the same page regarding Paul's first visit to Jerusalem. But here he specifically asked for a judgment regarding the central message that he preached to the Gentiles and found that there was no conflict between his gospel teaching and that of the other apostles. Especially when we consider that these were the most influential

---

[18] Koester, *Introduction*, 2:103.
[19] See Paul's efforts to take up offerings on behalf of poor believers (1 Cor 16:1–4; 2 Cor 8:1–15).

leaders in the early church, the value of such a positive verdict could hardly be overemphasized. They were all on the same page with regard to the most sacred proclamation in early Christianity.

Again we are reminded of C. H. Dodd's statement that Paul and the other early apostles all agreed when it came to the gospel message.[20] Paul made clear that the early gospel preaching was concerned with the person of Christ, His death, burial, resurrection, and appearances (1 Cor 15:3–4). Paul is clear about this in other places as well, where he also quotes other early creedal traditions (such as Rom 1:3–4; 10:9). Similarly, the book of Acts also defines the early apostolic preaching of the gospel as referring to the deity, death, and resurrection of Jesus.[21] Interestingly, many critical scholars also consider a number of these Acts texts to be other early traditions that predate the book itself. Dodd was one of the leading authorities here, and he found the same gospel specifics in these Acts texts as in the writings of Paul.[22]

After Paul cites the early creedal text in 1 Corinthians 15, he mentioned the other apostles and affirmed that they were preaching the same message of Jesus' resurrection appearances as he was (15:11; cf. vv. 12–15). His readers could get the same information from either source. Here we see the reverse side of Gal 2:1–10. There the three chief apostles affirmed Paul's gospel message. Here Paul asserts that they were teaching the same central message of the resurrected Christ that he preached.[23]

For ancient texts, perhaps never do we see this sort of cross-checking by the major authorities, all at such an early date. Howard Clark Kee amazingly asserts that this material is so strong that "it can be critically examined and compared with other testimony from eyewitnesses of Jesus, just as one would evaluate evidence in a modern court or

[20] Dodd, *Apostolic*, 16.
[21] For a number of these passages, see Acts 1:21–22; 2:22–36; 3:13–16; 4:8–10; 5:29–32; 10:39–43; 13:28–31; 17:1–3,30–31.
[22] Dodd, *Apostolic*, 17–31, especially 19, 24, 26, 31.
[23] For this agreement between Paul and the other apostles on the nature of the gospel message, see M. Hengel, *The Atonement* (Philadelphia: Fortress, 1981), 38, 69; J. P. Meier, *A Marginal Jew: Rethinking the Historical Jesus* (New York: Doubleday, 1987), 118; H. D. Betz, *Galatians: A Commentary on Paul's Letter to the Churches in Galatia*, Hermeneia Series (Philadelphia: Fortress Press, 1979), 76; B. Meyer, "Resurrection as Humanly Intelligible Destiny," *Ex Auditu* 9 (1993): 15; Bauckham, *Jesus*, 266.

academic setting."[24] We conclude that Paul, Peter, John, and James the brother of Jesus were the right people, at the right place, at the right time, all proclaiming the same message!

AD 30–35: Back to the Date of the Actual Events

After our brief backtracking in order to place Paul's later trip to Jerusalem in its proper perspective, we are now ready to move to the final scene. Here we want to ask about those who had knowledge of these historical events prior to Paul's own reception of the data, including the creedal formulation. After all, Paul's obtaining the knowledge of these events beyond his own appearance of the risen Jesus was not an end in itself. We must track backward to the original occurrences themselves.

Working backward from Paul, then, these accounts had already been cast into succinct oral summaries for use in teaching, especially when most people were apparently illiterate. Slightly prior to that are the original recollections and accounts of these occurrences by those who knew of them. As we have just seen, we know that the entire process could take place quickly, based on the difference between the events themselves, the preaching of this data, and its recording just a relatively short time later. Critical scholars readily concede that the early Christians believed certain events had taken place with regard to Jesus. Ultimately, these events either occurred or they did not.

Therefore, prior to Paul's trip to Jerusalem and his discussion with Peter and James, the brother of Jesus, regarding the gospel data (which was perhaps also the time when he received the original creedal tradition in 1 Cor 15), Paul was obviously not the first one to have this report. At least the other two apostles, presumably along with others, had to know the information before Paul did. Now we are getting close to the beginning, since both Peter and James are listed among those who saw the risen Jesus, as is especially clear in 1 Cor 15:4,7. The only more foundational data are the actual events themselves.

How should we date each of these strands? We have seen that Paul's first trip to Jerusalem is usually placed at 35 or 36, and Paul's

[24] H. C. Kee, *What Can We Know About Jesus?* (Cambridge: Cambridge University Press, 1990), 1–2.

conversion at three years before that, or about 32 or 33. Since Paul believed that he saw an appearance of the recently dead and now risen Jesus, the crucifixion would have occurred earlier still. But that event could not have happened long beforehand, as indicated by Paul's acquaintance with those who knew Jesus well, such as his brother James and his chief apostle Peter. Jesus' death had occurred shortly before the appearances. If any of the early confessions embedded in the Acts sermons[25] can also be granted as reliable reconstructions of the earliest preaching, then the resurrection was preached from the beginning, immediately after Jesus' death.

How early do critical scholars date this pre-Pauline creed? Even radical scholars like Gerd Lüdemann think that "the elements in the tradition are to be dated to the first two years after the crucifixion . . . not later than three years after the death of Jesus."[26] Similarly, Michael Goulder contends that Paul's testimony about the resurrection appearances "goes back at least to what Paul was taught when he was converted, a couple of years after the crucifixion."[27]

An increasing number of exceptionally influential scholars has recently concluded that at least the teaching of the resurrection, and perhaps even the specific formulation of the pre-Pauline creedal tradition in 1 Cor 15:3ff., even dates to AD 30! In other words, there never was a time when the message of Jesus' resurrection was not an integral part of the earliest apostolic proclamation.[28] No less a scholar than James D. G. Dunn even states regarding this crucial text: "This tradition, we can be entirely confident, was *formulated as tradition within months of Jesus' death*."[29]

Therefore, Paul received creedal material in Jerusalem just five years or so after Jesus' crucifixion that was actually formulated earlier,

---

[25] Such as those listed in endnote 21.

[26] G. Lüdemann, *The Resurrection of Jesus*, trans. J. Bowden (Minneapolis: Fortress, 1994), 38.

[27] M. Goulder, "The Baseless Fabric of a Vision," in G. D'Costa, ed., *Resurrection Reconsidered* (Oxford: Oneworld, 1996), 48.

[28] L. W. Hurtado, *How on Earth Did Jesus Become a God? Historical Questions About Earliest Devotion to Jesus* (Grand Rapids: Eerdmans, 2005), esp. 4; cf. Bauckham, *Jesus*, 264–68, 307–8; Wright, *Resurrection*, 319, 553–34, 583.

[29] J. D. G. Dunn, *Jesus Remembered*, vol. 1 of *Christianity in the Making* (Grand Rapids: Eerdmans, 2003), 825 (Dunn's emphasis).

perhaps dating all the way back to shortly after the death of Jesus. But regardless of where we date this creedal tradition itself, the underlying *content* of the gospel message regarding the death and resurrection of Jesus goes back to the beginning. In other words, it was the central message of the early apostolic church from its inception.

Conclusion: Bringing It All Together

The Gospels contribute many worthwhile items to a discussion of Jesus' resurrection. These texts fall well within the range of admissible sources, especially for the ancient world. However, by following the critical model and emphasizing the "authentic" epistles of the apostle Paul, we begin at a point perhaps 10 to 40 years before the Gospels. But this strategy also brings additional benefits, such as the early creedal traditions which Paul reports.

In the case of 1 Cor 15:3ff., critical scholars agree that Paul's reception of at least the content of this proclamation, and probably the creed itself, go back to the mid-AD 30s, when he spent two weeks with Peter and James, the brother of Jesus. But these two apostles had the material before Paul did, and the events behind the reports are earlier still.

This is probably the chief argument that persuades the majority of scholars today that the proclamation of Jesus' resurrection originated in the earliest church. Virtually all critical scholars think this message began with the real experiences of Jesus' earliest disciples, who thought that they had seen appearances of their risen Lord.[30] It did not arise at some later date. Nor was it borrowed or invented. As Bauckham asserts, "There can be no doubt that . . . Paul is citing the *eyewitness testimony* of those who were recipients of resurrection appearances."[31] This is the chief value of this argument. It successfully secures the two most crucial historiographical factors: (1) the reports of the original eyewitnesses, which are (2) taken from the earliest period. This is the argument that has rocked a generation of critical scholars. The historicity of Jesus' resurrection appearances is indeed strongly evidenced.

---

[30] For details, see G. R. Habermas, "Experiences of the Risen Jesus: The Foundational Historical Issue in the Early Proclamation of the Resurrection," *Dialog: A Journal of Theology* 45 (2006): 288–97.

[31] Bauckham, *Jesus*, 308.

Chapter 10

HOW SCHOLARS FABRICATE JESUS

Craig A. Evans

O ne of the characters in Dan Brown's *The Da Vinci Code* claims that in the three centuries or so following the death of Jesus, "thousands of documents" were penned chronicling the life of Jesus as a mortal. Readers are told that Emperor Constantine (who ruled 312–37) changed the historical record by commissioning a new Bible, which omitted Gospels that spoke of the humanity of Jesus and embellished Gospels that emphasized His divinity. The "earlier" Gospels, Brown's novel tells us, were outlawed, gathered up, and burned. Nevertheless, the true story of Jesus managed to survive in the Dead Sea Scrolls and in the old Gnostic books found in Egypt.

Most of these astonishing assertions are either false or grossly misleading, as all trained historians know. Constantine apparently did commission the production of 50 copies of Scripture (as Christian historian Eusebius reports), but he did not decide which Gospels to include and which to omit. Furthermore, the claim that the Dead Sea Scrolls preserve the truth regarding Jesus is ludicrous, for the scrolls mostly date from the first century BC and do not refer to Jesus or to anyone in His following. Many of the Gnostic books found in Egypt (at Nag Hammadi and elsewhere) do refer to Jesus and His disciples, but all of these books are *later not earlier* than the Gospels in the New Testament. The "true" story of Jesus is not preserved in these writings. Indeed, the Gospels of the New Testament present Jesus as truly human, while the Gnostic Gospels exalt Jesus' heavenly status and often deny the reality of His humanity. And, of course, there is not a shred of credible evidence that Jesus had a wife and children. Brown's fictional character could not have got his facts more mixed up. Brown's book is rife with these types of errors and blunders.

The single greatest factor that contributes to the kind of distortion that one encounters in Dan Brown's book is the fascination on the part of some scholars with a number of second- and third-century writings that for various reasons most early Christians never accepted as authoritative. The Jesus in these writings is noticeably different from the Jesus of the first-century New Testament Gospels. It is not surprising, then, that portraits composed on the basis of appeal to the later writings are different. In my view, which is shared by many historians and biblical scholars, these portraits are distortions. The radical scholars, whose work inspires authors like Dan Brown, do not offer careful reconstructions of the historical Jesus but fabrications that pander to this fad and that fad.

Of the many extracanonical Gospels that have been trotted out in recent years, not least the much talked about *Gospel of Judas*, those most cherished are the *Gospel of Thomas*, Egerton Papyrus 2, the *Secret Gospel of Mark*, and the so-called *Gospel of Peter*. These four sources received prominent attention in John Dominic Crossan's *Four Other Gospels: Shadows on the Contours of Canon.*[1] These sources have continued to receive scholarly attention, with respect to questions relating to the historical Jesus and the origin of the Jesus tradition and the New Testament Gospels. The *Gospel of Thomas* has enjoyed pride of place and is in fact the fifth Gospel in the Jesus Seminar's publication *The Five Gospels.*[2] *Thomas*, with which I begin, will receive more attention than the other extracanonical Gospel sources.

The Gospel of Thomas

The most celebrated extracanonical Gospel is the *Gospel of Thomas*, which survives in complete form in Coptic as the second tractate in

[1] J. D. Crossan, *Four Other Gospels: Shadows on the Contours of Canon* (New York: Harper & Row, 1985; repr. Sonoma: Polebridge, 1992).
[2] R. W. Funk, R. W. Hoover, and the Jesus Seminar, *The Five Gospels: The Search for the Authentic Words of Jesus* (Sonoma: Polebridge Press; New York: Macmillan, 1993).

Codex II of the Nag Hammadi library (NHC II,2) and partially in three Greek fragments in Oxyrhynchus Papyri 1, 654, and 655.[3] P.Oxy. 654 preserves *Gos. Thom.* prologue and sayings §1–7 and a portion of saying §30. P.Oxy. 1 preserves *Gos. Thom.* sayings §26–33. P.Oxy. 655 preserves *Gos. Thom.* sayings §24, §36–39, and §77. Although the point has been disputed, it seems that most scholars contend that *Thomas* was originally composed in Greek and that the Oxyrhynchus Papyri stand closer to the original form of the tradition. The issue of the original language of *Thomas* will be taken up below.

Most of the codices that make up the Nag Hammadi library have been dated to the second half of the fourth century, though of course many of the writings within these old books date to earlier periods. The codex that contains the *Gospel of Thomas* may date to the first half of the fourth century. In the case of the *Gospel of Thomas* itself (whose *explicit* reads: *peeuaggelion pekata thomas,* "the Gospel according to Thomas"), we have the three Greek fragments from Oxyrhynchus, which date to the beginning and middle of the third century. One of the fragments may date as early as 200. Many scholars allow that *Thomas* was composed as early as the middle of the second century. How much earlier is hotly debated. I will argue that *Thomas* dates no earlier than the end of the second century.

A few scholars still argue that the *Gospel of Thomas* contains primitive, pre-Synoptic tradition.[4] This is possible theoretically, but numerous difficulties attend efforts to cull from this collection of sayings or *logia* (114 in the apparently complete Coptic edition) material that can with confidence be judged primitive, independent of the New Testament Gospels, and even authentic. Quoting or alluding to

---

[3] For recent studies of the *Gospel of Thomas,* see M. W. Meyer, *The Gospel of Thomas: The Hidden Sayings of Jesus* (San Francisco: HarperCollins, 1992); S. J. Patterson, *The Gospel of Thomas and Jesus* (Sonoma: Polebridge, 1993); E. Pagels, *Beyond Belief: The Secret Gospel of Thomas* (New York: Random House, 2003).

[4] For a selection of studies by scholars who believe that the *Gospel of Thomas* contains primitive, pre-Synoptic tradition, see H. Koester, "Q and Its Relatives," in J. E. Goehring et al. (eds.), *Gospel Origins and Christian Beginnings* (J. M. Robinson Festschrift; Sonoma: Polebridge, 1990), 49–63, here 61–63; R. D. Cameron, "The Gospel of Thomas: A Forschungsbericht and Analysis," *Aufstieg und Niedergang der römischen Welt* II.25.6 (1988) 4195–251. See also S. L. Davies, "Thomas: The Fourth Synoptic Gospel," *BA* 46 (1983), 6–9, 12–14, who makes the astonishing claim that the *Gospel of Thomas* "may be our best source for Jesus's teachings" (p. 9).

more than half of the writings of the New Testament (i.e., Matthew, Mark, Luke, John, Acts, Romans, 1–2 Corinthians, Galatians, Ephesians, Colossians, 1 Thessalonians, 1 Timothy, Hebrews, 1 John, Revelation),[5] *Thomas* could well be a collage of New Testament and apocryphal materials that have been interpreted, often allegorically, in such a way as to advance second- and third-century mystical or Gnostic ideas. Moreover, the traditions contained in *Thomas* hardly reflect a setting that predates the writings of the New Testament, which is why Dominic Crossan and others attempt to extract an early version (or early versions) of *Thomas* from the Coptic and Greek texts that are now extant. Attempts such as these strike me as special pleading—that is, if the extant evidence does not fit the theory, then appeal to hypothetical evidence. The problem here is that we do not know if there ever was an edition of the *Gospel of Thomas* substantially different from the Greek fragments of Oxyrhynchus or the later Coptic translation from Nag Hammadi. Positing an early form of *Thomas*, stripped of the embarrassing late and secondary features, is a gratuitous move. The presence of so much New Testament material in *Thomas* should give us pause before accepting theories of the antiquity and independence of this writing.

Another telling factor that should give us pause before assuming too quickly that the *Gospel of Thomas* offers early and independent tradition lies in the observation that features characteristic of Matthean and Lucan *redaction* are also found in *Thomas*. First, we may consider a few examples involving Matthew. Logia §40 and §57 reflect Matt 15:13 and 13:24–30, respectively. This Matthean material derives from M and gives evidence of Matthean redaction. Other sayings in *Thomas* that parallel the triple tradition agree with Matthew's wording

---

[5] For a synopsis of parallels between the New Testament writings and the *Gospel of Thomas*, see C. A. Evans, R. L. Webb, and R. A. Wiebe, *Nag Hammadi Texts and the Bible: A Synopsis and Index* (New Testament Tools and Studies 18; Leiden: Brill, 1993), 88–144. Scholars who think *Thomas* is dependent on the New Testament writings include R. E. Brown, "The Gospel of Thomas and St John's Gospel," *New Testament Studies* 9 (1962–63): 155–77; B. Dehandschutter, "Recent Research on the Gospel of Thomas," in F. Van Segbroeck, et al. (eds.), *The Four Gospels 1992* (F. Neirynck Festschrift; Bibliotheca ephemeridum theologicarum lovaniensium 100; Leuven: Peeters, 1992), 2257–62; and M. Fieger, *Das Thomasevangelium: Einleitung, Kommentar und Systematik* (Neuetestamentliche Abhandlungen 22; Münster: Aschendorff, 1991).

(cf. Matt 15:11 = *Gos. Thom.* §34b; Matt 12:50 = *Gos. Thom.* §99), rather than with Mark's wording. Matthew's unique juxtaposition of alms, prayer, and fasting (Matt 6:1–18) appears to be echoed in *Gos. Thom.* §6 (= P.Oxy. 654 §6) and §14. In *Thomas* alms, prayer, and fasting are discussed in a negative light, probably reflecting Gnostic antipathy toward Jewish piety, which surely argues for viewing *Thomas* as secondary to Matthew. All of this suggests that *Thomas* has drawn upon the Gospel of Matthew.

There is also evidence that the *Gospel of Thomas* was influenced by the Gospel of Luke. The Lucan evangelist alters Mark's awkward "For there is nothing hidden except that it be revealed" (Mark 4:22) to "For there is nothing hidden that will not be revealed" (Luke 8:17). This edited version is found in *Gos. Thom.* §5–6, with the Greek parallel preserved in P.Oxy. 654 §5 matching Luke's text exactly, which counters any claim that Luke's text only influenced the later Coptic translation.[6]

Elsewhere there are indications that *Thomas* has followed Luke (*Gos. Thom.* §10 influenced by Luke 12:49; *Gos. Thom.* §14 influenced by Luke 10:8–9; *Gos. Thom.* §16 influenced by Luke 12:51–53, as well as Matt 10:34–39; *Gos. Thom.* §55 and §101 influenced by Luke 14:26–27, as well as Matt 10:37; *Gos. Thom.* §73–§75 influenced by Luke 10:2). Given the evidence, it is not surprising that a number of respected scholars have concluded that *Thomas* has drawn upon the New Testament Gospels.[7]

And finally, not long after the publication of the *Gospel of Thomas*, it was noticed that the new Gospel shared several affinities with Eastern,

[6] On Luke's influence on the *Gospel of Thomas*, see J. P. Meier, *A Marginal Jew: Rethinking the Historical Jesus*, vol. 1 (New York: Doubleday, 1991), 136; C. M. Tuckett, "Thomas and the Synoptics," *Novum Testamentum* 30 (1988): 132–57, esp. 146.

[7] Several scholars have concluded that the *Gospel of Thomas* draws upon the New Testament Gospels. See R. M. Grant, *The Secret Sayings of Jesus* (Garden City: Doubleday, 1960), 113; B. Gärtner, *The Theology of the Gospel According to Thomas* (New York: Harper, 1961), 26–27, 34, 42–43. Similar conclusions have been reached by H. K. McArthur, "The Dependence of the Gospel of Thomas on the Synoptics," *Expository Times* 71 (1959–60): 286–87; W. R. Schoedel, "Parables in the Gospel of Thomas," *Concordia Theological Monthly* 43 (1972): 548–60; K. R. Snodgrass, "The Gospel of Thomas: A Secondary Gospel," *Second Century* 7 (1989–90): 19–38; Tuckett, "Thomas and the Synoptics," 157; Meier, *A Marginal Jew*, 130–39. According to C. E. Carlston (*The Parables of the Triple Tradition* [Philadelphia: Fortress, 1975], xiii), "Many readings of the Gospel of Thomas and a considerable amount of time spent with the secondary literature . . . have not yet convinced me that any of the parabolic material in Thomas is clearly independent of the Synoptic Gospels."

or Syrian, Christianity especially as expressed in second-century traditions, including Tatian's harmony of the four New Testament Gospels, called the *Diatessaron*. This point is potentially significant, for the *Diatessaron* was the only form of New Testament Gospel tradition known to Syrian Christianity in the second century. We must carefully consider the implications of this evidence.

Proponents of the independence and first-century origin of the *Gospel of Thomas* are aware of at least some aspects of this writing's relationship to Syrian Christianity. Crossan and Stephen Patterson rightly acknowledge Edessa, eastern Syria, as the original provenance of *Thomas*. They point out, among other things, that the name "Judas Thomas" is found in other works of Syrian provenance, such as the *Book of Thomas the Contender* (NHC II,7), which begins in a manner reminiscent of the *Gospel of Thomas*: "The secret words that the Savior spoke to Judas Thomas, which I, even I Mathaias, wrote down" (138.1–3; cf. 142.7: "Judas—the one called Thomas"), and the *Acts of Thomas*, in which the apostle is called "Judas Thomas, who is also (called) Didymus" (§1; cf. §11: "Judas who is also Thomas"). The longer form of the name in the *Acts of Thomas* agrees with the prologue of the *Gospel of Thomas*, where the apostle is identified as "Didymus Judas Thomas." In the Syriac version of John 14:22, "Judas (not Iscariot)" is identified as "Judas Thomas." This nomenclature continues on into later Syrian Christian traditions.[8]

Despite these affinities with Syrian tradition, whose distinctive characteristics, so far as we can trace them, emerged in the second century, Crossan and Patterson (and others) are confident that the *Gospel of Thomas* in fact originated early. Patterson thinks *Thomas* must have existed before the end of the first century (though he allows for later editing). Crossan believes that the first edition of *Thomas* emerged in the 50s and the later edition, essentially the extant text, emerged in the 60s or 70s. In other words, the *Gospel of Thomas* in its first edition is

---

[8] On the apostle Thomas in Syrian Christian tradition, see H.-C. Puech, "The Gospel of Thomas," in E. Hennecke and W. Schneemelcher, eds., *The New Testament Apocrypha. Gospels and Related Writings*, vol. 1 (London: SCM Press; Philadelphia: Westminster, 1963), 278–307; Crossan, *Four Other Gospels*, 9–11; Patterson, *The Gospel of Thomas and Jesus*, 118–20; idem, "Understanding the Gospel of Thomas Today," in S. J. Patterson, J. M. Robinson, and H. G. Bethge, *The Fifth Gospel: The Gospel of Thomas Comes of Age* (Harrisburg, PA: Trinity, 1998), 37–40.

earlier than any of the New Testament Gospels. Indeed, even the later edition of *Thomas* may be earlier than the New Testament Gospels.[9]

Scholars have weighed in on both sides of this question, with many arguing that the *Gospel of Thomas* dates to the second century (e.g., early to mid) and with almost as many (several of whom are numbered among the members of the Jesus Seminar) arguing that *Thomas* dates to the first century. The latter usually date *Thomas* to the end of the first century but believe they can identify independent tradition that in some cases should be preferred to its parallel forms in the Synoptic Gospels.

This important question cannot be settled by taking a poll. We need to take a hard look at the *Gospel of Thomas*, especially as it relates to Syrian tradition. This text probably should not be dated before the middle of the second century. Indeed, the evidence suggests that *Thomas* was probably composed *in the last quarter of the second century*. Probably nothing in *Thomas* can be independently traced back to the first century. Let us consider the evidence.

In print and in public lectures, Crossan has defended the antiquity and independence of the *Gospel of Thomas* principally on two grounds: (1) He can find "no overall compositional design" in the Gospel, apart from a few clusters of sayings linked by catchwords; and (2) he finds several differences in the parallels with the New Testament Gospels that he believes cannot be explained in terms of Thomasine redaction. Patterson's arguments are similar.[10] As it turns out, the Syrian evidence answers both points.

Almost from the beginning a few scholars with Syriac expertise recognized the Semitic, especially Syriac, style of the *Gospel of Thomas*. This was, of course, consistent with what has already been said about the form of the name of the apostle. It was further noticed that at

---

[9] On the proposal that the *Gospel of Thomas* dates to the first century, see S. L. Davies, *The Gospel of Thomas: Annotated and Explained* (Woodstock, VT: Skylight Paths, 2004), 146–47; J. D. Crossan, *The Historical Jesus: The Life of a Mediterranean Jewish Peasant* (San Francisco: HarperOne, 1993), 427–30; Patterson, *The Gospel of Thomas and Jesus*, 118–20; idem, "Understanding the Gospel of Thomas Today," in Patterson, Robinson, and Bethge, *The Fifth Gospel*, 40–45. The editors of the Greek fragments of the *Gospel of Thomas* (i.e., P.Oxy. 1, 654, and 655) suggested that the original Greek text probably dated to AD 140, a date that Crossan, Patterson, and others find too late and based on untested and unwarranted assumptions.
[10] See Crossan, *Four Other Gospels*, 11–18.

points distinctive readings in *Thomas* agree with the Syriac version of the New Testament or with the earlier *Diatessaron* by Tatian.[11] It was also wondered if perhaps portions of *Thomas* originated in the Syriac language, instead of the Greek language, as was widely assumed.

In a recent study Nicholas Perrin has put this question to the test. He has analyzed the entire text of *Thomas*, retroverting the Coptic into Syriac and Greek. The results of his investigation are impressive. On the assumption that the *Gospel of Thomas* was originally written not in Greek or Coptic but in Syriac, which is not implausible given its Syrian provenance, more than five hundred catchwords can be identified linking almost all of the 114 sayings that make up this work. In fact, Perrin could find no linking catchwords for only three couplets (§56 and §57, §88 and §89, and §104 and §105). These exceptions are hardly fatal to Perrin's analysis, for the original Syriac catchwords could easily have been lost in transmission or in translation into Coptic.[12]

Moreover, Perrin is not only able to explain the order of the whole of *Thomas* in reference to catchwords; he is able to show in places the Gospel's acquaintance with the order and arrangement of material in Tatian's *Diatessaron*. The mystery of the order of the sayings that make up the *Gospel of Thomas* appears to have been resolved. Perrin concludes that the *Gospel of Thomas* is indeed dependent on the New Testament Gospels but not directly. *Thomas* depends on the New Testament Gospels as they existed in the *Diatessaron*, in Syriac.

[11] The *Diatessaron* (from Greek, meaning "through the four [Gospels]") blends together the four New Testament Gospels. See W. L. Petersen, *Tatian's Diatessaron: Its Creation, Dissemination, Significance and History in Scholarship* (*Vigiliae Christianae* Supplement 25; Leiden: Brill, 1994). In a comprehensive study G. Quispel observed that, in comparison with the Greek New Testament Gospels, the *Gospel of Thomas* and Tatian's *Diatessaron* share a large number of textual variants. Indeed, almost half of the sayings in *Thomas* give evidence of at least one such variant. See G. Quispel, *Tatian and the Gospel of Thomas: Studies in the History of the Western Diatessaron* (Leiden: Brill, 1975). Tatian (*c.* 120–180), a disciple of Justin Martyr (*c.* 100–165), composed the *Diatessaron*, probably in Syriac and probably in Syria, sometime between 172 and 174. The *Diatessaron* relies heavily on Matthew and may have been inspired by the earlier harmony of the Synoptic Gospels produced by Justin Martyr.

[12] On catchwords in the *Gospel of Thomas* and Syriac as the original language, see N. Perrin, *Thomas and Tatian: The Relationship between the Gospel of Thomas and the Diatessaron* (Academia Biblica 5; Atlanta: Society of Biblical Literature, 2002); idem, "NHC II,2 and the Oxyrhynchus Fragments (P.Oxy 1, 654, 655): Overlooked Evidence for a Syriac *Gospel of Thomas*," *Vigiliae Christianae* 58 (2004): 138–51.

The principal argument that Crossan and others have advanced in support of the literary independence of the *Gospel of Thomas* from the New Testament Gospels has been dealt a crippling blow. It is no longer justified to say that there is no discernible framework or organizing principle lying behind the composition of *Thomas*. There clearly is, if this writing of acknowledged Syrian provenance is studied in the light of the Syriac language.

Just as impressive is the number of specific contacts between the *Gospel of Thomas* and Syrian Gospel traditions and other Syrian religious traditions. Again and again we see where *Thomas* differs from the New Testament Gospels and where *Thomas* agrees with Syrian tradition. This point has not been sufficiently appreciated by Crossan and others.

Before concluding the discussion of the *Gospel of Thomas*, one other issue needs to be addressed. Stephen Patterson, James Robinson, and others have argued that the genre of the *Gospel of Thomas* supports an early date. Because *Thomas* is like Q, the sayings source on which Matthew and Luke drew, then *Thomas* in its earliest form may approximate the age of Q.[13] This argument is wholly specious not only because it does not take into account the extensive coherence with late second-century Syrian tradition, which has been reviewed above, or the lack of coherence with pre-70 Jewish Palestine; it fails to take into account the fact that other sayings collections, some in Syria, emerged in the second and third centuries. Among these is the rabbinic collection that became known as the *Pirqe 'Abot* ("Chapters of the Fathers") and the *Sentences of Sextus*. The latter is particularly significant because it originated in Syria in the second century, the approximate time and place of the emergence of the *Gospel of Thomas*. The evidence suggests that the *Gospel of Thomas* is another second-century collection that emerged in Syria.

The evidence strongly points to a late origin of the *Gospel of Thomas*. The association of the work with Judas Thomas, the arrangement and order of the sayings explained by hundreds of Syriac catchwords that

---

[13] On the argument that the sayings genre of the *Gospel of Thomas* is evidence of an early date, see J. M. Robinson, "LOGOI SOPHON: On the Gattung of Q," in J. M. Robinson and H. Koester, *Trajectories Through Early Christianity* (Philadelphia: Fortress, 1971), 71–113; Patterson, *The Gospel of Thomas and Jesus*, 113–18.

link the sayings, and the coherence of the readings in *Thomas* that differ from the Greek New Testament Gospels with the readings either in the *Diatessaron* or other Christian Syriac works from this period compellingly argue for a late second-century Syrian origin of the *Gospel of Thomas*. In short, the flood of factors point to the Eastern, Syriac-speaking church, a church that knows the New Testament Gospels primarily, perhaps exclusively, through Tatian's *Diatessareon*, a work not composed before AD 170, that persuades me that the *Gospel of Thomas* does not offer students of the Gospels early, independent material that can be used for critical research into the life and teaching of Jesus.

The Akhmîm Gospel Fragment (the Gospel of Peter?)

In a discussion of writings attributed to the apostle Peter, church historian Eusebius of Caesarea (*c.* 260–340) mentions a *Gospel of Peter*, which Serapion, bishop of Antioch (in office 199–211), condemned as heretical (*Hist. Eccl.* 6.12.3–6). Serapion quotes no portion of this Gospel, only saying that it was used by Docetists (who asserted, in the spirit of Gnosticism, that the Christ only *appeared* [Gk. *dokeō: "seem, appear"*] to be human and die, not in actuality). In the winter of 1886–87, during excavations at Akhmîm in Egypt, a codex was found in the coffin of a Christian monk. The manuscript comprises a fragment of a Gospel, fragments of Greek *Enoch*, the *Apocalypse of Peter*, and, written on the inside of the back cover of the codex, an account of the martyrdom of St. Julian. The Gospel fragment bears no name or hint of a title, for neither the *incipit* nor the *explicit* has survived. Because the apostle Peter appears in the text, narrating in the first person (v. 60 "But I, Simon Peter"), because it seemed to have a docetic orientation, and because the Gospel fragment was in the company of the *Apocalypse of Peter*, it was widely assumed that the fragment belonged to the *Gospel of Peter* mentioned by Eusebius.[14]

---

[14] The ninth-century Akhmîm Gospel fragment was published five years after its discovery, in U. Bouriant, "Fragments du texte grec du livre d'Enoch et de quelques écrits attribués à Saint Pierre," in *Mémoires publiés par les membres de la Mission archéologique française au Caire* 9.1 (Paris: Libraire de la Société asiatique, 1892), 137–42. Edited and corrected editions of the text can also be found in J. A. Robinson and M. R. James, *The Gospel According to Peter, and The Revelation of Peter* (London: C. J. Clay, 1892); H. von Schubert, *The Gospel of St. Peter* (Edinburgh: T. & T. Clark, 1893); and more recently in M. G. Mara, *Évangile de Pierre* (Sources

Critical assessments of the newly published Gospel fragment di-
verged widely, with some scholars claiming that the fragment was independent of the New Testament Gospels and others claiming that the
fragment is dependent on the New Testament Gospels.[15] Throughout
this debate no one seriously asked if the Akhmîm fragment really was
part of the second-century *Gospel of Peter*. It was simply assumed that
it was.

Then, in the 1970s and 1980s two more Greek fragments from
Egypt were published, P.Oxy. 2949 and P.Oxy. 4009, which with varying degrees of confidence were identified as belonging to the *Gospel
of Peter*. Indeed, one of the fragments was thought to overlap with
part of the Akhmîm fragment. The publication of these fragments renewed interest in the Gospel because many felt that the identity of
the Akhmîm fragment as the second-century *Gospel of Peter*, initially
accepted and later rejected by Serapion, was confirmed. Indeed, some
have suggested that the Fayyum Fragment, or P.Vindob. G 2325, is yet
another early fragment of the *Gospel of Peter*.[16]

In recent years Helmut Koester and a circle of colleagues and students have given new life to Gardner-Smith's position. According to
Koester, the *Gospel of Peter*'s "basis must be an older text under the
authority of Peter which was independent of the canonical gospels."

chrétiennes 201; Paris: Éditions du Cerf, 1973).

[15] Those who argue that the newly discovered Akhmîm Gospel fragment depends on the Synoptic Gospels include T. Zahn, *Das Evangelium des Petrus* (Erlangen: Deichert, 1893); H. B.
Swete, *EUAGGELION KATA PETRON: The Akhmîm Fragment of the Apocryphal Gospel of
St. Peter* (London and New York: Macmillan, 1893), xiii–xx. Robinson (*Gospel According to
Peter*, 32–33) speaks of "the unmistakeable acquaintance of the author with our Four Evange-
lists. . . . He uses and misuses each in turn." Those who argue that the fragment is independent
of the Synoptic Gospels include A. Harnack, *Bruchstücke des Evangeliums und der Apokalypse
des Petrus* (Texte und Untersuchungen 9; Leipzig: Hinrichs, 1893); A. Harnack and H. von
Schubert, "Das Petrus-evangelium," *TLZ* 19 (1894) 9–18; P. Gardner-Smith, "The Gospel of
Peter," *Journal of Theological Studies* 27 (1925–26): 255–71; idem, "The Date of the Gospel of
Peter," *Journal of Theological Studies* 27 (1925–26): 401–7.

[16] For reconstruction of P.Oxy. 2949, see R. A. Coles, "Fragments of an Apocryphal Gospel
(?)," in G. M. Browne et al. (eds.), *The Oxyrhynchus Papyri* (vol. 41; London: Egypt Exploration Society, 1972), 15–16 (+ pl. II). P.Oxy. 2949 may date as early as the late second century. The second fragment, P.Oxy. 4009, also probably dates to the second century. See D.
Lührmann and P. J. Parsons, "4009. Gospel of Peter?" in Parsons et al., eds., *The Oxyrhynchus
Papyri* (vol. 60; London: Egypt Exploration Society, 1993), 1–5 (+ pl. I). For the proposal that
the Fayyum Fragment also belongs to the *Gospel of Peter*, see D. Lührmann, with E. Schlarb,
Fragmente apokryph gewordener Evangelien in griechischer und lateinischer Sprache (Marburger
theologische Studien 59; Marburg: N. G. Elwert, 2000), 80–81.

Koester's student Ron Cameron agrees, concluding that this Gospel is independent of the canonical Gospels, may even antedate them, and "may have served as a source for their respective authors." [17] This position has been worked out in detail by Crossan who accepts the identification of the Akhmîm fragment with Serapion's *Gospel of Peter*. In a lengthy study that appeared in 1985, Crossan argued that the *Gospel of Peter*, though admittedly in its final stages influenced by the New Testament Gospel tradition, preserves an old tradition, on which all four of the canonical Gospels' Passion accounts are based.[18] This old tradition is identified as the *Cross Gospel*. Crossan's provocative conclusion calls for evaluation.

The author of the Akhmîm Gospel fragment apparently possessed little accurate knowledge of Jewish customs and sensitivities. According to 8.31 and 10.38 the Jewish elders and scribes camp out in the cemetery as part of the guard keeping watch over the tomb of Jesus. Given Jewish views of corpse impurity, not to mention fear of cemeteries at night, the author of our fragment is unbelievably ignorant. Who could write such a story only 20 years after the death of Jesus? And if someone did at such an early time, can we really believe that the Matthean evangelist, who was surely Jewish, would make use of such a poorly informed writing? One can scarcely credit this scenario.

There are worse problems. The Jewish leaders' fear of harm at the hands of the Jewish people (Akhmîm fragment 8.30) smacks of embellishment if not Christian apologetic. The "seven seals" (8.33) and the "crowd from Jerusalem and the surrounding countryside" that "came in order to see the sealed tomb" (9.34) serve an apologetic interest: the resurrection story is well attested. These details are probably secondary to the canonical tradition. The appearance of the expression, "the Lord's day" (*hē kyriakē*, 9.35), of course, is another indication of lateness (cf. Rev 1:10; Ign. *Magn.* 9:1), not antiquity. The centurion's

---

[17] On recent scholarly support of the antiquity of the *Gospel of Peter*, see H. Koester, *Introduction to the New Testament*, vol. 2: *History and Literature of Early Christianity* (New York: Walter de Gruyter, 1982), 163; cf. R. D. Cameron, *The Other Gospels: Non-Canonical Gospel Texts* (Philadelphia: Westminster, 1982), 78.

[18] On the theory that an early form of the *Gospel of Peter* lies behind the Passion narratives of the New Testament Gospels, see J. D. Crossan, *The Cross that Spoke: The Origins of the Passion Narrative* (San Francisco: Harper & Row, 1988), esp. 404.

confession (Akhmîm fragment 11.45) appears to reflect Matthean influence (Matt 27:54; cf. Mark 15:39; Luke 23:47).[19]

Finally, can it be seriously maintained that the Akhmîm fragment's
resurrection account, *complete with a talking cross and angels whose
heads reach heaven*, constitutes the most primitive account extant? Is
this the account that the canonical evangelists had before them? Or
is it not more prudent to conclude what we have here is still more
evidence of the secondary, fanciful nature of this apocryphal writing?[20]
Does not the evidence suggest that the Akhmîm Gospel fragment is
little more than a blend of details from the four canonical Gospels,
especially from Matthew, that has been embellished with pious imagination, apologetic concerns, and a touch of anti-Semitism?

The evidence strongly suggests that the Akhmîm Gospel fragment
is a late work, not an early work, even if we attempt to find an earlier
substratum, (gratuitously) shorn of imagined late accretions. But more
pressing is the question that asks if the extant ninth-century Akhmîm

---

[19] On the late and secondary nature of the Akhmîm Gospel fragment (or *Gospel of Peter*), see T.
W. Manson, "The Life of Jesus: A Study of the Available Materials," *Bulletin of the John Rylands
University Library* 27 (1942–43): 323–37; C. H. Dodd, "A New Gospel," in Dodd, *New Testament Studies* (Manchester: Manchester University, 1953), 12–52; and É. Massaux, *The Influence
of the Gospel of Saint Matthew on Christian Literature Before Saint Irenaeus*, ed. A. J. Bellinzoni (3
vols., New Gospel Studies 5.1–3; Macon: Mercer University Press, 1990–93), 2.202–14. Dodd
(p. 46) concludes that the Akhmîm fragment (which he accepts as the *Gospel of Peter*) "depends
on all four canonical Gospels, and probably not on any independent tradition."

[20] Crossan and others have not sufficiently probed the significance of the fantastic elements in
the Akhmîm Gospel fragment. The fragment describes the risen Jesus as so tall that his head
extended above the heavens and that the cross on which Jesus had been crucified exited the
tomb with him. These are the details of late not early tradition. On the great height of Jesus,
see *Shepherd of Hermas* 83.1 ("a man so tall that he rose above the tower"). The *Shepherd of
Hermas* was composed sometime between AD 110 and 140. The mid-second century addition
to 4 Ezra (i.e., 2 Esdras 1–2) describes the "Son of God" as possessing "great stature, taller than
any of the others" (2:43–47). The Akhmîm Gospel fragment's description of Jesus' head extending *above the heavens* probably represents a further and much later embellishment of these
traditions. The Akhmîm Gospel fragment's description of the cross that exits the tomb with
the risen Jesus, accompanied by angels, parallels late Ethiopic tradition, attested in two works,
whose original Greek compositions probably dated no earlier than the middle of the second
century. According to the *Epistula Apostolorum* (or *Letter of the Apostles*) §16, Jesus assures His
disciples: "I will come as the sun which bursts forth; thus will I, shining seven times brighter
than it in glory, while I am carried on the wings of the clouds in splendor with my cross going
on before me, then to earth to judge the living and the dead" (J. K. Elliott, *The Apocryphal New
Testament* [New York: Oxford University Press, 1993], 566). This tradition, with some variation, is repeated in the Ethiopic *Apocalypse of Peter* §1: "With my cross going before my face
will I come in my majesty; shining seven times brighter than the sun will I come in my majesty
with all my saints, my angels" (Elliott, *The Apocryphal New Testament*, 600).

Gospel fragment *really is* a fragment of the second-century *Gospel of Peter* condemned by Bishop Serapion in the early third century. The extant Akhmîm fragment does not identify itself, nor do we have a patristic quotation of the *Gospel of Peter* with which we could make comparison and possibly settle the questions. Nor is the Akhmîm Gospel fragment Docetic, as many asserted shortly after its publication. If the fragment is not Docetic, then the putative identification of the fragment with the *Gospel of Peter* is weakened still further. After all, the one thing that Serapion emphasized was that the *Gospel of Peter* was used by Docetists to advance their doctrines.[21] And finally, as Paul Foster has shown, the connection between the Akhmîm Gospel fragment and the small papyrus fragments that may date as early as 200–250 is tenuous.[22] Thus, we have no solid evidence that allows us with any confidence to link the extant Akhmîm Gospel fragment with a second-century text, be that the *Gospel of Peter* mentioned by Bishop Serapion or some other writing from the late second century. Given its fantastic features and coherence with late traditions, it is not advisable to make use of this Gospel fragment for Jesus research.

Papyrus Egerton 2

Papyrus Egerton 2 consists of four fragments. The fourth fragment yields nothing more than one illegible letter. The third fragment yields little more than a few scattered words. The first and second fragments offer four (or perhaps five) stories that parallel Johannine and

---

[21] There are serious questions about the alleged Docetism in the Akhmîm Gospel fragment. In 4.10 it says that Jesus "himself was silent, as having no pain." This does not say that Jesus in fact felt no pain; it implies that He was silent, even though the experience was indeed painful. Also, the cry from the cross, "My power, [my] power, you have abandoned me!" (5.19), is taken by some to indicate Docetism. But what we have here is probably no more than influence from a variant form of Ps 22:1, where one of the Greek recensions reads "strength" (or "power"), instead of "God." For further discussion on this issue, see J. W. McCant, *The Gospel of Peter: The Docetic Question Re-examined* (Atlanta: Emory University Press, 1978). There really is no compelling basis for seeing Docetic tendencies in the Akhmîm Gospel fragment.

[22] On the problem of identifying the early Greek fragments with the Akhmîm Gospel fragment, see P. Foster, "Are There Any Early Fragments of the So-Called *Gospel of Peter*?" *New Testament Studies* 52 (2006): 1–28. Foster shows that it is far from certain that the small Greek fragments P.Oxy. 2949, P.Oxy. 4009, and P.Vindob. G 2325 are from the *Gospel of Peter* mentioned by Bishop Serapion.

Synoptic materials. Papyrus Köln 255 constitutes a related fragment of the text.[23]

At many points these fragments parallel the New Testament Gospels. The first story is replete with allusions to the Fourth Gospel. Jesus' assertion in lines 7–10 could well be drawn from John 5:39, 45. The lawyers' reply in lines 15–17 appears to be taken from John 9:29, while Jesus' rejoinder in lines 20–23a[24] reflects John 5:46. The attempt to stone Jesus in lines 22–24 parallels John 10:31, while the declaration in lines 25–30 that they were unable to do so because His "hour had not yet come" echoes John 7:30 and 8:20. Reference to Jesus in line 30 as "the Lord" has a secondary ring. The second story is mostly Synoptic. The third story again combines Johannine and Synoptic elements. The opening statement in lines 45–47, "Teacher Jesus, we know that [from God] you have come, for what you are doing tes[tifies] beyond all the prophets," is based on John 3:2 and 9:29 (cf. also John 1:45; Acts 3:18). Egerton's use of "teacher" (*didaskale*) is secondary to John's transliteration *rabbi* and may be due to its appearance in Mark 12:14a ("Teacher, we know that you are true"). The question put to Jesus in lines 48–50 is taken from Mark 12:14b parallel but appears to have missed the original point. Jesus' emotion in line 51 recalls Mark 1:43, while his question in lines 52–54 recalls a form of the question found in Luke 6:46. The remainder of Jesus' saying, which is a paraphrase of Isa 29:13, echoes Mark 7:6–7 and parallel.

Crossan's analysis of these fragments leads him to conclude that Papyrus Egerton 2 represents a tradition that predates the canonical Gospels. He thinks that "Mark is dependent on it directly" and that it gives evidence of "a stage before the distinction of Johannine and Synoptic traditions was operative." Koester agrees with Crossan's second point, saying that in Papyrus Egerton 2 we find "pre-Johannine

---

[23] For the Greek text of the London fragments of Egerton Papyrus 2, see H. I. Bell and T. C. Skeat, *Fragments of an Unknown Gospel and Other Early Christian Papyri* (London: British Museum, 1935), 8–15, 26; idem, *The New Gospel Fragments* (London: British Museum, 1951), 29–33. The superscript numbers in the English translation indicate approximately the line breaks.

[24] Lines 22a and 23a, which are based on Papyrus Köln 255, are so designated, in order to distinguish them from lines 22 and 23 of Papyrus Egerton 2, fragment 1 recto. The same is done with lines 42a–44a, which also are based on Papyrus Köln 255, at the end of the same fragment, in order to distinguish them from lines 42–44 of Papyrus Egerton 2, fragment 2 recto.

and pre-synoptic characteristics of language [which] still existed side by side." He thinks it unlikely, *pace* Jeremias, that the author of this papyrus could have been acquainted with the canonical Gospels and "would have deliberately composed [it] by selecting sentences" from them.[25]

Theoretically Crossan and Koester could be correct in this assessment. However, some serious questions must be raised. *First,* several times editorial improvements introduced by Matthew and Luke appear in Egerton (e.g., compare Egerton line 32 with Mark 1:40; Matt 8:2; Luke 5:12; or Egerton lines 39–41 with Mark 1:44; Matt 8:4; Luke 17:14). There are other indications that the Egerton Papyrus is posterior to the canonical Gospels. The plural "kings" is probably secondary to the singular "Caesar" that is found in the Synoptics (and in *Gos. Thom.* §100). The flattery, "What you do bears witness beyond all the prophets," may reflect John 1:34,45 and is again reminiscent of later pious Christian embellishment that tended to exaggerate the respect that Jesus' contemporaries showed Him (see the examples in *Gos. Heb.* §2 and Josephus, *Ant.* 18.3.3 §64).

A *second* question arises in response to Koester's statement about the improbability that the author of the Egerton Papyrus "would have deliberately composed [it] by selecting sentences" from the canonical Gospels. But is this not the very thing that Justin Martyr and his disciple Tatian did? Justin Martyr composed a *Harmony* of the Synoptic Gospels and Tatian composed a harmony (i.e., the *Diatessaron*) of all four New Testament Gospels. If Justin Martyr and Tatian, writing in the second century, can compose their respective harmonies through the selection of sentences and phrases from this Gospel and that Gospel, why could not the author of the Egerton Papyrus do the same thing?

A *third* question arises out of Koester's suggestion that the mixture of Johannine-like and Synoptic elements is primitive, while their

---

[25] On claims that the Egerton Papyrus is early and independent of the New Testament Gospels, see Crossan, *Four Other Gospels,* 183. H. Koester, *Ancient Christian Gospels: Their History and Development* (Harrisburg, PA: Trinity, 1992), 207, 215; cf. idem, "Überlieferung und Geschichte," 1488–90, 1522. Jeremias, "Papyrus Egerton 2," in Schneemelcher (ed.), *New Testament Apocrypha,* 96. Crossan (*Four Other Gospels,* 86) argues that Mark is actually "directly dependent on the [Egerton] papyrus text."

bifurcation into the extant canonical forms is secondary. If Koester's suggestion is correct, then the Egerton Gospel does indeed derive from the middle of the first century, as Crossan in fact argues. It would have to be this early if it were to be used by the Synoptic evangelists. If this is the case, then one must wonder why we have no other fragment or any other evidence of the existence of this extraordinarily primitive Gospel. How is it that we do not have other papyri, extracanonical Gospels, or patristic quotations attesting this primitive pre-Synoptic, pre-Johannine unified tradition?

Examples can be found in Justin Martyr's quotations, which sometimes combine materials from two or more Gospels. From *Apologia I* 15.9 we read: "If you love those who love you [cf. Matt 5:46 = Luke 6:32], what new thing do you do [*unparalleled*]? For even the fornicators do this [Matt 5:46: "tax collectors"; Luke 6:32–33: "sinners"]. But I say to you [cf. Matt 5:44], pray for your enemies [cf. Matt 5:44: "love"] and love those who hate you [cf. Luke 6:27: "do good"] and bless those who curse you and pray for those who mistreat you [cf. Luke 6:28]." In *Apologia I* 15.10–12 Justin combines materials from Matthew and Luke to create a lengthy saying that his readers would take as a single utterance. Yet it is a conflation.

In *Apologia I* 16.9–13 Justin has assembled, based on memory, a "word" of Jesus that is in reality a pastiche of Synoptic materials, which at one point may also reflect Johannine influence. Although drawn from a variety of contexts, there is nevertheless a general thematic unity that holds these materials together. With respect to composition, the sayings in P.Eger.2 §1 and §3 are similar to Justin's dominical "word."

Another feature that tells against the antiquity and priority of the Egerton Papyrus is the story related in the badly preserved verso of fragment 2. Jesus apparently sows a handful of seed on the Jordan River, from which abundant fruit springs. The story is reminiscent of the kind of stories one finds in the late and fanciful apocryphal Gospels. For example, in the *Infancy Gospel of Thomas* we are told of the boy Jesus who sowed a handful of seed that yielded a remarkable harvest (*Infan. Thom.* 10:1–2 [Latin]).[26]

---

[26] The *Infancy Gospel of Thomas* may have originated as early as the late second century. The

Although the hypothesis of Crossan, Koester, and others remains a theoretical possibility, the evidence available at this time suggests that in all probability Papyrus Egerton 2 represents a second-century conflation of Synoptic and Johannine elements, rather than primitive first-century material on which the canonical Gospels depended. The presence of at least one apocryphal tale akin to those of the least historically viable traditions only strengthens this conviction.

The Secret Gospel of Mark

At the annual Society of Biblical Literature meeting in New York in 1960, Morton Smith announced that during his sabbatical leave in 1958, at the Mar Saba Monastery in the Judean wilderness, he found the first part of a letter of Clement of Alexandria (*c.* 150–215) penned in Greek, in what he suggests was an eighteenth-century hand, in the back of a sixteenth-century edition of the letters of Ignatius. In 1973 Smith published two editions of his find, one learned and one popular. From the start scholars suspected that the text was a forgery and that Smith was himself the forger. Many scholars, including several members of the Jesus Seminar, defended Smith and the authenticity of the Clementine letter.

Two quotations of a mystical or secret version of the Gospel of Mark made the alleged find controversial, quotations of passages not found in the public Gospel of Mark. In the first, longer passage Jesus raises a dead man and then later, in the nude, instructs the young man in the mysteries of the kingdom of God. The homoerotic orientation of the story is hard to miss.

Despite the fact that no one besides Smith has actually studied the physical document and that the paper and ink have never been subjected to the kinds of tests normally undertaken, many scholars have accepted the Clementine letter as genuine and its testimony that there really was in circulation, in the second century, a secret version of the Gospel of Mark as valid. Indeed, some scholars have suggested that *Secret Mark* may help us nuance the solution of the Synoptic problem,

Infancy Gospel of Thomas should not be confused with the *Gospel of Thomas*, found complete at Nag Hammadi and in three fragments at Oxyrhynchus.

and, of course, some scholars have suggested that *Secret Mark* is older and more original than public Mark.[27]

The sad thing is that all of this labor has been misspent; the Clementine letter and the quotations of *Secret Mark* embedded within it constitute a modern hoax, and Morton Smith almost certainly is the hoaxer. Several scholars have for years suspected this to be the case, but the clear, color, recently published photographs of the document,[28] have given experts in the science of the detection of forgeries the opportunity to analyze the handwriting of the document and compare it with samples of the handwriting of the late Professor Smith. The evidence is compelling and conclusive: Smith wrote the text. Stephen Carlson and Peter Jeffrey have compiled and analyzed the evidence, some of which is as follows:[29]

1. Magnification of the handwritten text reveals the telltale presence of what handwriting experts call the "forger's tremor." That is, the handwriting in question is not really *written*; it is *drawn*, in the forger's attempt to imitate a style of writing not his own. These telltale signs are everywhere present in the alleged Clementine letter.

[27] For a sampling of scholarship concerned with the *Secret Gospel of Mark*, see M. Smith, *Clement of Alexandria and a Secret Gospel of Mark* (Cambridge: Harvard University Press, 1973); idem, *The Secret Gospel: The Discovery and Interpretation of the Secret Gospel According to Mark* (New York: Harper & Row, 1973); F. F. Bruce, *The Secret Gospel of Mark* (Ethel M. Wood Lecture; London: Athlone, 1974); M. W. Meyer, *Secret Gospels: Essays on Thomas and the Secret Gospel of Mark* (Harrisburg, PA: Trinity Press International, 2003). An early and outstanding critical review of Smith's books was written by Q. Quesnell, "The Mar Saba Clementine: A Question of Evidence," *Catholic Biblical Quarterly* 37 (1975), 48–67. Quesnell's probing review raised many troubling questions about the authenticity of the Clementine letter.

[28] For good quality color photographs of the Clementine letter, see C. W. Hedrick, "Secret Mark: New Photographs, New Witnesses," *The Fourth R* 13/5 (2000): 3–16. Hedrick thought that his photographs supplied evidence supporting the authenticity of the Clementine letter. As it turns out, they had the opposite effect.

[29] For convincing evidence that the Clementine letter that contains quotations and discussion of *Secret Mark* is a hoax, see S. C. Carlson, *The Gospel Hoax: Morton Smith's Invention of Secret Mark* (Waco, TX: Baylor University Press, 2005); P. Jeffrey, *The Secret Gospel of Mark Unveiled: Imagined Rituals of Sex, Death, and Madness in a Biblical Forgery* (New Haven: Yale University Press, 2007). In his recent essay, "The Question of Motive in the Case against Morton Smith," *Journal of Biblical Literature* 125 (2006): 351–83, Scott Brown attempts to cast doubt on Carlson's proposals, particularly with regard to Smith's motives. The question of motive, apart from the discovery of a confession, will remain the most uncertain feature of this strange case. But the handwriting evidence, along with several other pieces of circumstantial evidence, admits to much less doubt.

2. Comparison of the style of the Greek of the handwritten text with Morton Smith's style of writing Greek (as seen in his papers and marginal notes in his books) has shown that Smith is the person who wrote (or "drew") the Clementine letter. For example, Smith had an unusual way of writing the Greek letters *tau, theta,* and *lambda.* These unusual forms occasionally intrude in what otherwise is a well-executed imitation of eighteenth-century style of Greek handwriting in the document in question.

3. Some of the distinctive themes in the document are in evidence in some of Smith's work published *before* the alleged find in 1958.[30]

4. The discolored blotch that is plainly visible in the lower left-hand corner of the final page of the printed text of the volume and in the lower left-hand corner of the second page of the handwritten text prove that the handwritten pages were originally part of the printed edition of the letters of Ignatius. These corresponding blotches, as well as many of the other blotches and discolorations that can be seen in the color photographs, are mildew. The presence of this mildew strongly suggests that the book in question was not originally a part of the library of Mar Saba, whose dry climate is not conducive to the production of mold and mildew in books. The mildew in the printed edition of the letters of Ignatius suggests that book spent most of its existence in Europe. We may speculate that in Europe, or perhaps in North America, the book was purchased and the Clementine letter was drawn onto the blank end papers. The book was then taken to

---

[30] Prior to the "discovery" of the letter of Clement and its quotations of *Secret Mark*, Smith linked the idea of a secret Christian doctrine, which he thinks is alluded to in Mark 4:11 ("To you has been given the secret of the kingdom of God"), to *t. Hag.* 2.1, which discusses forbidden sexual relationships in Leviticus 18. See M. Smith, *Tannaitic Parallels to the Gospels* (Journal of Biblical Literature Monograph Series 6; Philadelphia: Society of Biblical Literature, 1951), 155–56. Just prior to his visit to the Mar Saba Monastery in 1958, Smith published an article, in which he again makes mention of *t. Hag.* 2.1, only this time linking it to Clement of Alexandria. See M. Smith, "The Image of God: Notes on the Hellenization of Judaism, with Especial Reference to Goodenough's Work on Jewish Symbols," *Bulletin of the John Rylands University Library* 40 (1958): 473–512, here 507. This distinctive combination—the "secret of the kingdom of God," *t. Hag.* 2.1, a rabbinic passage that discusses forbidden sexual relationships, and Clement of Alexandria—is found only in Morton Smith's writings. The combination is also found in the Mar Saba letter, supposedly written by Clement of Alexander, in which the "secret of the kingdom of God" (a phrase from Mark 4:11) is taught to a young man clothed with only a linen cloth over his "naked" body, followed by mention of "naked [man] with naked [man]," which of course is one form of the forbidden sexual relationships.

the Mar Saba Monastery, where it was subsequently "found" in the library.

5. One of the Mar Saba documents cataloged by Smith is written in the same hand as the alleged Clementine letter. This document Smith dated to the *twentieth* century (not to the *eighteenth* century, as in the case of the Clementine letter). Moreover, the document Smith dates to the twentieth century is signed "M. Madiotes." This name is a pseudo-Greek name, whose root means "sphere" or globe," or, in reference to a person, "swindler" or "baldy." Carlson plausibly suggests that here Smith, who was bald, is facetiously alluding to himself (i.e., "M[orton] the baldhead").

6. The entire story—finding a long-lost document in the Mar Saba Monastery that is potentially embarrassing to Christianity—is adumbrated by James Hunter's *The Mystery of Mar Saba*.[31] Indeed, one of the heroes of the story, who helps to unmask the perpetrators and expose the fraud, is Scotland Yard Inspector Lord *Moreton*. The parallels between Morton Smith's alleged Mar Saba discovery and Hunter's Mar Saba mystery are fascinating. It should be added that Smith says in the preface to his publication of the Clementine letter that his invitation to visit Mar Saba came in 1941 (the year after the publication of Hunter's novel).

7. Carlson identifies very plausibly the motives behind Smith's playful deception. We need not go into these details in this context. They possess a great deal of explanatory power. It is hard not to reach the conclusion that Morton Smith penned *Secret Mark*.

Concluding Remarks

Many scholarly portraits and reconstructions of the historical Jesus are badly distorted through the use of documents that are late and of dubious historical value. The irony is that in trying to "go behind" the New Testament Gospels and find truth buried under layers of tradition and theology some scholars depend on documents that were

---

[31] J. H. Hunter, *The Mystery of Mar Saba* (New York and Toronto: Evangelical Publishers, 1940, and reprinted many times).

composed 60 to 100 years *after* the New Testament Gospels. This is a strange way to proceed.

Two of the four extracanonical Gospels reviewed in this paper originated in the second half of the second century. These are the *Gospel of Thomas* and the Egerton Papyrus. A third writing, the Akhmîm Gospel fragment, also cannot date earlier than the middle of the second century, if indeed *it is* the *Gospel of Peter* mentioned by Bishop Serapion at the beginning of the third century. But there are grave doubts that this document is the *Gospel of Peter*. The Akhmîm Gospel fragment may be part of an unknown writing from an even later period of time. In any case, scholars are in no position to extract from the Akhmîm fragment a hypothetical mid-first century Passion and resurrection narrative on which the first-century New Testament Gospels relied. Such a theory completely lacks a critical basis.

The remaining document—comprising quotations of the *Secret Gospel of Mark*, imbedded in a long-lost letter by Clement of Alexandria—is a modern hoax and therefore has nothing to offer critical scholarship concerned with Christian origins and the emergence of the Jesus and Gospel tradition. Yet this writing, along with the other texts, has been used in historical Jesus research.

The scholarly track record with respect to the use of these extracanonical Gospels is frankly embarrassing. In marked contrast to the hypercritical approach many scholars take to the New Testament Gospels, several scholars are surprisingly uncritical in their approach to the extracanonical Gospels. It is hard to explain why scholars give such credence to documents that reflect settings entirely foreign to AD pre-70 Jewish Palestine and at the same time reflect traditions and tendencies found in documents known to emerge in later times and in places outside of Palestine.

This kind of extreme scholarship, which in some manifestations hardly qualifies as critical, provides a context out of which the irresponsible pseudoscholarship and popular writing can emerge. Critical scholars need to challenge it head-on, underscoring its highly theoretical nature and tendency to indulge in special pleading. If extreme scholarship is not checked, the industry of fabricating strange and eccentric Jesuses will continue.

Chapter 11

HOW BADLY DID THE EARLY SCRIBES CORRUPT THE NEW TESTAMENT?

An Examination of Bart Ehrman's Claims[1]

Daniel B. Wallace

Introduction: The Radical Fringe Has Gone Mainstream

In the last 125 years or so, the major attack on the work of the earliest scribes of the New Testament has come from the far right, theologically speaking. Anti-intellectual crackpots have always generated far more heat than light, spewing forth anathemas on any who would dare to think that the oldest manuscripts may reasonably be assumed to represent fairly the original text. Occasionally such a viewpoint, though for the most part with more genteel language, is found in some bona fide scholars. From John Burgon, the antagonist to Westcott and Hort in the late nineteenth century, to Zane Hodges in the second half of the twentieth century, to Maurice Robinson today, an outspoken minority of exclusively *conservative* scholars has attempted to discredit the testimony of our oldest manuscripts by vilifying their character (or, at least, by seeing them as rather inferior witnesses to the original text).

---

[1] Thanks are due to Andreas Köstenberger, editor of the *Journal of the Evangelical Theological Society*, for his kind permission in allowing me to cannibalize my article, "The Gospel According to Bart: A Review Article of *Misquoting Jesus* by B. Ehrman," *Journal of the Evangelical Theological Society* 49 (2006): 327–49, for this chapter.

There has justifiably been a suspicion, however, that even the best of these conservative scholars starts with a theological agenda, whether stated or not—an agenda that dictates their conclusions.[2] Occasionally, those who work with the Greek text, and thus in some measure stand apart from the Bible-thumping preachers in America's backwaters, imbibe vitriol. David Otis Fuller, for example, in *Counterfeit or Genuine*, speaks of modern translations which, to a large degree, are based on the more ancient manuscripts, as "bastard Bibles."[3] Wilbur Pickering, former president of the Majority Text Society, in his master's thesis at Dallas Seminary declared that the most ancient manuscripts came from a "sewer pipe."[4] In his book *The Identity of the New Testament Text*[5]—a book which was the gold standard for many years for majority text advocates—Pickering states that "Aleph and B have lied" and that "Aleph is clearly a bigger liar than B,"[6] and that all the ancient manuscripts on which modern critical text are based are "convicted liars all."[7]

This sort of language might be expected from the ultraconservative wing because their method is dictated, from beginning to end, by their theological presuppositions. But in recent years the attack on the earliest witnesses has also come from the left side of the theological aisle. Just as within theologically conservative circles, there are prolific, though silly, liberal crackpots whose viewpoints should be paid no more attention than what a salmon should pay to a shiny bauble. And, to be sure, there are also New Testament scholars whose expertise is far removed from matters textual but who nevertheless freely opine that the state of the text is in such bad repair that we must abandon all hope of recovering anything remotely close to the original wording.

---

[2] For documentation, see D. B. Wallace, "Inspiration, Preservation, and New Testament Textual Criticism," *Grace Theological Journal* 12 (1992): 21–51; and idem, "The Majority Text Theory: History, Methods, and Critique," in *The Text of the New Testament in Contemporary Research: Essays on the* Status Quaestionis, in Studies and Documents, vol. 46, ed. B. D. Ehrman and M. W. Holmes (Grand Rapids: Eerdmans, 1994), 297–320.

[3] D. O. Fuller, ed., *Counterfeit or Genuine*[:] *Mark 16? John 8?* (2nd ed.; Grand Rapids: Grand Rapids International Publications, 1978), 10.

[4] W. Pickering, "An Evaluation of the Contribution of John William Burgon to New Testament Textual Criticism" (Th.M. thesis, Dallas Theological Seminary, 1968), 93.

[5] W. Pickering, *The Identity of the New Testament Text* (Nashville: Thomas Nelson, 1977).

[6] Ibid., 126.

[7] Ibid., 135.

The KJV-only crowd wants us to believe that the early manuscripts are all corrupt and that we should trust the later, more uniform majority. The radical liberals want us to believe that we can have no assurances about anything regarding the wording of the original text. Nothing is probable; everything is only possible. And this means that nothing can be affirmed. Ironically, both approaches are rather similar: they start with the result they are seeking to prove then address only the evidence that seems to support it. The results drive the method rather than vice versa. This is hardly an honest pursuit of truth.[8]

---

[8] M. Hengel, *Studies in Early Christology* (Edinburgh: T & T Clark, 1995), 57–58, makes a similar statement about the parallel dangers from "an uncritical, sterile apologetic fundamentalism" and "from no less sterile 'critical ignorance'" of radical liberalism. At bottom, the approaches are the same; the only differences are the presuppositions.

A good illustration of radical liberalism's critical ignorance about and abuse of textual criticism can be found in T. Freke and P. Gandy, *The Jesus Mysteries: Was the "Original Jesus" a Pagan God?* (New York: Three Rivers, 2001), 145. For this section of material, the authors rely on chap. 4, "How Reliable Are the Manuscripts of the Gospels?" of G. Stanton's *The Gospel Truth? New Light on Jesus and the Gospels* (Valley Forge, PA: Trinity, 1995), 33–48. First, they quote the pagan Celsus's complaint (as recorded in Stanton's book, 35) that Christians had deliberately tampered with the text of the NT. Their comment on Celsus's complaint is that "modern scholars have found that he was right. A careful study of more than 3,000 early manuscripts has shown how scribes made many changes" (Freke and Gandy, *Mysteries*, 145). The lone documentation to this sentence is Stanton's *Gospel Truth*, 35. But not only does Stanton mention nothing about 3,000 manuscripts on this page, not only are there nowhere close to 3,000 *early* manuscripts for the NT (let alone for any other ancient literature!), but Stanton himself does not agree with this assessment! Stanton goes on to quote Origen's response to Celsus that such alterations were made only by heretics. This quotation and Stanton's subsequent discussion are conveniently left out of Freke and Gandy's treatment. Freke and Gandy's selective quoting of the data seems to be driven by the results the authors wish to achieve rather than by an honest pursuit of truth. In the next paragraph they note: "Scholars also know that whole sections of the gospels were added later." They give the same example we mentioned in the last chapter—Mark 16:9–20. By whole sections apparently they mean one or two verses—and verses that have been excised in modern translations—because there is only *one* other large block of material that has affected modern translations of the NT, the story of the woman caught in adultery (John 7:53–8:11). And, although this passage is a favorite of many Christians, whether or not it is authentic makes no *doctrinal* significance. Yet Freke and Gandy are clearly giving the impression that we simply cannot trust anything about these manuscripts, that skepticism must rule our hearts. They have not represented either Stanton's treatment or that of other scholars, nor have they considered the evidence with anything that remotely resembles an honest handling of the data.

The same kind of irresponsible use of sources and results-driven approach can be found in a host of KJV-only literature. Chief among them is G. A. Riplinger's *New Age Bible Versions* (Shelbyville, TN: Bible & Literature Missionary Foundation, 1993). For an accessible critique, see J. White's "Why Respond to Gail Riplinger?" at http://www.bible.org/page.asp?page_id=664.

Things have changed in the last decade or so, however. By this I do not mean that the scholarship has improved or that the radical fringes have recanted of their circular reasoning. No, what has changed is that some respectable scholars have joined the ranks of the scornful. A trio of well-known, bona fide New Testament textual critics has for the last several years been trumpeting the same horn. Eldon Epp, David Parker, and Bart Ehrman—unquestionable authorities in textual criticism—have begun to show despair, or even disdain, about duplicating the autographic texts. Although they would certainly not agree with the KJV-only or even majority text crowd in their overall views of the text, they are similar in their questioning of the testimony of the early manuscripts. And they are doing it to such an extent that the average reader often sees these scholars as giving up on the quest for the autographs. Ehrman has been the most prolific and the most successful in bypassing peer review and appealing directly to the general reader. In particular, his wildly popular book, *Misquoting Jesus*,[9] has had a huge impact.

Most books on textual criticism sell in the hundreds; *Misquoting Jesus* has sold in the hundreds of thousands—and all within months of its release in November 2005. Interviews in the *The Washington Post*, National Public Radio, and Jon Stewart's *The Daily Show*, among many others, helped to bring visibility to the book in the public arena. Jon Stewart concluded his interview with Ehrman by stating, "I really congratulate you. It's a helluva book!" Within 48 hours, *Misquoting Jesus* was perched on top of Amazon. It "has become one of the unlikeliest bestsellers of the year."[10] Not bad for an academic tome on a "boring" topic!

One reason this book has done so well is that it appeals to the skeptic who *wants* reasons not to believe, who considers the Bible a book of myths. It's one thing to say that the stories in the Bible are legend; it's another to say that many of them were added centuries later. Although Ehrman does not say this, he leaves the impression that the original form of the NT was rather different from what the manuscripts now

---

[9] B. Ehrman, *Misquoting Jesus: The Story Behind Who Changed the Bible and Why* (San Francisco: HarperSanFrancisco, 2005).

[10] N. Tucker, "The Book of Bart: In the Bestseller 'Misquoting Jesus,' Agnostic Author Bart Ehrman Picks Apart the Gospels That Made a Disbeliever Out of Him," *Washington Post*, March 5, 2006, http://www.washingtonpost.com/wp-dyn/content/article/2006/03/04/AR2006030401369.html.

read. Those who have jumped on Ehrman's coattails include such dis-
parate groups as atheists and Muslim apologists—strange bedfellows,
indeed, but all united in their a priori assumption that the text of the
NT has been severely corrupted by the earliest scribes.

Misleading Statistics

Two of the undercurrents flowing through *Misquoting Jesus* are the
quality and quantity of the textual variants. "There are more variations
among our manuscripts than there are words in the New Testament,"
argues Ehrman.[11] Elsewhere he states that the number of variants is
as high as 400,000.[12] That is true enough but by itself is misleading.
Anyone who teaches NT textual criticism knows that this fact is only
part of the picture and that, if left dangling in front of the reader without explanation, is a distorted view. Once it is revealed that most variants are inconsequential—involving spelling differences that cannot
even be translated, articles with proper nouns, word order changes, and
the like—and that only a small minority of the variants alter the meaning of the text, the whole picture begins to come into focus. Indeed, less
than 1 percent of the textual variants are both meaningful and viable.[13]
The impression Ehrman sometimes gives throughout the book—and re-
peats in interviews—is that of wholesale uncertainty about the original
wording,[14] a view that is far more radical than he actually embraces.[15]

As to quantity of variants, consider the sentence, "Jesus loves
John." In Greek that statement can be expressed in a minimum of 16
different ways, though every time the translation would be the same
in English. And once we factor in different verbs for *love* in Greek, the
presence or absence of little particles that often go untranslated, and

---

[11] Ehrman, *Misquoting*, 90. This is a favorite statement of his, for it shows up in his interviews,
both in print and on the radio.

[12] Ibid., 89.

[13] For a discussion of the nature of the textual variants, see J. E. Komoszewski, M. J. Sawyer,
D. B. Wallace, *Reinventing Jesus: How Contemporary Skeptics Miss the Real Jesus and Mislead
Popular Culture* (Grand Rapids: Kregel, 2006). The section that addresses textual criticism,
comprising five chapters, is called "Politically Corrupt? The Tainting of Ancient New Testament Texts."

[14] For documentation, see Wallace, "Gospel According to Bart," 330–31, n. 16.

[15] See his statements in *Misquoting Jesus*, 55, 177, 207.

spelling differences, the possibilities run into the *hundreds.* Yet all of them would be translated simply as "Jesus loves John." There may be a slight difference in emphasis, but the basic meaning is not disturbed.

Now if a three-word sentence like this could potentially be expressed by hundreds of Greek constructions, how should we view the number of *actual* textual variants in the NT manuscripts? That there are only three variants for every word in the NT, when the potential is almost infinitely greater, seems trivial, especially when we consider how many thousands of manuscripts there are.

As Samuel Clemens said, "There are lies, damn lies, and statistics." Ehrman's emphasis on the quantity of variants while deemphasizing their nature, then speaking about the most problematic texts in the NT as though these were almost random examples from among thousands, looks increasingly like Clemens's third category.

The Orthodox Corruption of Scripture

The heart of *Misquoting Jesus* is chapters 5, 6, and 7. Here Ehrman especially discusses the results of the findings in his major work, *The Orthodox Corruption of Scripture.*[16] His concluding chapter closes in on the point he is driving at in this section: "It would be wrong . . . to say—as people sometimes do—that the changes in our text have no real bearing on what the texts mean or on the theological conclusions that one draws from them. We have seen, in fact, that just the opposite is the case."[17]

Cardinal Doctrines Affected by Textual Variants?

In chapters 5 and 6, Ehrman discusses several passages that involve variants allegedly affecting core theological beliefs. He summarizes his findings in his concluding chapter as follows:

> In some instances, the very meaning of the text is at stake, depending on how one resolves a textual problem: Was Jesus an angry man [Mark 1:41]? Was he completely distraught in the

---

[16] B. Ehrman, *The Orthodox Corruption of Scripture: The Effect of Early Christological Controversies on the Text of the New Testament* (Oxford: Oxford University Press, 1993).

[17] Ibid., 208.

face of death [Heb. 2:8–9]? Did he tell his disciples that they could drink poison without being harmed [Mark 16:9–20]? Did he let an adulteress off the hook with nothing but a mild warning [John 7:53–8:11]? Is the doctrine of the Trinity explicitly taught in the New Testament [1 John 5:7–8]? Is Jesus actually called "the unique God" there [John 1:18]? Does the New Testament indicate that even the Son of God himself does not know when the end will come [Matt. 24:36]? The questions go on and on, and all of them are related to how one resolves difficulties in the manuscript tradition as it has come down to us.[18]

Such a summary is intended to focus on the major problem passages that Ehrman has uncovered. Thus, following the well-worn rabbinic principle of *a maiore ad minus*,[19] or arguing from the greater to the lesser, we will address just these seven texts.

The Problem with Problem Passages

Three of these passages have been considered inauthentic by most NT scholars, including most *evangelical* NT scholars, for well over a century (Mark 16:9–20; John 7:53–8:11; and 1 John 5:7–8).[20] Yet Ehrman writes as though the excision of such texts could shake up our theological convictions. Such is hardly the case. (We will suspend discussion of one of these passages, 1 John 5:7–8, until the end.)

*The last twelve verses of Mark and the **pericope adulterae***. At the same time Ehrman implicitly raises a valid issue. A glance at virtually any English Bible today reveals that the longer ending of Mark and the *pericope adulterae* are to be found in their usual places. Thus, not only do the KJV and NKJV have these passages (as would be expected), but so do the ASV, RSV, NRSV, NIV, TNIV, NASB, ESV, TEV, NAB, NJB, and NET. Yet the scholars who produced these translations by and large do not subscribe to the authenticity of such texts. The rea-

---

[18] Ehrman, *Misquoting*, 208.

[19] See H. L. Strack, *Introduction to the Talmud and Midrash* (Atheneum, NY: Temple, 1978), 94, 96 for this hermeneutical principle known as *Kal Wa-homer*.

[20] An accessible discussion of the textual problem in these three passages can be found in the footnotes of the NET Bible (www.bible.org) on these texts.

sons are simple enough: they don't show up in the oldest and best manuscripts, and their internal evidence is decidedly against authenticity.[21] Why then are they still in these Bibles?

The answer to this question varies. For some they seem to be in the Bibles because of a tradition of timidity. There are seemingly good reasons for this. The rationale is typically that no one will buy a particular version if it lacks these famous passages. And if they don't buy the version, it can't influence Christians. Some translations have included the *pericope adulterae* because of a mandate from the papal authorities declaring the passage to be Scripture. The NEB and REB include it at the end of the Gospels rather than in its traditional location. The TNIV and NET have both passages in a smaller font with brackets around them. (Smaller type makes it harder to read from the pulpit.) The NET adds a lengthy discussion about the inauthenticity of the verses. Most translations mention that these pericopae are not found in the oldest manuscripts, but such a comment is rarely noticed by readers today. How do we know this? From the shock waves produced by Ehrman's book. In radio, TV, and newspaper interviews with Ehrman, the story of the woman caught in adultery is almost always the first text brought up as inauthentic, and the mention is calculated to alarm the audience.

Nevertheless, Ehrman has done a great service to the church by exposing the public to the inauthenticity of Mark 16:9–20 and John 7:53–8:11. Strong emotional baggage is especially attached to the latter text. For years it was my favorite passage that was not in the Bible. I would even preach on it as true historical narrative, even after I rejected its literary/canonical authenticity. And we all know of preachers who can't give it up even though they, too, have doubts about it. But there are two problems with this approach. First, in terms of popularity between these two texts, John 8 is the overwhelming favorite, yet its external credentials are significantly worse than Mark 16's. The same preacher who declares the Markan passage to be inauthentic extols the virtues of John 8. This inconsistency is appalling. Something

---

[21] For evidence that Mark intended to end his Gospel at 16:8, see D. B. Wallace, "Mark 16.8 as the Conclusion to the Second Gospel," in *Perspectives on the Ending of Mark: Four Views*, ed. D. A. Black (Nashville: B&H Academic, 2008). For arguments on the inauthenticity of John 7:53–8:11, see the textual critical notes in the NET Bible at this location as well as any critical commentary on John's Gospel.

is amiss in our theological seminaries when one's feelings are allowed to be the arbiter of textual problems. Second, the *pericope adulterae* is most likely not even *historically* true, at least in all its details. It was probably a story conflated from two different accounts.[22] Thus, the argument that one can proclaim it because the story really happened is apparently not completely valid.

In retrospect, keeping these two pericopae in our Bibles rather than relegating them to the footnotes seems to have been a bomb just waiting to explode. All Ehrman did was to light the fuse. One lesson we must learn from *Misquoting Jesus* is that those in ministry need to close the gap between the church and the academy. Professors and pastors have to educate believers. Instead of trying to isolate laypeople from critical scholarship, we need to insulate them. They need to be ready for the barrage because it is coming.[23] The intentional dumbing down of the church for the sake of filling more pews will ultimately lead to defection from Christ. Ehrman is to be thanked for giving us a wake-up call.

Not everything Ehrman has written in this book is of that ilk, but these three passages are. Again, we need to stress: these texts change no fundamental doctrine, no core belief. Evangelical scholars have rejected them as spurious for more than a century without disturbing one iota of orthodoxy.

The remaining four textual problems, however, tell a different story. Ehrman appeals either to an interpretation or to evidence that most scholars consider, at best, doubtful.

Hebrews 2:8–9. Translations are roughly united in how they treat Heb 2:9b. The NET is representative: "By God's grace he would experience death on behalf of everyone." Ehrman suggests that "by God's grace," *chariti theou*, is a secondary reading. Instead, he argues that "apart from God," or *chōris theou*, is what the author originally wrote. Only three Greek manuscripts have this reading, all from the tenth century or later. Codex 1739, however, is one of them, and it is a copy of an early and decent manuscript. *Chōris theou* is also found in several

---

[22] See B. D. Ehrman, "Jesus and the Adulteress," *New Testament Studies* 34 (1988): 24–44.

[23] Because of this need, several books written for a general audience but backed up with serious scholarship have been recently produced. Among them are C. Evans, *Fabricating Jesus*; D. Bock and D. B. Wallace, *Dethroning Jesus*; E. J. Komoszewski, M. J. Sawyer, and D. B. Wallace, *Reinventing Jesus*; B. Witherington, *What Have They Done with Jesus?* and many others.

fathers, one Vulgate manuscript, and some copies of the Peshitta.[24] Many scholars would dismiss such paltry evidence without further ado. If they bother to treat the internal evidence at all, it is because even though it has a poor pedigree, *chōris theou* is the harder reading and thus may require some explanation since scribes tended to smooth out the wording of the text. As well, something needs to explain the several patristic citations. But if a reading is an unintentional change, the canon of the harder reading is invalid. The hardest reading will be a nonsense reading, something that cannot be created on purpose. Although *chōris* is apparently the harder reading, it can be explained as an accidental alteration. It may be due either to a "scribal lapse"[25] in which an inattentive copyist confused *chōris* for *chariti*, or "a marginal gloss" in which a scribe was thinking of 1 Cor 15:27 which, like Heb 2:8, quotes Ps 8:6 in reference to God's subjection of all things to Christ.[26]

Without going into the details of Ehrman's defense of *chōris*, we simply wish to note four things. First, he overstates his case by assuming that his view is *certainly* correct. After three pages of discussion of this text in his *Orthodox Corruption of Scripture*, he pronounces the verdict: "The external evidence notwithstanding, Hebrews 2:9

---

[24] Ehrman says the reading "occurs in only two documents of the tenth century" (*Misquoting Jesus*, 145), by which he means only two *Greek* documents, 0243 (0121b) and 1739[txt]. These manuscripts are closely related and probably represent a common archetype. It is also found in 424[cvid] (thus, apparently a later correction in an eleventh century minuscule) as well as vg[ms] syr[pmss] Origen[gr (vr), lat] MSS[according to Origen] Theodore Nestorians [according to Ps-Oecumenius] Theodoret[1/2; lem] Ambrose MSS[according to Jerome] Vigilius Fulgentius. Ehrman does note some of the patristic evidence, underscoring an important argument, viz., "Origen tells us that this was the reading of the majority of manuscripts in his own day" (ibid.).

[25] So B. Metzger, *Textual Commentary on the Greek New Testament* (2nd ed.; Stuttgart: Deutsche Bibelgesellschaft, 1994), 595.

[26] Ibid. For similar arguments, see F. F. Bruce, *The Epistle to the Hebrews*, rev. ed., New International Commentary on the New Testament (Grand Rapids: Eerdmans, 1990), 70–71, n. 15. The point of the marginal gloss is that in Heb 2:8 the author quotes Ps 8:6, adding that "in the subjecting of all things to him, he left nothing outside of his control." In 1 Cor 15:27, which also quotes Ps 8:6, Paul adds the qualifier that God was excluded from the "all things" that were subjected to Christ. Metzger argues that the gloss was most likely added by a scribe "to explain that 'everything in ver. 8 does not include God; this gloss, being erroneously regarded by a later transcriber as a correction of [*chariti theou*],' was introduced into the text of ver. 9" (*Textual Commentary*, 595). For more information, see Wallace, "The Gospel According to Bart," 338, n. 38.

must have originally said that Jesus died 'apart from God.'"[27] Second, Ehrman's text-critical views are getting dangerously close to rigorous eclecticism.[28] The external data seem to mean less and less to him as he seems to *want* to see theological corruption in the text. Third, even though he is certain about his verdict, his late mentor, Bruce Metzger, was not. A year after *Orthodox Corruption* was published, Metzger's second edition of his *Textual Commentary* appeared. The United Bible Society (UBS) committee still gave the *chariti theou* reading the palm, but this time *upgrading* their conviction to an "A" rating. Finally, even assuming that *chōris theou* is the correct reading here, Ehrman has not made out a case that this is a variant that "affect[s] the interpretation of an *entire book* of the New Testament."[29] He argues that "[t]he less attested reading is also more consistent with the theology of Hebrews."[30] He adds that the author "repeatedly emphasizes that Jesus died a fully human, shameful death, totally removed from the realm whence he came, the realm of God. His sacrifice, as a result, was accepted as the perfect expiation for sin. Moreover, God did not intervene in his passion and did nothing to minimize his pain. Jesus died 'apart from God.'"[31] If this is the view of Jesus throughout Hebrews, how does the variant Ehrman adopts in 2:9 change that portrait? In his *Orthodox Corruption*, Ehrman says that "Hebrews 5:7 speaks of Jesus, in the face of death, beseeching God with loud cries and tears."[32] But that this text is speaking of Jesus "in the face of death" is not at all clear (nor does Ehrman defend this view). Further, he builds on this in his concluding chapter of *Misquoting Jesus*—even though he has never estab-

---

[27] Ehrman, *Orthodox Corruption*, 149 (italics added).

[28] By this I do not mean merely his adoption of *chōris theou* here. (After all, G. Zuntz, highly regarded as a brilliant and sober-minded reasoned eclectic, also considered *chōris theou* as authentic [*The Text of the Epistles: A Disquisition upon the* Corpus Paulinum [Schweich Lectures, 1946; London: Oxford University Press, 1953], 34–35].) Rather, I am referring to Ehrman's overall agenda of exploiting the apparatus for orthodox corruptions, regardless of the evidence for alternative readings. With this agenda Ehrman seems driven to argue for certain readings that have little external support. See P. Miller, "The Least Orthodox Reading Is to Be Preferred: A New Canon for New Testament Textual Criticism?" in a forthcoming book on NT textual criticism, title to be determined; edited by D. B. Wallace and published by Kregel.

[29] Ehrman, *Misquoting Jesus*, 132 (italics added).

[30] Ehrman, *Orthodox Corruption*, 148.

[31] Ibid., 149.

[32] Ibid.

lished the point—when he asks, "Was [Jesus] completely distraught in the face of death?"[33] He goes even further in *Orthodox Corruption*. I am at a loss to understand how Ehrman can claim that the author of Hebrews seems to know "of passion traditions in which Jesus was *terrified* in the face of death"[34] unless it is by connecting three dots, all of which are dubious—viz., reading *chōris theou* in Heb 2:9, seeing 5:7 as referring principally to the death of Christ and that His prayers were principally for Himself,[35] and then regarding the loud cries there to reflect his terrified state. Ehrman seems to be building his case on linked hypotheses, which is a poor foundation at best.

Mark 1:41. In the first chapter of Mark's Gospel, a leper approaches Jesus and asks Him to heal him: "If you are willing, you can make me clean" (Mark 1:40 NIV). Jesus' response is recorded in the Nestle-Aland text as follows: *kai splagchnistheis ekteinas tēn cheira auto ēpsato kai legei autō, Thelō, katharisthēti* ("and moved with compassion, he stretched out [his] hand and touched him and said to him, 'I am willing; be cleansed'"). Instead of *splagchnistheis* ("moved with compassion") a few Western witnesses[36] read *orgistheis* ("becoming angry"). Jesus' motivation for this healing apparently hangs in the balance. Even though the UBS[4] gives *splagchnistheis* a B rating, an increasing number of exegetes are starting to argue for the authenticity of *orgistheis*. In a *Festschrift* for Gerald Hawthorne in 2003, Ehrman made an impressive argument for its authenticity.[37] Four years earlier, a doctoral dissertation

---

[33] Ehrman, *Misquoting Jesus*, 208.

[34] Ehrman, *Orthodox Corruption*, 144 (italics added).

[35] The context of Hebrews 5, however, speaks of Christ as high priest; verse 6 sets the stage by linking Christ's priesthood to that of Melchizedek; verse 7 connects His prayers with "the days of his flesh," not just with His Passion. It is thus not unreasonable to see His prayers as prayers for His people. All this suggests that more than the passion is in view in Heb 5:7. The one datum in this text that may connect the prayers with the passion is that the one to whom Christ prayed was "able to save him from death." But if the prayers are restricted to Christ's ordeal on the cross, then the *chōris* reading in Heb 2:9 seems to be refuted, for in 5:7 the Lord "was *heard* [*eisakoustheis*] because of His devotion." How could He be heard if He died *apart from God*? The interpretive issues in Heb 5:7 are somewhat complex, yielding no facile answers. See W. L. Lane, *Hebrews 1–8*, Word Biblical Commentary (Dallas: Word, 1991), 119–20.

[36] D [ita d ff2 r1] Diatessaron.

[37] B. D. Ehrman, "A Leper in the Hands of an Angry Jesus," in *New Testament Greek and Exegesis: Essays in Honor of Gerald F. Hawthorne* (Grand Rapids: Eerdmans, 2003), 77–98.

by Mark Proctor was written in defense of *orgistheis*.[38] The reading has also made its way into the TNIV and is seriously entertained in the NET. We won't take the time to consider the arguments here. At this stage I am inclined to think it is most likely original. Either way, for the sake of argument, assuming that the "angry" reading is authentic, what does this tell us about Jesus that we didn't know before?

Ehrman suggests that if Mark originally wrote about Jesus' anger in this passage, it changes our picture of Jesus *in Mark* significantly. In fact, this textual problem is his lead example in chapter 5 ("Originals That Matter"), a chapter whose central thesis is that some variants "affect the interpretation of an *entire book* of the New Testament."[39] This thesis is overstated in general and particularly for Mark's Gospel. In Mark 3:5 Jesus is said to be angry, wording that is indisputably in the original text of *Mark*. And in Mark 10:14 He is indignant at His disciples.

Ehrman, of course, knows this. In fact, he argues implicitly in the Hawthorne *Festschrift* that Jesus' anger in Mark 1:41 perfectly fits into the picture that Mark elsewhere paints of Jesus. He says, for example, "Mark described Jesus as angry, and, at least in this instance, scribes took offense. This comes as no surprise; apart from a fuller under-standing of Mark's portrayal, Jesus' anger is difficult to understand."[40] Ehrman even lays out the fundamental principle that he sees running through Mark: "Jesus is angered when anyone questions his authority or ability to heal—or his desire to heal."[41] Now, for sake of argument, let's assume that not only is Ehrman's textual reconstruction correct, but his interpretation of *orgistheis* in Mark 1:41 is correct—not only in that passage but in the totality of Mark's presentation of Jesus.[42] If so, how then does an angry Jesus in 1:41 "affect the interpretation of an *entire book* of the New Testament"? According to Ehrman's own

---

[38] M. A. Proctor, "The 'Western' Text of Mark 1:41: A Case for the Angry Jesus" (Ph.D. diss., Waco: Baylor University, 1999). Even though Ehrman's article appeared four years after Proctor's dissertation, Ehrman was apparently unaware of Proctor's work.

[39] Ehrman, *Misquoting Jesus*, 132 (italics added).

[40] Ehrman, "A Leper in the Hands of an Angry Jesus," 95.

[41] Ibid., 94.

[42] For serious weaknesses in his *interpretation* of Mark's presentation of an angry Jesus, see Wallace, "The Gospel According to Bart," 341–42, n. 55.

interpretation, *orgistheis* only strengthens the image we see of Jesus in this Gospel by making it wholly consistent with the other texts that speak of his anger. If this reading is exhibit A in Ehrman's fifth chapter, it seriously backfires, for it does little to alter the overall portrait of Jesus that Mark paints. Here is another instance, then, in which Ehrman's theological conclusion is more provocative than the evidence suggests.

Matthew 24:36. In the Olivet Discourse Jesus speaks about the time of His own return. Remarkably, He confesses that He does not know exactly when that will be. In most modern translations of Matt 24:36, the text basically says, "But as for that day and hour no one knows it—neither the angels in heaven, *nor the Son [oude ho huios]*—except the Father alone." However, many manuscripts, including some early and important ones, lack *oude ho huios*. Whether "nor the Son" is authentic is disputed.[43] Nevertheless, Ehrman again speaks confidently on the issue.[44] The importance of this textual variant for the thesis of *Misquoting Jesus* cannot be overestimated. Ehrman alludes to Matt 24:36 in his conclusion, apparently to underscore his argument that textual variants alter basic doctrines.[45] His initial discussion of this passage certainly leaves this impression as well.[46] But if he does not mean this, then he is writing more provocatively than is necessary, misleading his readers. And if he does mean it, he has overstated his case.

What is not disputed is the wording in the parallel in Mark 13:32: "But as for that day or hour no one knows it—neither the angels in heaven, *nor the Son*—except the Father."[47] Thus, there can be no doubt that Jesus spoke of His own prophetic ignorance in the Olivet

---

[43] See the discussion in the NET Bible's note on this verse.

[44] *Orthodox Corruption*, 92: "Not only is the phrase [*oude ho huios*] found in our earliest and best manuscripts of Matthew, it is also necessary on internal grounds."

[45] Ehrman, *Misquoting Jesus*, 208 (quoted earlier).

[46] Ibid., 95: "Scribes found this passage difficult: the Son of God, Jesus himself, does not know when the end will come? How could that be? Isn't he all-knowing? To resolve the problem, some scribes simply modified the text by taking out the words 'nor even the Son.' Now the angels may be ignorant, but the Son of God isn't."

[47] Codex X, one Vulgate manuscript, and a few other unnamed witnesses (according to the apparatus of Nestle-Aland[27]) drop the phrase here.

Discourse. Consequently, what doctrinal issues are really at stake here? One simply cannot maintain that the wording in Matt 24:36 changes one's basic theological convictions about Jesus since the same sentiment is found in Mark. Not once in *Misquoting Jesus* does Ehrman mention Mark 13:32, even though he explicitly discusses Matt 24:36 at least six times, to the effect that this reading impacts our fundamental understanding of Jesus.[48] But does the wording change our basic understanding of *Matthew's* view of Jesus? Even that is not the case. Even if Matt 24:36 originally lacked "nor the Son," the fact that the Father *alone* (*ei mē ho patēr monos*) has this knowledge certainly implies the Son's ignorance (and the "alone" is only found in Matt 24:36, not in Mark 13:32). Again, this important detail is not mentioned in *Misquoting Jesus* or even in *Orthodox Corruption of Scripture*.

John 1:18. In John 1:18b, Ehrman argues that "Son" instead of "God" is the authentic reading. But he goes beyond the evidence by stating that if "God" were original the verse would be calling Jesus "the unique God." The problem with such a translation, in Ehrman's words, is that "the term *unique* God must refer to God the Father himself—otherwise he is not unique. But if the term refers to the Father, how can it be used of the Son?"[49] Ehrman's sophisticated grammatical argument for this is not found in *Misquoting Jesus* but is detailed in his *Orthodox Corruption of Scripture*:

> The more common expedient for those who opt for [(*ho*) *monogenēs theos*], but who recognize that its rendering as "the unique God" is virtually impossible in a Johannine context, is to understand the adjective substantivally [i.e., as a noun], . . . so that . . . the text should be rendered "the unique one, who is also God, who is in the bosom of the Father."
>
> . . . . It is true that *monogenēs* can elsewhere be used as a substantive (= the unique one, as in v. 14); all adjectives can. But the proponents of this view have failed to consider that it is never used in this way when it is immediately followed by a noun that agrees with it in gender, number, and case. Indeed

[48] Ehrman, *Misquoting Jesus*, 95, 110, 204, 209, 223 n. 19, 224 n. 16.
[49] Ibid., 162.

one must here press the syntactical point: when is an adjective *ever* used substantivally when it immediately precedes a noun of the same inflection? . . .

The result is that taking the term *monogenēs theos* as two substantives standing in apposition makes for a nearly impossible syntax, whereas construing their relationship as adjective-noun creates an impossible sense.[50]

Ehrman's argument assumes that *monogenēs* cannot normally be substantival, even though it is so used in verse 14, as he admits. Many critiques could be made of his argument, but chief among them is this: his absolutizing of the grammatical situation is incorrect. His challenge ("no one has cited anything analogous outside of this passage") was taken up by Stratton Ladewig, in a master's thesis at Dallas Seminary, as well as in an article I wrote for the *Journal of the Evangelical Theological Society*.[51] Suffice it to say here that there are, indeed, several examples in which an adjective that is juxtaposed to a noun of the same grammatical concord is not functioning adjectivally but substantivally.

Ehrman argues: "No Greek reader would construe such a construction as a string of substantives, and no Greek writer would create such an inconcinnity."[52] However, this assertion is simply not borne out by the evidence.[53] But if NT authors can create such expressions, this internal argument against the reading *monogenēs theos* loses considerable weight.

It now becomes a matter of asking whether there are sufficient *contextual* clues that *monogenēs* is in fact functioning substantivally. Ehrman has already provided both of them: (1) In John, it is unthinkable that the Word could become the *unique* God in 1:18 (in which He alone, and not the Father, is claimed to have divine status) only to have that status removed repeatedly throughout the rest of the Gospel. Thus, *assuming* that *monogenēs theos* is authentic, we are in fact almost driven to the sense that Ehrman regards as grammatically implausible but

[50] Ehrman, *Orthodox Corruption*, 81.

[51] Stratton Ladewig, "An Examination of the Orthodoxy of the Variants in Light of Bart Ehrman's *The Orthodox Corruption of Scripture*" (ThM thesis, Dallas: Dallas Theological Seminary, 2000); Wallace, "The Gospel According to Bart," 344–45.

[52] Ehrman, *Orthodox Corruption*, 81.

[53] See note 51 for references to texts that invalidate Ehrman's claims.

contextually necessary: "the unique one, himself God. . . ." (2) That *monogenēs* is already used in verse 14 as a substantive[54] becomes the strongest contextual argument for seeing its substantival function repeated four verses later. Immediately after Ehrman admits that this adjective can be used substantivally and is so used in verse 14, he makes his grammatical argument, which is intended to shut the coffin lid on the force of the connection with verse 14. But if the grammatical argument won't cut it, then the substantival use of *monogenēs* in verse 14 should stand as an important contextual clue. Indeed, in light of the well-worn usage in *biblical* Greek, we would almost expect *monogenēs* to be used substantivally and with the implication of sonship in 1:18.

Now, as our only concern here is to wrestle with what *monogenēs theos* would mean *if* it were original, rather than argue for its authenticity, there seems to be sufficient evidence to demonstrate a force such as "the unique one, Himself God" as a suitable gloss for this reading. Both the internal and external evidence are on its side; the only thing holding back such a variant is the interpretation that it was a modalistic reading.[55] But the basis for that is a grammatical assumption that we have demonstrated not to have weight. In conclusion, both *monogenēs theos* and *monogenēs huios* fit comfortably within orthodoxy; no seismic theological shift occurs if one were to pick one reading over the other. Although some modern translators have been persuaded by Ehrman's argument here, the argument is hardly airtight. When either variant is examined carefully, both are seen to be within the realm of orthodox teaching.

Suffice it to say that if "God" is authentic here, it is hardly necessary to translate the phrase as "the unique God," as though that might imply that Jesus alone is God. Rather, as the NET renders it (see also the NIV and NRSV), John 1:18 says, "No one has ever seen God. The

---

[54] A quick look at Lampe's *Patristic Greek Lexicon* also reveals that the substantival function of this adjective was commonplace: 881, def. 7, the term is used absolutely in a host of patristic writers.

[55] Modalism (or Sabellianism) is the heresy that God is *one* person who appears in three different modes (a unitarian view). This is in contrast to the orthodox Christian view—trinitarianism—which affirms that *three* persons exist in one being who share the same divine essence. For further discussion on the doctrine of the Trinity, see chap. 14.

only one, *himself God*, who is in closest fellowship with the Father, has made God known."

In other words, the idea that the variants in the NT manuscripts alter the theology of the NT is overstated at best.[56] Unfortunately, as careful a scholar as Ehrman is, his treatment of major theological changes in the text of the NT tends to fall under one of two criticisms: either his textual decisions are wrong, or his interpretation is wrong. These criticisms were made of his earlier work, *Orthodox Corruption of Scripture*, which *Misquoting Jesus* has drawn from extensively. For example, Gordon Fee said of this work that "[u]nfortunately, Ehrman too often turns mere *possibility* into *probability*, and probability into *certainty*, where other equally viable reasons for corruption exist."[57] Yet the conclusions that Ehrman put forth in *Orthodox Corruption of Scripture* are still offered in *Misquoting Jesus* without recognition of some of the severe criticisms of his work the first go-around.[58] For a book geared toward a lay audience, one would think that he would want to have his discussion nuanced a bit more, especially with all the theological weight he says is on the line. One almost gets the impression that he is encouraging the Chicken Littles in the Christian community to panic at data they are simply not prepared to wrestle with. Time and time again in the book, highly charged statements are put forth that the untrained person simply cannot sift through. And that approach resembles more an alarmist mentality than what a mature, master teacher is able to offer. Regarding the evidence, suffice it to say that *significant textual variants that alter core doctrines of the NT have not yet been produced.*

1 John 5:7–8. Finally, regarding 1 John 5:7–8, virtually no modern translation of the Bible includes the "Trinitarian formula," since scholars for *centuries* have recognized it as added later. Only a few late manuscripts have the verses. One wonders why this passage is even discussed in Ehrman's book. The only reason seems to be to fuel doubts. The passage made its way into our Bibles through political pressure, appearing for the first time in 1522, even though scholars then and

---

[56] For the case that the NT speaks clearly of Christ's deity, see R. Bowman and J. E. Komoszewski, *Putting Jesus in His Place: The Case for the Deity of Christ* (Grand Rapids: Kregel, 2007).

[57] G. D. Fee, review of *The Orthodox Corruption of Scripture* in *Critical Review of Books in Religion* 8 (1995): 204.

[58] For documentation, see Wallace, "The Gospel According to Bart," 347, n. 70.

now knew it was not authentic. The early church did not know of this text, yet the Council of Constantinople in AD 381 explicitly affirmed the Trinity! How could they do this without the benefit of a text that didn't get into the Greek NT for *another millennium?* Constantinople's statement was not written in a vacuum: the early church put into a theological formulation what they got out of the NT.

A distinction needs to be made here: just because a *particular* verse does not affirm a cherished doctrine does not mean that that doctrine cannot be found in the NT.[59] In this case anyone with an understanding of the healthy patristic debates over the Godhead knows that the early church arrived at their understanding from an examination of the data in the NT. The Trinitarian formula found in late manuscripts of 1 John 5:7 only *summarized* what they found; it did not *inform* their declarations.

Conclusion

In sum, *Misquoting Jesus* does not disappoint on the provocative scale. But it comes up short on genuine substance about Ehrman's primary contention. Scholars bear a sacred duty not to alarm layreaders on issues where they have little understanding. Indeed, even agnostic teachers bear this responsibility. Unfortunately, the average layperson will leave *Misquoting Jesus* with far greater doubts about the wording and teachings of the NT than any textual critic would ever entertain. A good teacher doesn't hold back on telling his students what's what, but he also knows how to package the material so they don't let emotion get in the way of reason. The irony is that *Misquoting Jesus* is supposed to be all about reason and evidence, but it has been creating almost as much panic and alarm as *The Da Vinci Code.* Is that really the pedagogical effect Ehrman was seeking? I have to assume that he knew what kind of a reaction he would get from this book, for he does not change the impression at all in his interviews. Being provocative, even at the risk of being misunderstood, seems to be more important to him than being honest even at the risk of being boring. But a good teacher does not create Chicken Littles.

[59] An error that the KJV-only crowd often makes.

Chapter 12

WHO DID JESUS THINK HE WAS?

Michael J. Wilkins

W ho did Jesus think He was? From a twenty-first century, evangelical Christian perspective, we might suppose that is almost a silly question. We believe that Jesus is the Son of God, the second person of the Trinitarian Godhead. And if we believe that of Jesus' identity, then surely He thought the same thing.

The Jesus of History and the Christ of Faith

Modern critics read the data of the New Testament differently by consistently making a distinction between what they refer to as the *Jesus of history* and the *Christ of faith*. By this they mean that the portrait of Jesus that surfaces from the Gospels, primarily the Synoptic Gospels (Matthew, Mark, and Luke), is different from the portrait of Jesus that surfaces from the rest of the New Testament.

They contend that the *Jesus of history* in the Synoptic Gospels gives the portrayal of Jesus' true identity. He grew up with typical human characteristics with a special calling of God (Luke 2:40,52), and He was a prophetic figure similar to John the Baptist (Luke 4:23). But they contend that He never explicitly called Himself Messiah, He silenced those who tried to give Him messianic status (Mark 1:2–25; 8:29–30), and He declared that He was different from His heavenly Father, who knew things about the future that He Himself did not know (Mark 13:32). Jesus knew that He was a special agent of God, but He did not claim that He was anything other than a prophet like those of the Old Testament.

They further contend that the Jesus depicted in the rest of the New Testament is the *Christ of faith*. The hopes of Jesus' mission were utterly devastated with His execution at the hands of the Roman authorities. But soon the followers of Jesus began to believe that Jesus' mission was not dead because it was alive in their minds and hearts. It was as though Jesus Himself were still alive. And if His mission was not dead, then He really was not only the Messiah of Israel but also the Messiah of all the nations. Jesus was still alive in their minds and hearts and was more exalted than ever, and by faith the early followers declared that He was the Christ, the Messiah, the Son of God (Acts 9:22; cf. Rom 1:3–4; Col 1:13–16).

Many modern critics contend that when the authors of the Gospels wrote the story of Jesus' life, they did so from the perspective of faith that Jesus was the Christ, the Son of God, but with the recognition that the Jesus of history did not make that claim, nor did He understand Himself to be such. When we find evidence of these kinds of claims in the Gospels, they are understood to be the Gospel writers interpolating later beliefs back into Jesus' ministry.

Peter's Declaration of Jesus' Identity as a Test-case

An example of this distinction is said to be found in the incident in Jesus' Galilean ministry where the apostle Peter acted as spokesman for the Twelve and declared that Jesus was the Christ, the Greek expression for "Messiah" (Mark 8:29–30; cf. Matt 16:16; 9:20).[1] Among Christians this has long been a benchmark for ascertaining the apostles' understanding of Jesus' identity and also for understanding Jesus' own self-understanding. But from early in the twentieth century up to recent years, modern critics have subjected Peter's declaration to radical critical examination, and many have

---

[1] The material in this section draws upon a forthcoming much larger study, "Peter and His Declaration of Jesus as Messiah," which I have undertaken for the Historical Jesus Study Group of the Institute for Biblical Research. My essay is one of 12 undertaking an analysis and defense of Jesus' historical mission, which are being collected and edited by D. Bock and R. Webb and to be published in the WUNT series (Tübingen: Mohr Siebeck).

declared it not to be a historical event. They contend that it must have been a later interpolation of the church's beliefs by the evangelists back into the narrative of Jesus' ministry, and so they view it as theological fiction.

Rudolf Bultmann viewed the incident as a legend of faith, a retrojection of the church's belief in the resurrection back into the Gospel accounts. He concludes, "The scene of *Peter's Confession* (Mk. 8:27-30) . . . is an Easter-story projected backward into Jesus' lifetime, just like the story of the Transfiguration (Mk. 9:2–8)."[2]

Hans Conzelmann rejected any note of historicity in the declaration: "Any assumption of a historical nucleus makes the texts incomprehensible. The scene is not a story, but a piece of christological reflection given the form of a story. Peter utters the creed of the community, 'You are the Messiah.'"[3]

This is similar to the more recent view of Robert Funk and the Fellows of the Jesus Seminar, who unhesitatingly indicate that the episode is largely or entirely fictive. In their view this is "a stylized scene shaped by Christian motifs."[4] They contend that the Caesarean declaration narrative is the product, in all likelihood, of later Christian imagination, and that the two events actually coincided—i.e., Peter had his Easter vision *and* came to the conclusion that Jesus was Messiah at the same time.[5] In their distinctive color-coding of Gospels material, the Fellows of the Jesus Seminar gave the incident a "black" reading, which indicates, "I would not include this narrative information in the primary database for determining who Jesus was," or, "This information is improbable. It does not fit verifiable evidence; it is largely or entirely fictive."[6]

---

[2] R. Bultmann, *Theology of the New Testament* (one vol. ed.; trans. Kendrick Grobel; New York: Charles Scribner's Sons, 1951), 26; cf. R. Bultmann, *The History of the Synoptic Tradition* (trans. John Marsh; 1931; rev. ed.; 1963; New York: Harper & Row, 1976), 257–59.

[3] H. Conzelmann, *An Outline of the Theology of the New Testament* (2nd ed.; 1968; trans. John Bowden; London: SCM, 1969), 130.

[4] R. W. Funk and the Jesus Seminar, *The Acts of Jesus: The Search for the Authentic Deeds of Jesus* (San Francisco: HarperSanFrancisco, 1998), 104.

[5] R. W. Funk, R. W. Hoover, and the Jesus Seminar, *The Five Gospels: The Search for the Authentic Words of Jesus* (New York: Macmillan, 1993), 75; Funk et al., *Acts of Jesus*, 104, 218, 303.

[6] Funk et al., *Acts of Jesus*, 36–37.

Burton Mack likewise contends that Peter's declaration, linked with the later actions of Jesus in the temple cleansing, are theological fiction. He maintains that "Mark's fiction of an anti-temple messiahship (a contradiction in terms) could have worked only after the temple had already been destroyed. The gospel theme must therefore be a post-AD 70 fabrication. Before that time the scenario would have appeared ridiculous."[7]

The Christ of History

Although modern critics have raised several problems regarding the historicity of Peter's declaration and Jesus' self-identity, the view that the incident is historical and reliable has much more to commend it than does the view that the declaration scene is a piece of fiction. As such, it gives us insight to the apostles' understanding of who they understood Jesus to be and who Jesus understood Himself to be.

When countering the claims of modern critics, it is often helpful to use common methodologies to provide a level playing field from which we can dismantle their conclusions with their own tools. One such strategy is to employ "criteria of authenticity" that modern critics themselves use to deny the authenticity of events in Jesus' life. Contending for a comprehensive understanding of the historical Jesus within the historical context are two prominent Jesus scholars, John Meier, a Roman Catholic scholar, and Craig Evans, an evangelical scholar. Both have given primary or valid criteria a relative ranking in effectiveness in attempting to evaluate the authenticity of events and sayings of Jesus.

---

[7] B. L. Mack, *A Myth of Innocence: Mark and Christian Origins* (Philadelphia: Fortress, 1988), 282–83. He surmises that after the failed Jewish War of the late sixties Mark fabricated the incident of Peter's declaration and the Passion prediction after the destruction of the temple in AD 70 in part to counter enthusiasm for messianic uprisings after the tragic events of the failed Jewish War.

John P. Meier[8]	Craig A. Evans[9]
Primary Criteria	*Valid Criteria*
1. Embarrassment	1. Historical Coherence
2. Discontinuity	2. Multiple Attestation
3. Multiple Attestation	3. Embarrassment
4. Coherence	4. Dissimilarity
5. Rejection and execution	5. Semitisms and Palestinian Background
	6. Coherence

Employing only briefly at least three of these criteria will lead to the conclusion that the Gospel writers recorded a historically authentic account of Peter's declaration that Jesus was the Christ/Messiah, and its authenticity affirms Jesus' self-identity as the Messiah of Israel, but a different kind of Messiah than even Peter expected.

1. Palestinian Background

In the first place the criterion that Evans titles "Semitisms and Palestinian background" is helpful. This criterion indicates that if the text describes events or concepts distinctive to early first-century Palestine, then one need not look to the later, more Hellenistic church for its origin.[10]

Mark tells us that Peter's declaration took place in Caesarea Philippi in "the villages of Caesarea Philippi." This is an odd expression, for the reader might have expected "the region of Caesarea Philippi" after the pattern found earlier (cf. Mark 5:1,17; 7:24,31; 8:10).[11] But Mark's expression strikes a strong note of reminiscence. Associating the declaration with this Gentile place strikes a chord of an actual memory of

---

[8] J. P. Meier, "Criteria: How Do We Decide What Comes from Jesus?" *A Marginal Jew: Rethinking the Historical Jesus—Volume One: The Roots of the Problem and the Person* (Anchor Bible Reference Library; New York: Doubleday, 1991), 167–95.

[9] C. A. Evans, "Recent Developments in Jesus Research: Presuppositions, Criteria, and Sources," *Jesus and His Contemporaries: Comparative Studies* (Leiden: Brill, 2001), 1–49; esp. 13–26.

[10] Evans, *Jesus and His Contemporaries*, 22–23; cf. Meier, *A Marginal Jew*, 1:180.

[11] Matthew has "into the parts [*eis ta merē*] of Caesarea Philippi," focusing on the villages that would be included in the larger district, as he did in 15:21; cf. BADG 633; W. D. Davies and D. C. Allison Jr., *A Critical and Exegetical Commentary on the Gospel According to Matthew*, vol. 2: A Commentary on Matthew VIII–XVIII (Edinburgh: T&T Clark, 1991), 616.

an event in an unexpected locale. There is little evidence for a tendency in Palestinian Jewish-Christian circles to add to the Gospel records a reference to a city outside Palestine.[12]

This geographical notation occurs unexpectedly in the narrative but demonstrates the evangelists' attention to historical detail. Jesus continued His outreach to Jews living in the villages of that region which was part of the former geographical northern tribes of Israel, a detail that lends plausibility to the evangelists' historical record. Jesus was drawing the ill attention of Herod Antipas in the region of Galilee; so moving away from Galilee provides a bit of a respite out of Herod's political jurisdiction. Peter's declaration that Jesus is the Christ, and in Matthew's wording, the Son of the living God (Matt. 16:16), is a striking messianic contrast to the stone, pagan god Pan that was worshiped in the region.

The awkwardness of the expression as a whole, the unexpectedness of the reference to Caesarea of Philippi, and moving in a northerly direction that is the opposite direction from Jerusalem, to which the following pericopes point, argue for the historicity of the topographical setting of the entire incident.[13] James Dunn comments, "There are several indications that Mark has been able to draw on a well-rooted memory, with the variations between the Synoptists characteristic of performance flexibility."[14]

2. Embarrassment

A second criterion may be even more helpful. It is called the criterion of "embarrassment," which indicates that if a saying or event created embarrassment or theological difficulties for the church and for the evangelist himself, it is unlikely to have been invented by the early church.[15] As Meier says, "The point of the criterion is that the early

---

[12] H. F. Bayer, *Jesus' Predictions of Vindication and Resurrection: The Provenance, Meaning, and Correlation of the Synoptic Predictions* (WUNT 2/20; Tübingen: J. C. B. Mohr [P. Siebeck], 1986), 155; C. A. Evans, *Mark 8:27–16:20* (WBC 34b; Nashville: Thomas Nelson, 2001), 10, 13.

[13] Bayer, *Jesus' Predictions*, 155; R. H. Gundry, *Mark: A Commentary on His Apology for the Cross* (Grand Rapids: Eerdmans, 1993), 425–26.

[14] J. D. G. Dunn, *Jesus Remembered*, vol. 1: *Christianity in the Making* (Grand Rapids: Eerdmans, 2003), 644–45.

[15] For discussion see Evans, *Jesus and His Contemporaries*, 18–19; Meier, *A Marginal Jew*,

church would hardly have gone out of its way to create material that only embarrassed its creator or weakened his position in arguments with opponents."[16]

The criterion of embarrassment authenticates the declaration incident in a significant way. After Peter makes his declaration, Jesus responds by commanding Peter and the others to tell no one (Mark 8:30). Then in the sequel, which is firmly tied to the declaration by each of the Synoptics, Jesus gives His first Passion prediction (Mark 8:31); but Peter responds to the prediction by rebuking Jesus; and at this, Jesus turns and rebukes Peter, saying, in identical language in both Mark and Matthew, "Get behind me, Satan!" (Mark 8:33 NIV; Matt 16:23).

This has been recognized by many scholars as a classic case for the use of the criterion of embarrassment because if Mark or Matthew or the early church had created the declaration scene in order to elevate Peter, why would they disgrace Peter with a story about his opposition to Jesus' Passion prediction? Whatever had been gained by the declaration proper was lost in Jesus' calling him Satan.

The evangelists did not shrink from recording an incident that is embarrassing to Peter, the leader of the twelve apostles, which adds credibility to their intentions to record incidents the way they occurred. Although Peter is commended for his God-inspired declaration that Jesus is the Christ/Messiah, and in Matthew is designated to play a primary leadership role in the establishment of the church, when Jesus reveals an aspect of His messianic ministry, suffering and dying, that is incongruent with Peter's still-developing conception, he is declared by Jesus to be a Satan-inspired hindrance to Jesus' fuller messianic mission. The historical credibility of the evangelists' record of this incident is heightened by their willingness to include material that is embarrassing to Peter.

3. Historical Coherence

Third, and perhaps most importantly, the evangelists' accounts of Peter's declaration demonstrate authenticity because the incident has

1:168–71.
[16] Meier, *A Marginal Jew*, 1:168.

coherence historically with both the developing messianic ministry of Jesus and the final events of Jesus' life that led to His crucifixion. Here we employ the criterion of "historical coherence," which looks at the larger pattern of Jesus' historical circumstances and the principal features of His life. This criterion looks to one of the most striking things about Jesus' earthly life, His violent death, and attempts to understand the whole of His life in the light of that final event.[17] As Meier states, "A Jesus whose words and activities did not threaten or alienate people, especially powerful people, is not the historical Jesus."[18]

This is one of the most crucial pieces of evidence for establishing the authenticity of the incident surrounding Peter's declaration because virtually all scholars, including modern critics, acknowledge that Jesus was crucified at the hands of the Romans. If so, what led to His crucifixion, and specifically, what led to His crucifixion as the "King of the Jews" as all four of the Gospels record,[19] is critical for understanding what Jesus' mission on earth was all about.

Here we look briefly at three incidents to see how the episode of Peter's declaration coheres historically with Jesus' earlier developing mission and with His later execution.

Relationship to John the Baptist

John the Baptist and Jesus were inextricably linked in their messages declaring that the kingdom of God was at hand (cf. Matt 3:2; 4:17). John pointed to Jesus as the one who would bring imminent eschatological judgment. From a religious perspective this was perceived as a spiritual revival of repentance. But from a political perspective it was perceived as a threat of sedition. Josephus tells us that Herod Antipas arrested and executed John because he feared that the enthusiasm of his followers would lead to sedition (Josephus, *Antiquities* 18.5.2 §116–19).

---

[17] This criterion especially asks what words and activities fit in with and explain Jesus' trial and crucifixion as "King of the Jews," which Evans contends is "the single most important feature that must be taken into account in any work that wishes to be taken seriously"; cf. Evans, *Jesus and His Contemporaries*, 13–14.

[18] Meier, *A Marginal Jew*, 1:177.

[19] Matt 27:37; Mark 15:26; Luke 23:38; John 19:19.

John expected imminent eschatological judgment, but this only led to his imprisonment. So prior to his execution, he questioned Jesus about His identity as the Coming One (Matt 11:2–3; Luke 7:18–20). Jesus responded that in His ministry of healing and preaching the good news John should draw an appropriate conclusion that He was indeed the Coming One (Matt 11:2–6; Luke 7:21–23). But Jesus deflected John's expectation that He would bring imminent eschatological judgment. Instead, Jesus' messianic ministry as the Coming One included being anointed with the Spirit to herald the kingdom of God and bring healing and preaching the good news (Matt 11:2–6; Luke 4:16–23; 7:21–23; cf. Isa 35:5–6). But the ruling authorities linked Jesus' mission with John's expectation of judgment and laid plans to execute Jesus as they did John.

Calling and Sending the Twelve

Jesus carried on and furthered John's prophetic announcement of the arrival of the kingdom of God, but in doing so He called and sent out the Twelve on a mission. This was a statement of hope of restoration or reunification to national Israel, but it was also a threat of condemnation to those who did not repent. In His preaching of the arrival of the kingdom of God, Jesus linked His anointing by the Spirit with His miraculous ministry as a demonstration that the kingdom had arrived in His ministry and that He was operating with divine authority (cf. Matt 12:28; Luke 11:20). The mission of the Twelve was to spread this message with the hope to gain the land and its people for the kingdom of God. With this calling and sending it implies a politically royal dimension because it is a vision for the nation.[20] The Twelve represent the new leadership needed to replace the failing religious leadership of Israel. Later Jesus will declare that the kingdom will be taken away from the leadership of Israel and given to the nation producing the fruits of it (cf. Matt 21:43). This does not make Him into a primarily political Jesus, but the national dimension in the light of the announcement of the kingdom of God and the calling and sending of the Twelve is significant and could not be ignored by the leaders of Israel. The beginnings of accusations formed that Jesus was a threat

[20] Cf. S. McKnight, "Jesus and the Twelve," *Bulletin of Biblical Research* 11/2 (2001): 203–31.

to the national security with His vision of establishing the kingdom of God, however misguided those accusations may have been.

Acclaimed as Prophet and King

The nature of Jesus' messianic ministry was also demonstrated in the ways He rejected attempts by the crowds to acclaim Him as the militaristic and political king of Israel (John 6:13–14). Other popular persons of Jesus' day had indeed roused up crowds to confront Rome and attempt to bring back the glories of the days of King David, but Jesus had no such intention for His messianic ministry. He continues to focus on the realities of the arrival of the kingdom of God in the power of the Spirit. But the crowds will continue to misunderstand Jesus' messianic intentions, and their pent-up desire for a messianic deliverer will attract the attention of the Roman occupation.

In one scene Jesus' preaching and healing and working great miracles elicited responses from the crowd acclaiming Him as "the Prophet who is to come into the world" (John 6:14 NIV). But Jesus rejects this acclaim because it included a frenzied desire to make Him king (John 6:15). Jesus is here connected with the tradition that regarded Moses as a king as well as a prophet.[21] Jesus rejects this attempt to turn Him into the kind of leader that the crowd desires.[22] Raymond Brown asserts:

> We believe that in these verses John has given us an item of correct historical information. The ministry of miracles in Galilee culminating in the multiplication (which in John, as in Mark, is the last miracle of the Galilee ministry) aroused a popular fervor that created a danger of an uprising which would give authorities, lay and religious, a chance to arrest Jesus legally.[23]

---

[21] Cf. Deut 18:18; 33:5; 4QTest (175) 5–8. C. S. Keener, *The Gospel of John: A Commentary* (Peabody, MA: Hendrickson, 2003), 669–71.

[22] P. N. Anderson, *The Christology of the Fourth Gospel: Its Unity and Disunity in the Light of John 6* (rpt; 1996; Harrisburg, PA: Trinity Press International, 1997), 177. Of the 16 times that the term *basileus* ("king") occurs in John's Gospel, it never is used by Jesus to refer to Himself.

[23] Raymond E. Brown, *The Gospel According to John: Introduction, Translation, and Notes* (2 vols; Anchor Bible Commentary 29; Garden City, NY: Doubleday, 1966), 1:249–50.

In the whole context of Jesus' ministry, He was viewed as a threat to the authority of the religious establishment. After Herod Antipas executed John the Baptist, he had already taken notice of Jesus for His widespread ministry (Matt 14:1–12; Mark 6:14–29; Luke 9:7–9). Jesus began to withdraw from Galilee because of Antipas's attention to Him.[24]

Josephus tells us that in first-century Palestine wilderness prophets who promised signs like Moses' usually gained large followings and hailed their leaders as a prophet or deliverer, and they were often interpreted as political insurrectionists.[25] In that time of varied messianic expectations, it is not hard to imagine that the lines between prophetic and royal hope became blurred among some of the people. Many among the crowd understood Jesus in this potentially political light,[26] especially when Jesus' own preaching and activity—focused on the kingdom of God—aroused pent-up hopes for the return of the Davidic glories. It is a matter of history, however, that Jesus rejects the popular, earthly kingship that the people desire.[27] Nonetheless, even though Jesus rejects attempts to make Him into a political/militaristic king, misconceptions of His mission would lead to His execution by the Romans as the "King of the Jews."

Accepting the title "Messiah"—with Qualification

Peter's declaration that Jesus is the Christ/Messiah coheres remarkably with the broader historical portrait of Jesus' unique messianic ministry and His tragic, yet victorious messianic death in crucifixion. Peter rightly declares that Jesus' true identity is that of the Christ/Messiah because it coheres with what Peter had seen Jesus developing in His messianic ministry. Yet Jesus instructs Peter and the others not to broadcast that declaration (cf. Matt 16:20; Mark 8:30; Luke 9:21). Jesus does not warn the disciples to be silent because He considered it incorrect. Jesus accepted the declaration, but He did so with two qualifications. In the first place, Jesus expressed caution in the public

---

[24] Matt 14:13; cf. Mark 6:31–32; Luke 9:10.

[25] E.g., Josephus *War* 2.261–63; *Ant* 17.273–74; 20.97–98; 169–71.

[26] Cf. Anderson, *Christology of the Fourth Gospel*, 177–79; Keener, *John*, 1:670–71.

[27] B. Lindars, *The Gospel of John* (New Century Bible Commentary; Grand Rapids: Eerdmans, 1972), 244.

use of the title Messiah/Christ because the crowds, the religious establishment, and the Roman government will mistakenly assume that Jesus was establishing a militaristic kingship. But Jesus did not reject the title Messiah as declared by Peter.

In the second place, Jesus accepts Peter's declaration, but He will need to clarify to Peter and the Twelve that He was a different kind of Messiah than even they understood Him to be. So Jesus reveals that suffering and dying were included in His messianic ministry (Mark 8:31). This is a historical inevitability in the light of the religious and political opposition and also fulfilled the prophecies of Messiah who would be the Suffering Servant (e.g., Isaiah 53). Peter only partially understood Jesus' intent in His messianic ministry because when Jesus revealed this aspect of His messianic mission, Peter wanted to deter Him and force Jesus into his own conception of Messiah (Mark 8:32). But such deterrence was not from God, and Peter is declared to be a tool of Satan in that move (8:33). Jesus is Messiah, but He is to be a suffering and dying and raised Messiah, something that even His closest followers could not yet fully grasp.

The criterion of historical coherence establishes the authenticity of Peter's declaration of Jesus as Messiah within His overall historical mission and crucifixion. Peter has a growing recognition of Jesus' unique messianic ministry, which surpasses the crowds' understanding. Yet it was not fully developed. Jesus understands the swelling historical inevitability of His arrest and execution, which will be in accord with the divine prophetic inevitability of His sacrificial death.

Widely varied messianic expectations were found in Judaism at the time of Jesus' ministry. Jesus deflected any attempts by those around Him to conform to their expectations and instead carefully articulated and demonstrated the ways He was the Messiah. Although the arrival of the kingdom of God in the person of Jesus was not one involving armies and weapons of war, it nonetheless was misunderstood by the common people, the religious authorities, and the political and military regime to the extent that it resulted in His execution. Larry Hurtado concludes, "Jesus' execution had to have been based on one or more charges of a very serious nature, perhaps involving a threat to public order, which would certainly correspond to a perceived royal-messianic claim, whether made by him or his followers."[28] Jesus' historical mission was a fulfillment of Old Testament prophecies that God would send Messiah to bring liberation and peace to His people. But it was a different kind of liberation and peace than the majority of people hoped to see occur.

Jesus' Self-Understanding

I have painted with broad strokes the portrayal of modern critics and their inadequate distinction between the Jesus of history and the Christ of faith. I have demonstrated that in His historical mission Jesus understood Himself to be the Messiah but one who confounded not only the crowds and His enemies but also His own closest companions. All of the Gospel writers point us in this direction, but we briefly conclude with Matthew's historical focus on Jesus' self-understanding in the final days of His life.[29]

From the beginning of this Gospel, which announced the arrival of Jesus as the son of David, the son of Abraham (Matt 1:1), Matthew has carefully detailed Jesus as the Messiah who fulfills Israel's expectations and the nations' hopes. As the spotlight of history focuses on the events of the cross, Matthew draws attention to Jesus as Messiah, but in a tragically ironic way as one who baffled His own followers, disappointed the crowds, and enraged the religious leaders. He will be a crucified Messiah. With four strokes of his narrative brush, Matthew fills in the details and the colors of his portrait of Jesus as the crucified Messiah. Derek Tidball explains: "He wants our attention to be held by who it was that was pinned in such a humiliating and fatal way to a stake on the hill of Golgotha. It is a portrait which in a myriad of ways tells us about the real identity of the central figure and so of his mission."[30] Matthew highlights four specific features of Jesus as the crucified Messiah that run throughout the Passion Narrative.

---

[28] L. W. Hurtado, *Lord Jesus Christ: Devotion to Jesus in Earliest Christianity* (Grand Rapids: Eerdmans, 2003), 57.

[29] This is adapted from M. J. Wilkins, *Matthew* (NIV Application Commentary; Grand Rapids: Zondervan, 2004), 844–45.

[30] D. Tidball, *The Message of the Cross: Wisdom Unsearchable, Love Indestructible* (The Bible Speaks Today; Downers Grove: InterVarsity, 2000), 134.

1. Prophesied Deliverer. As the anticipated Messiah, Jesus fulfills Scripture that prophesied His actions during the final hours that led to the cross for the deliverance of His people. It is divinely appointed time (26:18), His hour of prophesied reckoning (26:24,45). The people of Israel anticipated a deliverer, but Jesus will deliver them in ways that not all expected. He will be stricken (26:31), fulfilling the prophecies of a slain, stricken Messiah who brings healing and deliverance from iniquity to His people (Isa 53:4–12; Zech 12:9–14). Later rabbis interpreted these verses to mean that they should expect a slain Messiah (*b. Sukkah 52a*). But for many this will be a real stumbling block because the events of the crucifixion point to Jesus' self-understanding of His divine incarnation as the Son of God (26:46,54).

2. Sacrificial Servant. As the fulfillment of the prophecies of a crucified Messiah, Jesus will spill His blood as the Servant who is the willing sacrifice to bear the sins of humanity. He raises the Passover cup of redemption and declares, "This is my blood of the covenant, which is poured out for many for the forgiveness of sins" (Matt 26:28 NIV). He is the fulfillment of the symbolism of the Passover lamb as He becomes the Servant of the Lord who bears the sins of humanity (Isa 53:12). The events of the cross are not pleasant. They are bloody. And modern sensibilities want to clean them up to make them more palatable. But to do so minimizes the awfulness of sin and its requisite eternal penalty which makes necessary the bloody punishment. The initiation of the Lord's Supper points forward to the crucifixion, requiring us to steel ourselves to understand the profound necessity of Jesus the sacrificial Servant as a crucified Messiah.

3. Willing Lord. Throughout His ministry Jesus exercised control over the forces of nature and the spirit world. That control does not cease as He goes to the cross. He is not a victim of these circumstances but a willing Lord. His anointing by the worshiping woman expressed more than any could really comprehend because He is truly the anointed Davidic Messiah who is David's Lord (22:43). Yet the woman's act unknowingly anointed Him for death (26:12) as the obedient Son of His heavenly Father (26:44). Jesus sovereignly initiates the prophesied new covenant, but it is through the cup of wrath that He willingly accepts (26:28,39–44).

4. Humble King. Jesus was worshiped as He was born "king of the Jews" (2:2, 11); and He will be mocked as He is crucified "king of the Jews" (27:29). Both times find Jesus in the humblest of settings. The first was the humble setting of a poor Bethlehem home, the second in the humiliation of the powerful Roman Praetorium. But Jesus knows who He is and what He has come to accomplish. He doesn't have to prove anything to anyone because He knows that He is indeed the King of the Jews (27:11). The humiliation of His incarnation brought the arrival of the kingdom of heaven to those who dared to respond to His invitation (4:17). The humiliation of His crucifixion brings the redemption of humanity to those who dare to respond to His inauguration of the new covenant in His blood (26:28). But the humiliation of His death is also a poignant promise that His kingdom will soon manifest itself with power and glory when He comes again (26:29; cf. 13:41–42; 24:30–31).

So who did Jesus think He was? Messiah, to be sure, but far more than even His closest followers understood. He is the divine Son of God who offers Himself as the suffering and dying and rising Messiah, bringing life to all who heed His call to the kingdom of God. Jesus' intentional messianic mission uniquely focused on the establishment of the kingdom of God for all people, which declares the good news that they can be set free from the tyranny of sin and death and brought into newness of life in the power of the Spirit.

Part 3

THE COHERENCE OF CHRISTIAN DOCTRINE

Chapter 13

THE COHERENCE OF THEISM

Charles Taliaferro and Elsa J. Marty

P hilosophers have long been concerned with the coherence of the concept of God. The stakes are high. Atheist philosophers from ancient Greece onward have sought to show that the idea of God or gods makes no sense. Other philosophers have found that the concept of God or gods is supremely intelligible. God has been described as the most real being (*ens realissimum*), and some philosophers (beginning with Anselm of Canterbury in the twelfth century) have argued that if the *idea* of God is coherent, we may legitimately reason through logical premises that God actually exists. There is a long history of philosophical debate about the concept of God, which has been well thought through and elaborated upon over time. As the seventeenth-century philosopher Henry More once observed, the idea of God is pregnant with rich possibilities and virtues.

New Atheism, a movement led by people like Richard Dawkins, Daniel Dennett, Sam Harris, and Christopher Hitchens, however, treats the concept of God as an ill-designed hypothesis, based on what they think is fear, ignorance, and wishful thinking. Often hostile and militant in their attacks, they cannot comprehend how an intelligent person could possibly believe in the existence of God. Yet their depictions of theism are, in our view, simplistic caricatures. It is as though they have completely overlooked the millennia of sincere, dedicated, and nuanced philosophical reflection on the concept of God. In *The God Delusion*, for example, Richard Dawkins describes "the God

Hypothesis" as the thesis that "there exists a superhuman, supernatural intelligence who deliberately designed and created the universe and everything in it, including us." Later in the book he asserts that "goodness is no part of the definition of the God Hypothesis, merely a desirable add on."[1] Apart from Dawkins's absurd stipulation that the concept of God is the concept of a "superhuman" (as if God were some kind of supersized Homo sapiens), the idea that goodness is a mere "add on" with respect to God utterly misses the whole central idea of God. Most fundamentally, the concept of God is one of a reality that merits our highest praise and deepest faith.

Philosophers have worked hard to refine the concept of God as unsurpassably good and worthy of praise because that is the key to recognizing the attributes that make God, God: God's necessary or underived existence, incorporeality, omnipotence, essential goodness, omniscience, omnipresence, and eternity. Each one enhances the others. Consider omnipotence without omniscience. Arguably, a being without omniscience would have less power than one with omniscience. The attributes of God are therefore not a patchwork of arbitrary characteristics. Each one is, rather, interconnected, and together they form a coherent whole. Appreciating this helps one avoid the more crude depiction of God one finds in Dawkins's work. Dawkins's conception of goodness as a mere add-on shows the failure of the New Atheists to comprehend the concept of theism. Philosophers do not arbitrarily pick and choose what attributes they would like God to have. Theism makes sense as a coherent whole; one does not add and subtract aspects of God at will.

In this chapter we seek to defend the coherence of the concept of God. We begin with a brief word on how to discern coherency in arguments regarding theism and proceed to outline six divine attributes, or properties, involved in the concept of God: necessary existence, incorporeality, essential goodness, omnipotence, omniscience, and eternity. With respect to each, we offer a brief account of at least one skeptical challenge and a reply. We conclude with reflections on what may be called the flexibility of theism.

---

[1] R. Dawkins, *The God Delusion* (Boston: Houghton Mifflin Co., 2006), 31, 106.

We, the authors, come from the Christian tradition and make sense of God in light of Jesus the Christ. The divine attributes inherent in the concept of God are generally agreed upon by theists from other religious traditions as well. Our aim in this essay is simply to defend from a philosophical standpoint the coherence of theism and thereby defend the coherence of a concept that is central to both Christian and other theistic traditions. Specific Christian teachings about God as Triune and God incarnate further enrich the philosophy of God beyond what may be a general theism, and we comment on this at the end of our chapter.

A Coherent Method for Recognizing Coherent Concepts

The concept of a being or state of affairs is coherent if it is possible that the being or state of affairs exists or obtains. If the concept of God is coherent, for example, it is possible that God exists. Determining the coherence of a central religious idea such as God is not the same, however, as determining the coherence or incoherence of some theoretical or mathematical proposition or idea. Number theory and logical consistency may be all that is needed to determine the coherence of some theorem. However, with respect to certain more metaphysical claims, such as the claim that persons can survive the death of their bodies, more than logical consistency will be required; we will need to test relevant concepts such as being a person, having a body, and personal identity. Engaging in various thought experiments in which we try to imagine (picture, describe, conceive of) persons without bodies, we come to see that this state of affairs is not a *bona fide* possibility. In thinking about theism, we will need not only logical consistency, clarity, and powers of imagination but also a sound sense of values. This will come to the fore when we discuss the divine attributes of power, knowledge, and essential goodness below. We will also make use of an important insight from feminist thinkers to refine the philosophy of power at work in the concept of omnipotence.

Of all the values that would be useful to note at the beginning of our inquiry, probably the most important is humility. When it comes to the concept of God in theistic tradition, we are approaching the concept of a being who is both immanent and transcendent. God is believed to be immanent insofar as God is the omnipresent Creator, without whose ongoing causal sustaining power the cosmos would not exist. But God is also believed to be transcendent in the sense that God is more than we are able to grasp. In theology, the positive statements we can make about God are part of what is known as cataphatic theology or the *via positiva* (the positive way), while the denial that we can fully grasp the divine is part of apophatic theology or the *via negativa* (the negative way). In what follows we are engaged in the *via positiva*; but although we defend the intelligibility of the concept of God as necessarily existing and so on, we also want to acknowledge in the end that (if theism is right), God is more than we can fully grasp. And this calls for a sense of humility, not stemming from what the New Atheists think of as infantile fear or the love of mystery but from a sense of the overwhelming, awesome nature of God.

Let us now explore a set of divine attributes and consider the cause for or against their coherence.

Necessary Existence

Philosophers in the Islamic tradition have been especially committed to articulating the thesis that God's existence is the concept of a reality that is not contingent. One way they (and later, Christian thinkers) express the concept is by claiming that God's essence (what it is to be God) contains existence. With respect to everything else in this world, *essence* (what a thing is) is distinct from *existence* (the fact of a thing existing or not existing). At one time horses did not exist, and one day horses will likely cease to exist. (Astrophysicists conjecture that when the sun uses up all of its hydrogen four billion years from now, the earth will vaporize.)

The concept of God, however, is not contingent because (if there is a God), God never came into existence nor can God cease to exist. God's essence is existence. To be God is to exist. To ask why God exists would be like asking, "Why is red, red?" The color red simply *is* red. The redness of red is simply a matter of the law of identity: A is A, or every thing is itself. Similarly, *if there is a God*, then there is a being whose reality is not derived from another force (a super God) and whose nonexistence is implausible.

Dawkins has complained that if theists are allowed to posit the necessary existence of God, then he ought to be allowed to posit necessary existence of the cosmos. There are two problems with this. First, theists do not begin with some arbitrary concept, x and then add on necessary existence. Their reasoning, rather, is that necessary existence is part of the existence of God. If someone were to report, "Oh, God existed at noon today and then perished at 2:00 PM," we would normally think the person was joking. The concept of God simply *is* the concept of a being that cannot be vulnerable to nonexistence. Second, there does not appear to be anything in the cosmos or about the cosmos that involves necessary existence. The fact that science must observe the world in order to explain it is evidence that the world could have been different. The concept of the cosmos is contingent; various scientific theories explaining the way that the world works may have conditional necessity (a quark must have a certain electric charge, given the prevailing laws of physics), but nothing in or about the cosmos is essentially necessarily existent, nor are the laws of physics themselves necessary. There are current laws of the conservation of energy, but none of them provides any reason to think that energy itself necessarily exists. The mere endurance of some force or event over time, even if it is without beginning, does not itself constitute necessary existence.

Consider the following objection, however. Can't we *conceive* of a cosmos without God? If so, it seems that it is possible that God does not exist. If it is possible that God does not exist, then God's existence is not necessary.

Reply: Conceiving of the nonexistence of God is more difficult than it may appear at first glance. I can conceive of a cosmos without conceiving of the truth 1+1=2, but it does not necessarily follow that I am conceiving of a cosmos in which 1+1 does not equal 2. If one can see that God's existence is impossible the way one can see that $1+1 \neq 3$, then there is no problem with grasping the possibility of God's not existing. But short of an argument that God's existence may be known to be impossible, the objector would need to do two things: (1) conceive of God and (2) conceive of *that God's* not existing. This, we suggest, is difficult because (by definition), acknowledgment of God's existence is necessary to conceive of God's nonexistence. To conceive of God's nonexistence without conceiving of God would be like conceiving of water without hydrogen or oxygen. You may *think* that you could have water sloshing around in a container while clever scientists rename all the oxygen and hydrogen atoms, but because water *is* H_2O, this is not a *bona fide* possibility. God's existence, unlike that of the cosmos, is necessary.

Incorporeality

God is sometimes portrayed in the Scriptures of the monotheistic traditions in terms of a material embodiment: Adam and Eve "heard the sound of the Lord God walking in the garden" (Gen 3:8).[2] But virtually all philosophical theists interpret these passages as metaphors to describe God, who is a nonphysical reality—a being not identical with any material object. "God is spirit" (John 4:24). Traditional Christians believe God became incarnate (embodied), but this is not the same thing as believing that God's *being* turned into a corporeal object. (The problem with thinking that God became a physical object is that identity is strict and symmetrical. If A is identical with B, then B is identical with A. If God is identical with a physical body in the first century, then God has always been identical with that body, which means, absurdly, that that body has always existed. For this reason traditional Christians see Jesus as God incarnate or—literally—enfleshed and in that sense fully human rather than holding that God became numerically identical with an animal body.)[3]

Some philosophers have argued that there might be a powerful, knowledgeable, good god only if this being has a body like Zeus or Thor because an incorporeal agent is a contradiction of terms. Don't all coherent ideas about agents require embodied, material beings?

The difficulty with this objection is that there does not appear to be anything about being an agent (a subject who intentionally brings about events) that ipso facto requires any kind of body. Agents are not

[2] Scripture quotations are from the Holman Christian Standard Bible.
[3] See C. Taliaferro and S. Goetz, "The Prospects for Christian Materialism," *Christian Scholar's Review* 37/3 (2008): 303–21.

necessarily physical or embodied. Even if we humans are essentially embodied (we cannot exist without our bodies), it does not follow that *every* conceivable (or unconceivable) being is corporeal.

Besides, even in our own case, it is difficult to establish that our power of agency (our desire and ability to bring about some event) is itself physical. We can observe *what happens* in the brain when a person desires to think about mathematics, but arguably that is not to observe the person's *desire* to think about mathematics. Contemporary brain science has not shown how our subjective experience (our thinking, sensing, and emotions) can be the same thing as our brain processes. There is good evidence of correlation, but correlation is not identity. And even if it turns out that our mental states and activities are the same things as our brain activity, this does not rule out the possibility of other agents being incorporeal agents.

Some philosophers further oppose the concept of an incorporeal agent on the grounds that any explanation of events by such an agent would be empty or void of significance because of their inability to be subjected to scientific observation or explanation. Matthew Bagger, one of the New Atheists and a professor of religion at Brown University, argues that we simply cannot *ever* resort to theistic accounts:

> [W]e can never assert that, in principle, an event resists natu-
> ralistic explanation. A perfectly substantiated, anomalous
> event, rather than providing evidence for the supernatural,
> merely calls into question our understanding of particular
> natural laws. In the modern era, this position fairly accurately
> represents the educated response to novelty. Rather than in-
> voke the supernatural, we can always adjust our knowledge of
> the natural in extreme cases. In the modern age in actual in-
> quiry, we never reach the point where we throw up our hands
> and appeal to divine intervention to explain a localized event
> like an extraordinary experience.[4]

Bagger appeals to what we moderns assume in all other contexts of explanation, and none of these seems to allow for an appeal to God (or

---

[4] M. Bagger, *Religious Experience, Justification, and History* (Cambridge: Cambridge University Press, 1999), 13.

what Bagger calls "the supernatural"). Jan Narveson, a Canadian philosopher, offers a more pointed, direct assault on theistic explanations, which he sees as empty of content. We cite him at length:

> It ought to be regarded as a major embarrassment to natural theology that the very idea of something like a universe's being "created" by some minded being is sufficiently mind-boggling that any attempt to provide a detailed account of how it might be done is bound to look silly, or mythical, or a vaguely anthropomorphized version of some familiar physical process.
>
> It is plainly no surprise that details about just *how* all this [creation] was supposed to have happened are totally lacking when they are not, as I say, silly or simply poetic. For the fundamental idea is that some infinitely powerful mind simply willed it to be thus, and, as they say, Lo!, it was so! . . . "How are we supposed to know the ways of the infinite and almighty God?" it is asked—as if that put-down made a decent substitute for an answer. But of course it doesn't. If we are serious about "natural theology," then we ought to be ready to supply content in our explication of theological hypotheses just as we do when we explicate scientific hypotheses. Such explications carry the brunt of explanations. Why does water boil when heated? The scientific story supplies an analysis of matter in its liquid state, the effects of atmospheric pressure and heat, and so on until we see, in impressive detail, just how the thing works. An explanation's right to be called "scientific" is, indeed, in considerable part earned precisely by its ability to provide such detail.[5]

If Narveson and Bagger are correct, a theistic explanation of the cosmos is not a live option.

Against Narveson and Bagger one may reply that there are two general kinds of explanations for events: intentional accounts (which invoke values, designs, purposes), and nonintentional accounts (which

[5] J. Narveson, "God by Design?" in *God and Design: the Teleological Argument and Modern Science*, ed. N. A. Manson (London: Routledge, 2003), 93–94.

lack values, designs, and purposes). So, for example, scientific accounts of heat, light, gravity, and chemical bonds consist of nonintentional causal explanations. An account of the speed of light contains no recourse to desire, purpose, or value. Intentional explanations are essential, however, if one wants to explain our writing and your reading of this book. Some eliminativists (materialists who avoid appeals to mental activities) have proposed that *all* explanations must (in the end) avoid intentionality, but we shall assume (as most philosophers today hold) that an account of your reading this book must include some beliefs, desires, and intentions (a curiosity about religion, a desire to think critically about it, and so on).

If there are such intentional explanations, there must be what some philosophers call *basic actions*. These are acts one does for reasons, but one does them directly and without the mediation of other acts. You might do one thing (get your friend's attention) by doing another (calling out to her), but some acts are not mediated. Your calling out to your friend because you want to meet her may require a host of factors to come into play in a full explanation (factors including social expectations, language use, personality type, etc.). But some acts will be not further accountable by other acts. When you called, you did not do so by your willing that certain neurons fire or that your nervous system react in some way; you simply did the act.

When Narveson complains that theistic explanation lacks certain mechanisms and causal elements, his complaint cuts against intentional explanations in ordinary human (and other animal) activities. In everyday, *bona fide* explanations of human agency, there are basic acts that are not further reducible into "impressive detail." (It should also be noted that if there must always be an answer to "how things work" in physical causation, there can be *no basic physical causes*. This seems counter to many views of causation in the physical world and threatens an infinite regress.) If divine intentions are basic, so are some human intentions even though the latter are exercised by beings with animal bodies. This implies that Narveson is not successful in ruling out the possibility of theistic accounts.

If Narveson is not successful, then it is hard to see how Bagger could be. In his characterization of naturalism in *Religious Experience,*

Justification, and History, where he seeks to rule out all theistic explanations, he explicitly does *not* commit himself to materialism or to the emptiness of intentional explanations. If he allows intentional explanations in principle, it is difficult to see why an appeal to our "modern" sensibilities and values can exclude theism in principle. Recall Bagger's treatment of what is natural, cited earlier. His use of "natural" is surprisingly broad, for his definition appears to allow for a natural world that is radically nonmaterialistic (perhaps even idealist, according to which reality consists of mental states) or pan-psychic (the view that all of reality has mental properties) so long as God is not included. But if the natural can include such capacious reference to the mental and the intentional, how can it rule out, as a general principle, an appeal to divine intentionality?

Essential Goodness

In the Scriptures of Judaism, Christianity, and Islam, the divine is a reality of unsurpassable greatness with unrivaled sovereignty as Creator and as a moral compass for human life, worthy of our highest allegiance, awe, loyalty, and worship. The goodness of human and other life and the good of the whole creation seem to be derived from the goodness of God. The Psalms (authoritative for Judaism and Christianity) proclaim God's great goodness (e.g., Pss 31:19; 106:1) and describe God's work and being as perfect (Ps 19:7; Matt 5:48), for example, while the Qur'an depicts God as mighty wisdom and truth, deserving all praise (Sura 31). Some passages in the Scriptures of the monotheistic traditions imply that God can do no evil, e.g., "It is impossible for God to lie" (Heb 6:18). The idea that God is essentially good follows from the idea that God is maximally excellent. A being capable of falling into evil and wickedness is not excellent.

Some theists, however, do not accept the notion that God is essentially good, offering against it "the argument from praise."

1. An agent does a praiseworthy act when the agent does the act but could have done otherwise.
2. If God is essentially good, then God cannot be praised for doing only good acts, for God could not do otherwise.

3. Therefore, either God is not praiseworthy or not essentially good.

One reply to this is that while God's essential goodness entails that "God does no evil" or, even more strongly, "God can do no evil," it does not fix *all* divine action. That is, while creating a cosmos may be good, God does not have to do it. If God did not create the cosmos, no thing or person would have been harmed. The creation itself is commonly regarded in theistic tradition as a gift, and a giver may rightly be praised for giving such a gift. Praising and worshiping God are not limited to what may be called moral praise. When one feels and expresses awe before God, this can be similar to (but vastly greater than) the awe one feels before sublime, breathtaking natural phenomena (an awesome mountain, an exploding star, the birth of a child, and so on). The awe felt is not about moral behavior, but it is still about abundant value.

If God is essentially good and the final cause, then where does evil come from? The problem of evil is a constant concern for philosophers, and unfortunately we do not have space here to address it adequately. Some philosophers attribute it to the freedom of the will, others to the relativity of our subjective perceptions, others to the fact that God's constant interference in the form of miracles would result in massive irregularities in life, etc. One point worth mentioning, however, is that if the problem of evil makes sense, then you are well on your way to accepting essential goodness as integral to the concept of God. After all, the problem of evil would not be a "problem" without the concept of an essentially good God.

More objections to God's essential goodness arise when it is paired with the following two divine attributes: omnipotence and omniscience. We discuss these objections in the following sections.

Omnipotence

The idea that God is all-powerful is an early, foundational principle of monotheism. Part of what distinguished monotheistic religious traditions was their creation stories. Unlike the stories of the gods of Mesopotamia and the Greco-Roman world, in which creation involved violence, even disembowelment, the God of monotheism creates singularly, with unrivaled power. In Genesis creation is portrayed in terms of divine commands in the form of speech or in terms of mediated and unmediated action. An action is mediated when another agent is involved (God heals in response to petitionary prayer).

Puzzles arise with respect to omnipotence, however, in two ways: internally and externally. Internal puzzles concern only the attribute itself, whereas external puzzles emerge when the attribute is paired with other divine attributes, such as essential goodness. The most famous of the internal difficulties is framed in terms of a task that an omnipotent being cannot perform. Here is one version, sometimes called "The Paradox of the Stone."

1. An omnipotent being is able to do any act.
2. If God is omnipotent, God can create a stone so heavy that no one can lift it.
3. If God is omnipotent, God can lift any stone.
4. But if God can lift any stone, then God cannot create a stone so heavy that no one can lift it.
5. And if God can create a stone so heavy that no one can lift it, then there could be a stone that not even God can lift.
6. There is at least one act God cannot do.
7. Hence, God is not omnipotent. (Some will argue more radically that since God must be omnipotent to be God, this proves that God does not exist.)

The most common way to address this puzzle is by refining premise 1 to: An omnipotent being is a being able to do any *possible* act. There cannot be a stone so heavy that a being who can lift any stone cannot lift it. It only appears possible if we are actually picturing a less powerful being than God. We, as human beings, can build objects so heavy that we cannot lift them, but a being like God who can do anything possible cannot (for logical reasons) create an object that God cannot lift.

We think this is a decisive reply to "The Paradox of the Stone." There is no need to undertake philosophical acrobatics, as some philosophers do, by arguing that God can do what is logically incoherent or could choose to limit God's powers (create a stone and choose to be unable to lift it). Part of the problem with this argument, by the way, is that by insisting that omnipotence should include the ability to do the logically incoherent, it removes our ability to think about these matters at all.

A more vexing problem with omnipotence arises when the attribute is paired with other divine properties, especially essential goodness, which (contrary to Dawkins's hypothesis) we believe is no mere add-on in theistic religious traditions.

Consider the following difficulty.

1. An omnipotent being is able to do any logically possible act.
2. An essentially good being is not able to do evil.
3. Because God is essentially good, God cannot do any logically possible act.
4. Therefore, God is not omnipotent.

The argument might be reformulated by comparing God with a Godlike being that is not essentially good, whom we may call Molech.

1. If God is essentially good, God is not able to do evil.
2. There cannot be a being more powerful than God.
3. There could be a being, Molech, with all God's properties except essential goodness.
4. If Molech exists, Molech can do any act God can do, plus any evil act.
5. In this case Molech would be more powerful than God.
6. Conclusion: God is not essentially good, or more radically there is no God.

Various logical maneuvers have been used in replying to these arguments. For example, it has been argued that an essentially good being can do evil to accomplish a greater good, but this would (presumably) only permit certain acts. It has also been argued that God has the ability *to do evil* but *cannot do evil*. (Imagine someone like Mother Teresa: she had the power to push an innocent person under a bus, but given her character, she could not do so.)

We suggest that the more promising reply to these difficulties is to contend that the ability to do evil is not a power that is proper to a maximally excellent being, as has been argued by Augustine (354–430), Boethius (480–526), and Aquinas (1224/5–1275). For free human creatures, our ability to do wrong might be an essential reflection (or the necessary complement) of our ability freely to do good, but for a God with unsurpassable excellence, the ability to do evil is a liability, a condition of vulnerability to corruption and degradation. The power of God is best thought of not in terms of bare power but of perfect, praiseworthy power.

An emphasis on *perfect* power in a philosophy of God also accords with feminist objections to the concept of God as sheer power. The early modern feminist Mary Wollstonecraft (1759–97) complained that men tend to privilege brute power in their concept of God:

> Man, accustomed to bow down to power in his savage state, can seldom divest himself of this barbarous prejudice, even when civilization determines how much superior mental is to bodily strength; and his reason is clouded by these crude opinions, even when he thinks of the Deity.—His omnipotence is made to swallow up, or preside over his other attributes, and those mortals are supposed to limit his power irreverently, who think that it must be regulated by his wisdom.[6]

Wollstonecraft counseled, instead, giving primacy to the goodness of God. Here again we see the benefits of considering the divine attributes in their interconnectedness as a coherent whole. God's essential goodness leads us to a more nuanced understanding of the nature of God's omnipotence, which can also have implications for the way we humans understand our own uses of power.

The appeal to perfect power and essential goodness has been used by some Christian philosophers to articulate the ideal unity of wills in the Trinity. Both Richard Swinburne and Stephen T. Davis have contended that supreme goodness is exemplified in the Trinity by ideal self-love, the love of another, and the love of two for a third. The topic

---

[6] M. Wollstonecraft, *A Vindication of the Rights of Women* (Mineola, NY: Dover Publications, 1996), 45.

is too broad to develop fully here, but we note that the concept of perfect power has been a fruitful one for constructive contemporary philosophical theology.[7]

Omniscience

The thesis that God is all-knowing has generated weighty philosophical attention, especially with regard to the scope of divine knowledge. The chief focus has been on "future free contingents," future events that are genuinely contingent, not predetermined, such as result from the exercise of free choice. Freedom means *the possibility of doing something with the ability to do otherwise.* But what if God knows perfectly and precisely that you will give to Oxfam tomorrow? If so, the future seems fixed. If God knows what you will do tomorrow, you cannot do otherwise. But if the future is fixed, how can you be free?

There are several replies:

The first is simply to claim that the objection falsely assumes that divine knowledge you will freely give to Oxfam tomorrow undermines your freedom. If you freely will do *x* tomorrow and had the power to do otherwise, the foreknowledge of what you will freely do does not at all imply that you could not do otherwise. To adopt an analogy from ancient Greek philosophy, if you foreknow which chariot will win the race tomorrow, your foreknowledge does not determine the winner. An objector might protest that you could know the victor only if the race is fixed, but two points can be made against this objection when applied to God: first, God's mode of knowing may be profoundly different from human foreknowledge (see the section on eternity below) and, second, since our knowledge of past free action does not in any way undermine the actor's freedom, why should knowledge of the future?

The second reply to our initial challenge invokes a radically comprehensive portrait of divine knowledge. According to some philosophers, God possesses what is called "middle knowledge," knowing what all possible creatures would do under any condition. Knowing what circumstances you are in at any point in your life, God knows

[7] See S. T. Davis, *Christian Philosophical Theology* (New York: Oxford University Press, 2006).

how you will exercise your agency and your power to do otherwise. This exalted understanding of divine knowledge was formulated by the sixteenth-century philosopher Luis de Molina and is defended today by Thomas Flint and William Craig.

A third, different (and controversial) reply is that omniscience does not cover future free contingents. If you have not yet given to Oxfam, whether you will or will not do so is not fixed or determined. But if it is not known what you will do, "omniscience" can cover only "all possible knowledge." If there is no possible knowledge of what will occur in future free contingencies (though many theologians would dispute this), an omniscient being would not be bound or expected to know the future.

Let us consider another objection to divine omniscience. A formal version of the argument involves what is called "concept empiricism."

1. According to concept empiricism, to grasp the concept of a sensation or an emotion, a being must have experienced it. To grasp properly the concept *red*, you would need to have experienced the color red; to grasp vulnerability, you must have been vulnerable; to grasp sadism, you must have felt sadistic.

2. Thesis: God is omniscient. God, for example, knows the concepts red, vulnerability, and sadism.

3. Thesis: God is also omnipotent, incorporeal, and essentially good.

4. If premise 1 is true, premises 2 and 3 cannot both be true. If God is incorporeal, God has no sensory cognitive faculties and so cannot experience *red*. If God is omnipotent and thus possesses perfect power, God cannot experience vulnerability. If God is essentially good, God cannot experience sadistic emotions. If God cannot experiences such sensations and emotions, God cannot know them and thus God cannot be omniscient.

This is an interesting argument indeed. The first premise is intuitively plausible. After all, if you knew everything about the concept of *red* (the retinal and brain conditions essential to seeing red, the relevant wavelengths, and so on), but had no sensation of seeing red, you would *not know what red looks like*.

The conclusion can be challenged by objecting to its understanding of the relation of the divine attributes to the emotions and sensations. Many theists claim that an all-powerful God who creates genuinely free creatures might have to limit divine power in order for them to be genuinely free and thus would experience a kind of self-imposed restraint or weakness. If creatures can genuinely and freely resist God's love, wouldn't a loving God experience vulnerability?

A similar case is made with regards to the relationship between essential goodness and sadism (or any other emotion that is wrong or unjust). The objection that God cannot experience an emotion that is unjust ignores the possibility that unjust emotions are complex states made up of morally acceptable components wrongly combined or wrongly directed. Arguably, a morally perfect being who hates no one can grasp what it is like to hate persons by grasping the concepts of persons and hate (there is nothing wrong with hatred *per se*, as in the case of hatred of evil). A good God could grasp the concept of sadism by grasping such concepts as pleasure, pain, subordination, and power. (Incidentally, the supposition that a person must himself be tainted or vicious if he grasps *what it is like to be vicious* would condemn many truly great artists. In Shakespeare's construction of Iago in the play *Othello*, did he somehow himself share in Iago's venomous malice? Not necessarily.)

But apart from these ways of replying to the argument from concept empiricism, one may well challenge the first premise (that a being must have an experience of *x* to understand *x*).

First, there is no proof that an incorporeal agent cannot experience sensations. In fact, a number of philosophers today (but not a majority) think that sensations are mental properties and not identical to the products of the senses (of the retina, for example) or brain states, though they are caused by both. If this is possible, the argument fails because God could (in theory) experience sensations.

Second, even if human creatures cannot grasp *x* without experiencing *x*, is this a self-evident principle that governs all possible forms of knowing? Presumably one does not always need to be in a state of *x* to know *x*: I do not need to be a square to know about squares, to be hot to know that something is hot, or to be hateful to know that someone is hateful, and so on. Conceptual empiricism seems to be built on a premise that knowing something involves a kind of melding in which the *x* that is known is somehow made integral to the knowing subject, as though *x* comes to define or mark the knower. Something like this was in fact proposed by David Hume, who held that ideas of sensations were faint or faded sensations. But there seems to be little reason to accept this. An idea about, say, economic recession, is not a faded sensation of any kind. There are limits to what we humans can visualize. We cannot form a visual image of an object with a thousand sides, but we can conceive of such an object and reflect on its properties.

Eternity

The idea that God transcends, or is beyond, temporal change has a rich history. To some extent, the great monotheistic traditions inherited a Platonic concept of reality and value, according to which that which is most real and valuable (for Plato, this was described as "the good") is incorruptible and not subject to the alteration, fragmentation, and decay that comes about through time. Some philosophers have held that God must be eternal because otherwise God is in some way a prisoner of time and unable to enjoy the unity of life that should mark supreme perfection.

A contemporary advocate of God's eternity, Brian Leftow, makes the case this way: the life of a temporal being has what he calls "inner limits," in which parts of the being's life are separate from others. Such limitations have their advantages for beings living in time but with God would mark a splintering and fragmentation that does not befit the fullness and perfection of the divine. A perfect being would have its full being or reality in a complete state rather than spread out in a past that is gone and in a future that has yet to arrive.

The thesis that God is eternal may appear at odds with scriptural narratives in which God first does one act and then another. Most theologians in the three monotheistic traditions treat such references to God as highly analogical or metaphorical because the Hebrew and Christian Bibles and the Qur'an describe God from *our point of view*. We cannot help thinking of God as acting successively in time (first doing one thing, then another), and yet God does not in fact act this way. Some explain this by arguing that God eternally wills succession, that *God wills that there will be changes but God's will itself does not change*. God's inner being is therefore changeless or immutable, not subject to alteration, fragmentation, and decay. God may have a temporal dimension by being *at* all times or (as Christians believe) in the incarnation, as Jesus Christ in first-century Palestine, but God's inner being is transcendent. God's life is *tota simul*, or all at once, as Boethius famously described it.

This understanding of God has at least two benefits. The belief that God transcends time provides a promising way to address the problem of freedom and foreknowledge discussed earlier. If God is in some sense beyond time, what is for us past and future may be present to God. God therefore does not so much *foreknow* future acts, as God grasps them in a divine present moment. God's transcendence of time has the additional benefit of allowing that God created time. If God is temporally extended (meaning that God has a past, present, and future), God cannot be independent of time and therefore cannot be the creator of time.

There is an enormous literature arguing over whether God is temporally eternal or temporal but without beginning. Consider just one objection and reply.

According to what may be called *the objection from simultaneity*, the relation of simultaneity is transitive. A transitive relationship allows one to transfer a relation: if you are taller than Socrates and Socrates is taller than Plato, then you are taller than Plato. In terms of temporal relations, we seem to have transitivity. That is, if I am writing at the same time you are running and you are running at the same time Chris is singing, I am writing at the same time Chris is singing. If God exists simultaneously with Nero's burning Rome and with your whistling, then Nero is burning Rome at the same time you are whistling.[8] If you are whistling at the same time Nero is burning Rome, we have an obvious absurdity, and so God cannot be eternal.

Defenders of God's eternity have replied that the argument from simultaneity fails because simultaneity is transitive for temporal crea-

---

[8] A. Kenny, *The God of the Philosophers* (Oxford: Oxford University Press, 1979), 38–39.

tures like us but not for God, for whom all times are present. The life of God is not, as it were, lived instant by instant but in an extended, timeless present. As Leftow puts it; "An eternal God is God present with the whole of time by His life's being stretched out alongside it."[9] Once one consistently grasps what is involved in thinking of an eternal being, one can see that the simultaneity objection unfairly transfers temporal relations to the atemporal.

The Flexibility of Theism and the Importance of Experience

In this overview of attributes, objections, and replies, one can begin to see the difficulty of establishing the *incoherence* of theism. Many options are available to the theist in refining the concept of God. If, for example, an argument from simultaneity were reworked effectively, a theist can always revise her understanding of eternity and hold that God is not atemporal but everlasting or without beginning. (Richard Swinburne and Nicholas Wolterstorff adopt this alternative.) And, as we noted earlier, one can address the apparent conflict between freedom and omniscience on multiple levels. Although there is not room to develop a fuller philosophy of God here, we suggest that a crucial point where flexibility is essential concerns integrating our concept of God with the experience of suffering and oppression. Along with a number of other philosophical theists, we believe that a loving God affectively responds to and is in solidarity with those unjustly oppressed. We think that a combination of biblical testimony, religious experience, and reflections on value theory and love should lead us to see God as affectively responsive to the cosmos that God sustains and loves. Theism has sufficient openness so that one may be a classical theist and affirm God as impassible (not subject to passion) and immutable (not subject to change), but one may also be a Christian theist [10] and hold that God is passible (God does have love as a passion) and God's will for the creation involves an engaging, intimate divine-human interplay.

---

[9] B. Leftow, *Time and Eternity* (Ithaca: Cornell University Press, 1991), 117.
[10] In an effort to emphasize the divine interaction with the creation, some thinkers have adopted the view of process philosophy or panentheism.

What we are calling the flexibility of theism is especially important as we move beyond a general theistic worldview and take serious God's Triune nature and the incarnation. For the Christian, God is not like a stagnant, impersonal principle. All the divine attributes are involved in the dynamics of the incarnation and the interrelationship of love within the Godhead, where love is not in ignorance but through complete knowledge and where such inner love comes to fruition through power in the creation.

Exploring reasons for recognizing the truth of theism is immediately relevant to exploring reasons for recognizing the coherence of theism. Some of the best reasons for thinking x is possible are the reasons for thinking x is actual. Several other chapters in this book take up such positive arguments. For our part, we note that merely entertaining the possibility of theism can open oneself up experientially to the possibility of a living encounter with God. As Peter Donovan observes:

> A religious believer who looks on the world as a domain in which God may possibly manifest himself (in one way or another) has the potential for a whole range of significant experiences not open to the person without such a world-view. He does not just view the world in a religious way. He lives within it, and acts and responds and experiences its events and happenings (including his own feelings and states of mind) with the possibility in his mind that in doing so he may be coming in touch not just with the world and other people in it, but with the activity and manifestations of God.[11]

Advancing theoretical arguments against the New Atheists over the coherence of God is merely the beginning of inquiry. The next step is to explore the possibility of encountering God's existence with humility, mindful that the divine attributes such as omniscience are not less than we can conceive, but rather such attributes and indeed God's being are far greater in profundity and richness than we can imagine.[12]

[11] P. Donovan, *Interpreting Religious Experience* (New York: Seabury, 1979), 81.
[12] We are grateful to Ms. Elizabeth Clark for criticism on an earlier version of this chapter and to Tiepolo for his faithful companionship.

Chapter 14

IS THE TRINITY A LOGICAL BLUNDER?
GOD AS THREE AND ONE

Paul Copan

Any Christian who has interacted with Muslims or Jehovah's Witnesses will eventually hear questions such as: How can God be three and one? Or, If Jesus was God, to whom was He crying out from the cross, "My God, My God, why have You forsaken Me?" (Matt 27:46).[1] Unfortunately, in our age of vanishing biblical literacy, the average Christian's understanding of the Trinity is minimal or even heterodox. This ignorance is tragic for several other reasons: many fail to recognize Christianity's unique doctrine of God; they are therefore unable to defend Christian orthodoxy; and they perhaps are not being assisted within the Christian community to worship God "in . . . truth" (John 4:24). First, trinitarianism distinguishes the Christian faith from other versions of theism—namely, Judaism and Islam, which are unitarian; many Christians seem unaware of this unique and central tenet of their faith in the triune God as Father, Son, and Spirit. Second, Christians tend to be inept at responding to the antitrinitarian thought and argumentation of Muslims, Jehovah's Witnesses, or Mormons; many are incapable of articulating an effective doctrinal response to alternate theological perspectives, not to mention defining and appreciating their own. Third, the Christian's worship is often uninformed and misguided because of this doctrinal

[1] Unless otherwise noted, Scripture quotations are from the Holman Christian Standard Bible.

ignorance; I have heard elders and even pastors thank the Father for dying on the cross or refer to the Holy Spirit as "It."

Challenges exist not only *within* the church but also *outside* it. In our post-September 11 world, we commonly hear the slogan, "Christians and Muslims worship the same God." Yes, Arab Christians used the term *Allah* for the triune God long before the time of Muhammad, and many of them still do! However, these two Abrahamic faiths diverge sharply regarding the nature of God: Muslims reject the tri-unity of God as heretical and blasphemous; this is *shirk*—ascribing partners to God.

The New Atheists have taken their potshots at Christian doctrine and the concept of God. Richard Dawkins, for instance, seems to have little patience with (or, I might add, understanding about) Trinitarian discussions in church history:

> Rivers of medieval ink, not to mention blood, have been squandered over the "mystery" of the Trinity, and in suppressing deviations such as the Arian heresy. Arius of Alexandria, in the fourth century, denied that Jesus was *consubstantial* (i.e. of the same substance or essence) with God. What on earth could that possibly mean, you are probably asking? Substance? What "substance"? What exactly do you mean by "essence"? "Very little" seems the only reasonable reply.[2]

To add to such challenges, popular Western culture tends wrongly to assume that "God" refers to a *supreme person*. Not a few Christian philosophers—I won't mention any names—have referred to God as "a person." This is misleading. *Three persons*—Father, Son, and Spirit—fully share in the *one true God's* identity. From eternity there has existed not one solitary *person* but a God-in-relation, three divine persons fully loving and enjoying one another. Personal relationships did not come into existence when God created finite personal beings (angels and humans). Relationship has *always* existed in this triune divine family. Christians should not think of God apart from His self-revelation as triune, and this should inform us in our worship of God and in our life in the world. Unlike many philosophical conceptions

---

[2] R. Dawkins, *The God Delusion* (Boston: Houghton Mifflin Co., 2006), 54.

of God as "wholly Other," an "Unmoved Mover," "First Cause," or the "Ground of all being," the Christian understanding rejects such non-relational abstractions in favor of a God who is personal, intrinsically relational, and history engaging. This tri-personal God, though "over all" (*transcendent*), is also "in all" (*immanent*) and "not far from each one of us" (Acts 17:27).

Three Dangers to Avoid

The Athanasian Creed (c. AD 500) attempts to make sense of the biblical data that affirm God's threeness and oneness:

> Now the catholic faith is that we worship One God in Trinity and Trinity in Unity, neither confounding the Persons nor dividing the substance. For there is one Person of the Father, another of the Son, another of the Holy Spirit. But the Godhead of the Father, of the Son, and of the Holy Spirit, is One, the Glory equal, the Majesty coeternal. . . . And yet not three eternals but one eternal, as also not three infinites, nor three uncreated, but one uncreated, and one infinite. So, likewise, the Father is almighty, the Son almighty, and the Holy Spirit almighty; and yet not three almighties but one almighty. So the Father is God, the Son God, and the Holy Spirit God; and yet not three Gods but one God. . . . For like as we are compelled by Christian truth to acknowledge every Person by Himself to be both God and Lord; so are we forbidden by the catholic religion to say, there be three Gods or three Lords. . . . So there is one Father not three Fathers, one Son not three Sons, and one Holy Spirit not three Holy Spirits.

In the history of Christianity, the Western church (Catholic and Protestant) has stressed God's *unbreakable oneness of God's being* whereas the Eastern Orthodox church has emphasized the *distinctiveness of the three persons*. That said, orthodox Christian formulations of the Trinity should attempt to avoid *overemphasizing/denying* one of three

Trinitarian fundamentals; doing so could lead to doctrinal significant error:[3]

- Overemphasizing *threeness* leads to tritheism—a version of polytheism (many gods). This error, which is found in one version of Mormonism, *denies God's oneness* (monotheism).
- Overemphasizing *oneness* leads to modalism—that God is just one person who appears in different modes or manifestations (e.g., as Father in the Old Testament, Son in the New Testament, and Spirit during the New Testament church age). This unitarian (as opposed to trinitarian) view of God is characteristic of much liberal theology which, for example, rejects Jesus' divinely authoritative status; it *denies God's threeness*.
- Rejecting *equality* leads to subordinationism. In this case the three persons do not *possess alike* the divine nature but are a kind of hierarchy. According to Jehovah's Witnesses, the Father alone is God; Jesus is "a god" and the first creature God made; and the Holy Spirit is not personal but merely a force. This subordinationist error *undermines the equality of the divine persons*.

By contrast, the orthodox doctrine of the Trinity emphasizes that only one God exists (oneness). This God exists eternally in three distinct persons—Father, Son, and Spirit (threeness). Also, these persons are fully equal in their essential divine attributes and perfections (equality).

[3] R. Nicole, "The Meaning of the Trinity," in P. Toon and J. D. Spiceland, eds., *One God in Trinity* (Westchester, IL: Cornerstone, 1980), 1–4.

The Divine Family

From eternity, the triune God has existed. Indeed, the self-sufficient Trinity of Father, Son, and Spirit have existed in their free, mutual self-giving and self-receiving love. Relationship or communion is intrinsic to this "household" (or economy) of divine persons who, though distinct from one another, are inseparably united in other-oriented love. This divine inter- (and inner-) connection of mutuality, openness, and reciprocity has no individualistic competition among the family members but only joy, self-giving love, and transparency. Rather than being some isolated self or solitary ego, God is supremely relational in His self-giving, other-oriented nature. Within God is intimate *union* as well as *distinction*, an unbreakable communion of persons. The persons of the Godhead can be *distinguished* but not *separated*. God is both *community* and *unity*.[4]

Although some analogies of the Trinity can be problematic (e.g., water's three states, which implies modalism), other analogies may prove more accurate, useful, and illuminating. Consider the mythological three-headed dog Cerberus that guards Hades's gates. Though a single organism (substance), one dog (not three dogs), he has three distinct centers of awareness, each with the same canine nature. (In the world we have comparable analogies in, say, two-headed snakes or even inseparable Siamese twins; in such cases we have distinct centers of awareness within one unified organism.) Likewise, God is one immaterial soul (substance) with three distinct centers of consciousness, rationality, will, and agency (persons) who are deeply and necessarily interconnected, and they share the same unique divine nature.

Because a relational God exists and chooses to create humans in His image, relationality is central to *our* identity as humans. No wonder the Ten Commandments divide into two tables—our relationship to God and our relationship to fellow human beings. Jesus Himself summarizes our twofold duty: "love the Lord your God" and "love your neighbor" (Mark 12:30–31). We have been made for communion with God first and foremost, but how we regard fellow human beings

---

[4] D. B. Hart, *The Beauty of the Infinite: The Aesthetics of Christian Truth* (Grand Rapids: Eerdmans, 2003), 174.

reflects our spiritual condition (1 John 4:20). We recognize what love is by the model of the self-giving God in Christ (1 John 3:16).

Christians have long pondered the mystery of the Trinity, and we're not here trying to demystify the God whose nature and purposes can't be reduced to tidy formulas or manageable boxes. We should celebrate the unfathomable God, who's under no obligation to human demands to clarify everything about Himself (Deut 29:29). And why think our puny minds could grasp these "secret things" (NASB) anyway?

Paul reminds us that we know partially and lack the clarity about God's nature and ways (1 Cor 13:9; cf. Isa 55:9). "The great things of the gospel" (as theologian Jonathan Edwards put it) *are* astonishing, but *mystery* or *partial knowledge* doesn't imply *contradiction*. Let's keep this in mind as we consider the divine Trinity.

Toward a Clearer Understanding of the Trinity

What *do* the Scriptures mean when they tell us that God is both *three* and *one?* If Father, Son, and Spirit are divine persons, aren't there three Gods rather than one? Classical New England Unitarians—who stressed the fatherhood of God, the brotherhood of man, and the neighborhood of Boston (!)—and their ilk have suggested that Christians just can't count: 1+1+1 equals 3! Anthropologist Pascal Boyer, a naturalist who claims that religion is simply a matter of brain function and survival enhancement, is disdainful of religious believers. He claims that they don't think critically, don't check out evidence, and believe what can't be falsified. He adds that Christians seem particularly gullible and can't think correctly. Boyer specifically mentions the "irrational" doctrine of the Trinity. As it turns out, Boyer himself isn't displaying the appropriate critical thinking and evidence-checking he claims believers are lacking: ironically, he presents a doctrine that *no* orthodox Christian believes—"that three persons are one person."[5] No, the Christian believes that there are three necessarily inseparable persons (not "one person") who share one divine nature and substance.

---

[5] P. Boyer, *The Naturalness of Religious Ideas: A Cognitive Theory of Religion* (Berkeley: University of California Press, 1994), 6; cf. P. Boyer, *Religion Explained: The Evolutionary Origins of Religious Thought* (New York: Basic Books, 2001), 300.

Without trying to reduce God to human formulas and grids, how can we, in faithful humility, better grasp this central Christian doctrine of the Trinity? Perhaps the following considerations can assist us.

First, Scripture reveals both a oneness to God and a threeness. Jesus' first followers were religious Jews, orthodox monotheists. They were firmly committed to God's unique *oneness* in contrast to the polytheism of the surrounding nations. Twice daily they would recite the *Shema* ("Hear, O Israel"), declaring God's *oneness:* "The LORD our God, the LORD is one" (Deut 6:4; cf. Mark 12:29). An early Christian creed (AD 53) affirms Jesus' sharing in the divine identity as the "one Lord" (1 Cor 8:4–7), while steadfastly declaring that "there is no God but one." Even the demons hold to an orthodox monotheistic belief (Jas 2:19).

God's *threeness* is also apparent. In the Great Commission (Matt 28:18–20), Jesus tells His disciples to go and make disciples of all nations, "baptizing them in the *name* [not *names*] of the Father and of the Son and of the Holy Spirit." At Jesus' baptism, a reenactment of the exodus, Father and Spirit are also present (Matt 3:16–17). Paul's benediction expresses God's threeness: "May the grace of the *Lord Jesus Christ*, and the love of *God*, and the fellowship of the *Holy Spirit* be with you all" (2 Cor 13:14 NIV; cf. 1 Cor 12:4–6). So while God is one, three self-distinctions exist within the Godhead.

Second, God is one in essence or nature but three in person. Three and one aren't in contradiction here; to be in conflict, *the same category or relationship* must be involved. But *threeness* pertains to persons; *oneness* pertains to God's nature or essence. There isn't one divine nature *and* three divine natures; there aren't three persons *and* one person in the Godhead.

A nature is *what makes a thing (or person) what it is.* God has certain characteristics that make Him what He is. He can't *not* exist and is all-good, for example. And just as the Earth's billions of humans possess a common nature that sets them apart from angels and aardvarks, the triune persons are equally and fully God, sharing in the same nature though at a much deeper, more unified level than humans. Crucial to overcoming the contradiction charge in the doctrine of the Trinity is distinguishing between the only one divine *nature* and the three *persons* who possess it. There aren't three Gods, but one.

When Jehovah's Witnesses or Muslims ask Christians, "If Jesus was divine, to whom did he cry, 'My God, My God, why have You forsaken Me?' (Matt 27:46)," these questioners assume that if Jesus is God, then it is impossible that another can share the same divine nature. We can reject this without inconsistency and even respond, "If the *Father* is God, to whom is He speaking when He says *to the Son*, 'Your throne, O God, is forever' or "You, Lord, . . . laid the foundation of the earth'" (Heb 1:8,10 NASB)?

Third, to distinguish between person and nature, we must keep in mind two ways to use "is"—identity versus predication. Mark Twain is the pen name for Samuel Langhorne Clemens, the 26-cigars-a-day smoker and author of *The Adventures of Tom Sawyer.* Twain does not have characteristics that Clemens does not have. In other words, when we say, "Samuel Langhorne Clemens is Mark Twain," we can just as easily reverse the names: "Mark Twain is Samuel Langhorne Clemens." Each of those statements indicates identity: Mark Twain = Samuel Langhorne Clemens (and vice versa). The names, which refer to the same person, are fully interchangeable and thus identical.

When it comes to the Trinity, to say "Jesus is God" *isn't* identical to "God is Jesus." *Unlike* the Mark Twain example, "Jesus" *doesn't exhaust* what it means to speak of "God." *Jesus* and *God* are *not identical.* According to the Bible, Father and Spirit are called divine, just as Jesus is.[6] In the statement "Jesus is God," we use *is* to *describe* or *predicate*, not to identify or equate: Jesus is God in that He shares in the nature that only two other persons share; so there isn't just one person who can properly be called God.

Again, threeness pertains to persons, and oneness pertains to nature or essence. There is only *one* divine *nature*, but three *persons* share in it. For God to be God, He must possess certain qualities or properties— being all-knowing, all-powerful, and all-good. Only Father, Son, and Spirit participate in this divine nature and can thus be called "God." Each of these *three persons* is also a center of consciousness, responsi-

---

[6] On the Trinity's biblical foundations, see P. Copan, *"That's Just Your Interpretation"* (Grand Rapids: Baker, 2001).

bility, and activity and is *distinct* from the other; for example, Jesus *isn't* the Father; the Father *isn't* the Spirit. So there's simply no logical contradiction when Christians say, "Three *persons*, one *divine nature*."

Fourth, the members of the Trinity share the same being—not simply the same nature. That is, God is one substance (Lat. *substantia*) that exists (or subsists) on its own; God is His own self-contained entity. The Triune God isn't a mere assemblage of three divine beings (which would be polytheism—the belief in many gods), who happen to have a common purpose. Think back to the analogy of the three-headed Cerberus. The three centers of consciousness exist or are contained in one organism, a self-contained being. In the case of God, a *personal* being, we have three persons who similarly exist in one *soulish* being. God is not three beings but one. Just as one head of Cerberus is not a being, so none of the persons of the Trinity is *a* being. Just as one of the dog's heads cannot exist apart from connection (subsistence) with the other two in a single organism, likewise none of the persons of the Trinity can exist in being without the other. So this is radically different from polytheism/tritheism, in which we have distinct beings that are capable of existing on their own. The necessary unity of Father, Son, and Spirit is like the angles of a triangle. If we remove one angle, we no longer have a triangle; all three must be in place.

Fifth, the Triune persons are deeply interrelated or mutually indwell one another, sharing a necessary, unbreakable relational oneness. We earlier noted that humans possess a common nature. You and I have the same nature as Socrates and Plato. This nature makes us what we are, human. When it comes to God, we need further clarification. Though I share the same human nature with, say, my students, they are separate and distinct from me; it's possible for me to exist without them or vice versa. The members of the Trinity, however, are inseparably related. One can't exist without the other two. As we've seen, a triangle can't exist if we take away one of its angles since by definition a triangle is tri-angular. Likewise, God by definition is Triune. Unlike Unitarians, we can't have just the Father without Son or Spirit. The triune persons are necessarily and permanently interrelated.

Greek theologians used the term *perichoresis* (in Latin, *circumincessio*) to describe the Trinity's necessary interrelationships. Jesus spoke of being "in" the Father and the Father "in" Him to describe their unique relationship (cf. John 10:30,38; 17:21). There's a "mutual abiding" in the Godhead—unlike human relationships, however close they may be. The relationship of Father, Son, and Spirit is not some miscellaneous collection of distinct persons who just happen to share some generic divine essence ("God-ness") so that they can be classed together.[7] Rather, they *mutually, inseparably share* in the life of one another in a remarkable way—a life without isolation, insulation, secrecy, or fear. They enjoy a penetrating, transparent, mutual knowledge of the other as other, as co-other, and as loved other.[8] So while the divine persons each fully possess the same nature (each one can rightly be called "God"), more fundamental is their sharing a common, mutually indwelling unbreakable life together.

Consider the analogy of *the mutual interaction of the soul and the body.* The Scriptures speak of a *deep unity* between body and soul: the body interacts continually and deeply with the soul and the soul with the body. If I feel nervous in my soul, my stomach starts churning. If I cut off my arm, my soul must make certain adjustments in light of this loss. So there's a kind of mutual indwelling or interdependence in this body-soul relationship. The soul may temporarily separate from the body at death—the believer's absence from the body means being at home with the Lord (2 Cor 5:6–9). But there's normally a deep, interactive unity between them; they act as one.

Sixth, because the members of the Trinity share the same essence and mutually indwell one another, they also act as one and not in isolation from one another. All that the three divine persons do, they do as one. Whether creating, revealing, or redeeming, the three persons of the Trinity necessarily act as one. For example, when God creates, Father, Son, and Spirit are involved (e.g., Gen 1:1–2; John 1:3). Or when Jesus is raised from the dead, He is said to be raised by the Father (Gal 1:1; cf. Acts 2:24,32) and the Spirit (Rom 1:4), but Jesus declares that He has authority not only to lay down His life but also to take it up again (John 10:18; cf. 2:19: "I will raise it up"). The persons of

---

[7] C. Plantinga, "The Threeness/Oneness Problem of the Trinity," *Calvin Theological Journal* 23 (1988): 51; C. Plantinga, "The Perfect Family," *Christianity Today* 28 (March 4, 1988), 27.
[8] C. Plantinga, "The Perfect Family," 27.

the Trinity also indwell believers (John 14:16,18,23; Rom 8:9). Even though each person has a distinct center of awareness or consciousness and a distinct will, only one harmonious will is expressed in divine action. Rather than acting as three independent persons (as with Greek and Roman gods), each member of the Godhead is equally present in every divine action.[9]

In the depth of His being, God is *relational*. God is relating within Himself, and He is relational toward us. This God is *for us*. He has created us to *love* Him and to *cling* to Him (Deut 10:20; 13:4)—like a husband and wife must cling to each other (Gen 2:24). When God came to this planet, He sat at tables with the marginalized and outcasts of society, showing God's deep interest in them. When the Spirit brings us into God's family, He pours God's love into our hearts (Rom 5:5), giving us the confidence that we're God's adopted children (Rom 8:15; Gal 4:5).

These three divine persons are one in at least five important ways: (1) They share the same being (compare the three-headed being Cerberus). (2) They share in the same divine nature. (3) They mutually indwell one another (*perichoresis*), being bound together in relationship. (4) They necessarily act in perfect harmony. (5) Only one harmonious will is expressed in their actions. As we look at the story of Scripture, we can gather that, first, only one God exists and, second, three persons can legitimately be called "God." The Holy Trinity is indeed a mystery but not an incoherent one.

The Philosophical and Practical Relevance of the Trinity

The doctrine of the Trinity is not simply coherent and biblically rooted. Its incredible richness can direct us to live and think wisely not only within a loving, relating Christian community but also within society as public citizens and within a pluralistic global village as witnesses to the great things of the gospel.

In the *public square* of Western democracies, people tend to view God as a singular, unitary person who is a rule-setting monarch endowed with sheer power to impose His arbitrary standards on

[9] Hart, *The Beauty of the Infinite*, 182.

humans.[10] Obviously, many distrust and resist the idea of a God who only commands, calls for obedience, and judges the resistant. The doctrine of the Trinity, however, can explode this barren ethical arrangement. What if people viewed God as Triune, relating, self-giving, and other-centered by nature? What if God's rule includes not coercion or bullying but a desire for friendship with humans? What if God reveals and commands so that humans, by His grace, may freely "choose life" (Deut 30:19) and experience it "abundantly" (John 10:10 NASB)? And what if, rather than portraying a unilateral, top-down arrangement, we can present a relational God who wants none to perish but all to experience the holy warmth of His company (2 Pet 3:9)? Thus, if people continue to resist God's wooings (Acts 7:51), they will not only damage themselves, but they have the capacity to separate themselves from God's grace, and God will reluctantly allow them to go their own way forever. In the public square Christians should proclaim a relating God who is the foundation for ethics and personal responsibility, for human dignity and rights, for reason and truth, and for tolerance and cooperation.

Furthermore, Trinitarian doctrine can give the Christian valuable insights in *dialogue with other religions*. Today's "unknown God" (cf. Acts 17:22–23) is "something out there" that's unknown and unknowable; "It" may be the cause of the universe's existence and remarkable arrangement, but that's about all, we're told. Yet surely we can go further. Although Eastern or New Age philosophies often espouse an abstract, impersonal view of the Ultimate Reality, why think an *impersonal* entity or force offers a secure basis for the *personal* virtues—love, humility, kindness, compassion—elevated within such views? How can "It" serve as a foundation for human rights and personal dignity? In the monistic all-is-one philosophies of the East, there are no real I-You relationships, no distinctions between the compassionate and the pitied, between good and evil. All differences are illusory (*maya*). And why think this impersonal "God" is responsible for creating and sustaining the world we experience? It can't create anything that's

---

[10] Some comments here are taken from L. Newbigin, "Trinity as Public Truth," in *The Trinity in a Pluralistic Age: Theological Essays on Culture and Religion*, ed. K. J. Vanhoozer (Grand Rapids: Eerdmans, 1997), chap. 1.

not God or act on anything since there's nothing to act on.[11] Even if Eastern religions stress *duties* or *societal roles* rather than *rights*, their emphasis on not harming others but respecting them still takes human worth and dignity for granted, an assumption that an impersonal metaphysic/Ultimate Reality can't easily accommodate.

We naturally give priority to persons over impersonal objects in our everyday lives: "The most important things in life aren't things," we're told. Why then favor some Eastern ideal of "nothingness" (*sunyata*) or pure consciousness (Brahman) that's beyond personality or beyond good and evil? By contrast, the triune God offers a more fruitful context to ground and make sense of loving human relationships and interpersonal virtues, in addition to the existence of a finite universe.

Also, *feminist philosophers* have objected to a power-asserting "male," "hierarchical" conception of God in Western philosophy. But the biblical God, who makes male *and* female in His image, is a relational, personal being without gender. And although male pronouns are typically used to refer to God, Scripture contains metaphors of God's mother-like actions and emotions as tender, care-giving, compassionate, and protecting: giving birth to Israel (Deut 32:18); a nursing mother (Ps 131:2); a mother in labor (Isa 42:4); a mother bear and lioness (Hos 13:8). In addition, God's essentially other-oriented relationality goes a long way in addressing certain concerns and misconceptions feminists raise regarding an autocratic, dictatorial male deity.

Finally, the Trinity contributes to a resolution of *the problem of the One and the Many*—what philosopher William James called philosophy's most central problem. The ancient philosopher Heraclitus said that ultimate reality is *many* and *changing*—that is, *no unity*. On the other hand, the philosopher Parmenides claimed that reality is *one* and *unchanging*—that is, *no plurality*. We live not in a *multiverse* but a *universe*, a unity that holds diverse things together, and the three-in-one God furnishes us with resources to account for both unity and plurality.[12]

[11] F. G. Kirkpatrick, *A Moral Ontology for a Theistic Ethic: Gathering the Nations in Love and Justice* (Burlington, VT: Ashgate, 2003), 56.

[12] C. Gunton, *The One, the Three, and the Many* (Cambridge: Cambridge University Press, 1993).

Chapter 15

DID GOD BECOME A JEW?
A DEFENSE OF THE INCARNATION

Paul Copan

"The Word became flesh, and dwelt among us" (John 1:14)—this Word that not only was "with God" but "was God" (John 1:1).[1] The self-existent triune God created a good world, but His creatures turned away and became exiled and alienated from Him. But this was not the last word on the matter. God comes to us and communicates Himself to us through the Word, Jesus of Nazareth, to restore His creation and to form a new chosen people through Him. He is the second Adam and the beloved Son and the true Israel, which national Israel had failed to be. According to orthodox Christian doctrine, God became human—a first-century Jew—to restore His people and, indeed, all humanity to Himself.

The historic Christian faith has maintained that *two natures*, divine and human, exist fully in the person of Jesus of Nazareth; He is "perfect God, perfect man subsisting of a reasoning soul and human flesh," as the Athanasian Creed (c. AD 500) states it. The Chalcedonian Creed (AD 481) affirms that

> our Lord Jesus Christ [was and is] at once complete in Godhead and complete in manhood, truly God and truly man, consisting also of a reasonable soul and body; of one substance with the Father as regards his Godhead, and at the

[1] Unless otherwise noted, Scripture quotations are from the New American Standard Bible.

218

same time of one substance with us as regards his manhood; like us in all respects, apart from sin . . . recognized in two natures, without confusion, without change, without division, without separation; the distinction of natures being in no way annulled by the union.

As they do with the doctrine of the Trinity, liberal theologians, Muslims, Jehovah's Witnesses, and others assert that this God-in-flesh doctrine is incoherent. The all-knowing, all-powerful, all-good God is so utterly unlike humans, who are ignorant, frail, and flawed. The philosopher of religion and religious pluralist John Hick claims that Jesus of Nazareth, though "intensely conscious of God's holy and loving presence," was "wholly human." Eventually, the "Jesus cult" developed into the "cult of the risen Christ, transfigured and deified."[2] Jesus scholar Marcus Borg maintains that Jesus *couldn't* have said, "I am the way, and the truth, and the life" (John 14:6) or "I am the Light of the world" (John 8:12); psychologically sane people don't say such things.[3] Of course, the question remains: If early Christians put these words into Jesus' mouth, why would they make up an embarrassing, psychologically challenged Jesus? Borg's argument only postpones the question.

Is it absurd to affirm the incarnation? As with the doctrine of the Trinity, the incarnation is a mystery whose power and majesty cannot be reduced to a set of truth statements or formulas. The mystery of godliness is indeed great (1 Tim 3:16), but this does not mean the incarnation is irrational or illogical. In the spirit of Christian philosopher Thomas Morris's book *The Logic of God Incarnate*,[4] this essay will attempt to show that the incarnation, though a mystery, is a *coherent* one. I shall (1) briefly review the scriptural affirmations of Jesus' humanity and divinity, (2) highlight three important distinctions to help us understand the incarnation, and (3) examine the question of Jesus' temptation in light of His divinity.

[2] J. Hick, *The Fifth Dimension: An Exploration of the Spiritual Realm* (Oxford: One World, 1999), 234–36.

[3] In M. J. Borg and N. T. Wright, *The Meaning of Jesus: Two Visions* (San Francisco: HarperSanFrancisco, 1999), 149.

[4] T. V. Morris, *The Logic of God Incarnate* (Ithaca, NY: Cornell University Press, 1986; rpt. Wipf and Stock, 2002).

The Scriptures on Jesus' Humanity and Divinity

The Bible resoundingly affirms the *humanity* of Jesus. Second- and third-century Gnostic heresies—reflected in later noncanonical gospels such as *Thomas* and *Judas*—rejected the goodness of the physical creation, downplayed earthly history in favor of eternal truths and spiritual enlightenment; they denigrated the material body while exalting an immaterial soul. The Gnostic pseudogospels portray an otherworldly "Christ." By contrast the earlier, canonical Gospels present Jesus as fully *human*. Jesus is the Word become flesh (John 1:14). He is the "man" by whom came the resurrection of the dead (1 Cor 15:21). He is also the "second Adam" (1 Cor 15:45). This "man" is the "mediator between God and man" (1 Tim 2:5 HCSB) who is "revealed in the flesh" (1 Tim. 3:16) and who suffered and died on the cross (1 John 5:8).

What of Jesus' *divinity?* University of Edinburgh's Larry Hurtado argues that, contrary to all expectation, belief in Jesus' deity emerged as "a veritable 'big bang,' an explosively rapid and impressively substantial development in the earliest stage of the Christian movement."[5] What is the biblical evidence for His divinity?

Philippians 2:6–11, an early Christian hymn, provides strong evidence not only for the preexistence of the Son of God[6] but also for Jesus' equality with God the Father.

> [He], although He existed in the form of God, did not regard equality with God a thing to be grasped, but emptied Himself, taking the form of a bond-servant, and being made in the likeness of men. Being found in appearance as a man, He humbled Himself by becoming obedient to the point of death, even death on a cross. For this reason also, God highly exalted Him, and bestowed on Him the name which is above every name, so that at the name of Jesus every knee will bow, of those who are in heaven and on earth and under the earth,

[5] L. W. Hurtado, *Lord Jesus Christ: Devotion to Jesus in Earliest Christianity* (Grand Rapids: Eerdmans, 2003), 135.

[6] For a defense of the Son of God's preexistence (against positions taken by biblical scholars such as James D. G. Dunn), see D. McCready, *He Came Down from Heaven: The Preexistence of Christ and the Christian Faith* (Downers Grove, IL/Leicester, UK: InterVarsity/Apollos, 2006).

and that every tongue will confess that Jesus Christ is Lord,
to the glory of God the Father. (Phil 2:6–11)

Further support for Jesus' divinity comes from key Old Testament
references to Yahweh ("the LORD") that are used to refer to Jesus "the
Lord" in the New Testament:

- every knee will bow to *Yahweh* (Isa 45:23; to *Jesus* in Phil.
  2:10);
- to call on the name of *Yahweh* brings salvation (Joel 2:31–32;
  cf. the name of *Jesus* in Acts 2:20–21; Rom 10:13);
- a forerunner prepares the way for *Yahweh* (Isa 40:3; for *Jesus* in
  Matt 3:3);
- *Yahweh* is my shepherd (Ps 23:1; the shepherd is *Jesus* in John
  10:11);
- Isaiah sees *Yahweh's* glory (Isa 6:1–5,10; *Jesus'* glory in John
  12:41);
- *Yahweh* is the first and the last (Isa 44:6; 48:12; 51:12; the first
  and last is *Jesus* in Rev 1:17; 2:8; 22:13).

In addition, Jesus takes on divine prerogatives; that is, He assumes
the role and authority typically taken by Yahweh. He *forgives sin*, not
only displacing the temple but assuming God's authoritative domain
(Mark 2:5,7). He's the *judge* of the world (Matt 25:31–46; cf. 2 Cor
5:10). He is *prayed to* (Acts 7:59–60; 1 Cor 16:22; 2 Cor 12:9) and
He receives worship (John 20:28, where He is called "My Lord and
my God!"). He calls Himself the "Son of Man"—the exalted figure of
Daniel 7 who shares authority with the Ancient of Days (Mark 14:62).
He is explicitly called "God" (John 1:1,18; 20:28; Acts 20:28; Rom
9:5; Titus 2:13; Heb 1:8; 2 Pet 1:1; 1 John 5:20). A helpful acrostic
that summarizes the various aspects of Jesus' deity is *H-A-N-D-S:* Jesus
shares in the *Honors* due to God, the *Attributes* of God, the *Names* of
God, the *Deeds* of God, and the *Seat* of God's throne.[7]

We're familiar with the trilemma popularized by C. S. Lewis. Jesus
is not merely a "good moral teacher" (as merely good moral teachers
don't make such "outrageous" identity claims as having all authority

---

[7] Taken from E. Komoszewski and R. Bowman Jr., *Putting Jesus in His Place* (Grand Rapids:
Kregel, 2007).

or being the final judge of all humanity): Jesus was either a liar, a lunatic, or Lord of all. There is another alternative, however—legend. But Lewis was well aware of this possibility, and it was one he readily dismissed. He knew about miracle-denying New Testament critics, even theologians, who considered the incarnation to be a myth or legend, a human fabrication. Lewis was capable of distinguishing between legend and history, and he wrote of these scholars: "I distrust them as critics. They seem to me to lack literary judgment, to be imperceptive about the quality of the texts they are reading." Though studying the New Testament from their youth up, they lack the needed literary experience and so miss "the obvious things" about these texts: "If [the critic] tells me that something in a Gospel is legend or romance, I want to know how many legends and romances he has read, how well his palate is trained in detecting them by flavour; not how many years he has spent on that Gospel."[8] As Lewis affirms, Jesus' miracles and authoritative identity-claims in the Gospels are reliably recorded history; they are not the stuff of legends. Indeed, the notion that Jesus' death and resurrection are copycat beliefs from existing pagan dying-and-rising god myths from the Mediterranean world is simply implausible. As N. T. Wright asserts, efforts to find parallels between Christianity and these mystery religions "have failed, as virtually all Pauline scholars now recognize," and to do so "is an attempt to turn the clock back in a way now forbidden by the most massive and learned studies on the subject."[9]

Interestingly, while disputes had broken out in the earliest Christian communities over circumcision, spiritual gifts, or the place of the Mosaic Law, *no* disagreement exists in the New Testament writings regarding Jesus' lofty status as Lord of all. The fiercely monotheistic Jew, Paul, writing an early Christian creed (early AD 50s), Christianizes the *Shema* ("Hear, O Israel") of Deut 6:4–6, declaring Jesus is the one "Lord" of Israel and the Creator of all—"by whom are all things, and

---

[8] C. S. Lewis, "Fern-Seed and Elephants," in *Fern-Seed and Elephants and Other Essays on Christianity*, ed. Walter Hooper (London: Collins, 1975), 106–7.
[9] N. T. Wright, *What Saint Paul Really Said* (Grand Rapids: Eerdmans, 1997), 172–73. For a recent, comprehensive critique of the Jesus-legend argument, see P. R. Eddy and G. A. Boyd, *The Jesus Legend: A Case for the Historical Reliability of the Synoptic Tradition* (Grand Rapids: Baker Academic, 2007).

we exist through Him" (1 Cor 8:6). Jesus shares in the divine identity. The Hebrew Bible anticipates that Yahweh will come to Zion, defeat evil, and restore His people, gathering the scattered exiles into a new, redeemed community; and the early Christians affirm that this happened in the Christ event; Yahweh's kingdom breaks in by the person of Jesus of Nazareth.

The Incarnation: Three Important Distinctions

Having reviewed some of the biblical evidence, I would like to explore what I find to be a fruitful, reasonable, and biblically rooted model that helps us make sense of God's becoming man. Again, this is not an attempt to eliminate the incarnation's mystery but to argue that it isn't illogical. In unpacking this model, I want to make three distinctions.

1. The distinction between nature *and* person. A thing's *nature* or *essence* makes it what it is; it wouldn't exist if it lacked these features. We all have human-making features—the capacity to choose or act, to be conscious, to communicate, to feel, to hold beliefs—even if we aren't presently using those capacities, say, when we're asleep or comatose. God has characteristics that make him God. By *person*, we mean *a center of (self-)consciousness, will, activity, and responsibility.* Those who are persons include human and angelic individuals as well as the maximally great divine Persons within the Trinity—Father, Son, and Spirit.

What then is the *relation* between *person* and *nature?* A person *has* a nature; you and I *possess* something that makes us what we are, the same human *nature.* Jesus of Nazareth, though *one* Person, is fully God and fully human. He uniquely possesses *two* natures—one identical to *our human nature* and the other nature *divine.*

2. The distinction between what is "fully" (essentially) human and what is "merely" (commonly) human. Humans commonly have arms, legs, hair, and eyes; but even without these we can still be fully human. Also, humans commonly, even universally, commit moral wrongs; but despite Alexander Pope's statement, "To err is human," sinning isn't essential to being human. After all, Adam and Eve were created sinless;

Jesus was sinless; and in the afterlife believers will be sinless as well. Death, too, though common, doesn't define or partly define human beings. Enoch (Gen 5:24) and Elijah (2 Kgs 2:11) didn't die even though death has touched all other human beings. You get the idea.

This *essentially/fully* human and *commonly/merely* human distinction reminds us that certain human features we assume to be *essential* (part of our nature) often aren't essential after all; they may just be *common*. This distinction can help us see that a divine-human incarnation is possible: *what is essential to human nature doesn't exclude the possibility of being fully divine.* The *image of God* figures into our discussion at this point: human beings were made "a little lower than *God*" (Ps 8:5) to co-rule creation and to commune with God (Gen 1:26–27). Christ Himself, the new Adam, *is* the image of God (2 Cor 4:4; Col 1:15). As our representative, He both fulfills the human vocation in reflecting God's image and also graciously empowers us to live as humans were intended to live.

In *limited form* we share in certain attributes or properties with God—personality, relationality, rationality, morality, freedom, creativity—that enable us to fulfill our vocation. Certain essential human characteristics are derived from divine characteristics: *human nature is thus a subcategory of the divine.*

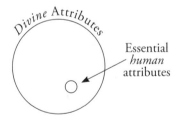

So the divine-human union in Jesus of Nazareth becomes possible. Biblical scholar F. F. Bruce puts it well: "It is because man in the creative order bears the image of his Creator that it was possible for the Son of God to become incarnate as man and in His humanity to display the glory of the invisible God."[10] According to one theologian, "If human beings are made in the image and likeness of God (Gen.

---

[10] E. K. Simpson and F. F. Bruce, *The Epistles of Paul to the Ephesians and to the Colossians* (New International Commentary on the New Testament, Grand Rapids: Eerdmans, 1957), 194.

1:26–7), there must be something divine about every human being. If, and this is our case, the divine Logos could assume a humanity, there must be something human about God."[11] Even though the essentially human and the divine are poles apart in terms of greatness, *they aren't necessarily mutually exclusive.* Though we are *limited* or *finite* in ourselves, finitude *doesn't define us as* human: Jesus aside, this *common/ universal* human characteristic isn't a *necessary* one.[12]

3. *The distinction between Jesus' two consciousnesses or levels of awareness—His developing first-century Jewish, human consciousness and the eternal, divine consciousness.* Imagine a spy on a dangerous mission, carrying in his mind top-secret information valuable to the enemy. To avoid divulging answers in case he's caught and tortured, he takes along a limited-amnesia producing pill with an antidote for later use. If the spy uses the amnesia pill, he would *still* possess the vital information in his mind; given these temporary conditions required to carry out his mission, he chooses to limit his access to the information that's stored up in his mind.

Similarly, during Jesus' mission to earth, He *still possessed* the full, undiminished capacities of divine knowledge and power, and He had access to those capacities as necessary for His mission. But before the foundation of the world, Father, Son, and Spirit freely determined together that the Son would limit or restrain the use of those powers to accomplish His overall mission (John 17:5,22–26). So (1) Jesus gave up having access to knowing, say, the time of His return (Matt 24:36) and, as we'll see, knowing that it was impossible for Him to sin or to be vulnerable to temptation (cf. Jas 1:13). However, (2) He didn't *lose* essential divine attributes; rather, He *voluntarily, temporarily suppressed* or *gave up access to* using certain divine capacities and powers He possessed all along. Like a father holding back the full force of his powers

---

[11] G. O'Collins, *Christology* (Oxford: Oxford University Press, 1995), 233.

[12] If humans are *created* or *finite,* did Jesus become a creature? No, He *took on* human nature and a human body. While both *are* God's creations, this doesn't mean that they are *necessary* to being human. Are humans *necessarily* finite? We can deny that both *creaturehood* and *being finite* are *necessary* or *essential* characteristics of human beings since God couldn't become something contrary to His nature. T. Senor, "The Incarnation and the Trinity," in *Reason for the Hope Within,* ed. Michael J. Murray (Grand Rapids: Eerdmans, 1999), 247. I am also borrowing here from Morris, *The Logic of God Incarnate.*

while playing soccer or baseball with his kids, so the Son of God, before coming to earth, determined to *restrain* His divine capacities.[13]

To illustrate how we can coherently talk about two levels of awareness, consider what it's like to come out of a dream in which we're *simultaneously* still dreaming *but also* conscious that it's a dream, at once "within" the dream and "outside" it. Or think of the two levels of awareness involved in self-deception: a person knows what's right but convinces himself to suppress his conscience. These examples of two levels of awareness—not two egos or selves, however—working together or overlapping in one person can perhaps give us some idea of the workings of the incarnate Christ's mind.

We can usefully compare Jesus' *two levels of awareness* ("minds") with *our* two levels of awareness—the *subconscious* and *conscious*: Jesus' *human* awareness can be likened to our *conscious*, and His *divine* awareness is analogous to our *subconscious*. When God the Son took on human form, *His fully aware eternal, His divine consciousness, His (comm) union with Father and Spirit, and His sustenance of the universe didn't cease but rather continued uninterrupted.* Yet in His limited, developing human consciousness, Jesus grew and developed with an earthly, first-century, Aramaic-speaking, Jewish awareness of the world. Reading the Scriptures, He saw with increasing clarity His messianic status. He struggled, experienced the range of human emotions, and deepened in obedience and submission to His Father's will (cf. Luke 2:52; Heb 2:18; 5:8).[14]

Jesus' human consciousness *significantly interacted* with His divine consciousness and wasn't cut off from certain heavenly illuminations like the glow of divine light that streams through a cloth curtain.[15] Jesus, however, *didn't regularly rely on His divine consciousness* while on earth but primarily operated in His human consciousness, just like us, with the added depth of divine awareness. Being fully human, Jesus

---

[13] G. Hawthorne, *The Presence and the Power* (Dallas: Word, 1991), 218.

[14] R. T. France, "The Uniqueness of Jesus," *Evangelical Review of Theology* 17 (Jan. 1993): 13.

[15] G. Hawthorne, *The Presence and the Power*, 212, 216. R. L. Reymond writes: "There is no confusion [in the crucifixion] of the divine and human natures of Christ. It is not the divine nature as such which is crucified; it is the divine person, because he is also human, who is crucified." "Incarnation" in *Evangelical Dictionary of Theology*, ed. W. A. Elwell (Grand Rapids: Baker, 1984), 556–57.

freely and fully depended on the Spirit's power as He sought to carry out His Father's purpose.

These three distinctions provide a helpful framework for addressing questions such as: (1) If Jesus was God, who was running the universe when He was a baby or on the cross? (2) How could God die? (3) If God "so loved the world," why did He send His Son rather than come Himself? This two-levels-of-awareness incarnational model helps us see that Jesus experienced the ongoing mutually indwelling trinitarian life, still governing the universe as a baby while dying on the cross. And He died as a mere, not essentially, human being; the divine nature wasn't crucified but the divine person, who is also human.[16] The mutual life of the Trinity suggests that each divine person experienced pain at the crucifixion; Jesus didn't suffer alone. Rather, "God was in Christ reconciling the world to Himself" (2 Cor 5:19).

If Jesus Was God, How Could He Be Tempted?

In the incarnation God comes close to us; He comes alongside us in our weakness, even enduring difficult temptations and struggles: "We do not have a high priest who cannot sympathize with our weaknesses, but One who has been tempted in all things as we are, yet without sin" (Heb 4:15).

The natural follow-up question to our discussion is, *If Jesus was God, how could He be tempted?* Because of God's intrinsic goodness (Jas 1:18), He can't be led into sin or overpowered by an outside force: "Let no one say when he is tempted, 'I am being tempted by God'; for God cannot be tempted by evil, and He Himself does not tempt anyone" (Jas 1:13). But wasn't the incarnate Christ tempted to depart from His Father's will, to take the easy way out (Matt 4:1–11)? Doesn't His temptation mean He can "come to the aid of those who are tempted" (Heb 2:18)? But doesn't this imply Jesus *could have* sinned? And if *not*, then wasn't His temptation simply playacting? As we'll see, the Bible portrays Jesus' temptations as a genuine anguished struggle; there is no playacting involved here. Let's explore further.

---

[16] R. L. Reymond, "Incarnation" in *Evangelical Dictionary of Theology*, 556–57. Cf. Acts 20:28: "The church of God which He purchased with His own blood."

First, the "merely/commonly" versus "fully/essentially" human distinction reminds us that the ability to sin isn't part of the definition of "human." The impossibility of humans' sinning in the new heaven and earth won't diminish their full humanity. Though common among human beings, the ability to sin isn't essential to our humanity. For Jesus to be fully human, He didn't need to have the ability to sin.

Second, for His redemptive mission on earth, the Son of God voluntarily set aside having access to knowing certain things; one such item was the awareness that He couldn't sin. The Gospels portray Jesus' supernatural knowledge of people's thoughts and details about future events. But Jesus is also ignorant of certain things such as the timing of His return (*parousia*, lit. "presence"): "But of that day and hour no one knows, not even the angels of heaven, nor the Son, but the Father alone" (Matt 24:36). We could also add Jesus' ignorance about the fig tree (Mark 11:13) and the hemorrhaging woman who touched him (Mark 5:30–33) or His amazement at a Gentile centurion's faith (Matt 8:10).

Likewise, Jesus' mission included intentionally surrendering the knowledge that *He, being divine, couldn't ultimately deviate from His Father's will.* In Gethsemane He prayed, "My Father, if it is possible, let this cup pass from Me; yet not as I will, but as You will" (Matt 26:39). Theologian Gerald O'Collins asserts that Jesus' growth in self-knowledge and self-identity and in struggling in prayer "supports the conclusion that the divine reality was not fully and comprehensively present to the [human] mind of Jesus."[17]

For temptation to be meaningful, Jesus, unable to sin, must have been unaware that sinning was impossible. *Jesus was unaware of the time of His own return so why not of the impossibility of sinning?* In His preincarnate state, the Son of God (with Father and Spirit) determined to give up temporary access to being aware of *both* of these things as part of His mission. He voluntarily limited access to expressing certain divine attributes (in being weak, hungry, and tired)—as well as having access to His divine knowledge (ignorance of His second coming and His invulnerability to sin), though He at any time could have chosen to be aware of them. Jesus thus identifies with us by experiencing *real*

[17] G. O'Collins, *Interpreting Jesus* (Ramsey, NJ: Paulist, 1983), 186.

temptations and limitations. If Jesus' human awareness saw the divine reality in all its clarity, being obedient, struggling in prayer, He could not have experienced true temptation.[18]

The incarnate Son's temptations *were* real; acting on them seemed a genuine possibility to Him. Though *unique*, His situation is *conceivable:* Imagine entering a room and closing the door behind you. Unbeknownst to you, the door has an automatic two-hour time lock. You consider leaving once or twice, but you freely decide to read for the full two hours, after which you leave the room. Would you have been able to leave earlier? No. But why did you *stay* in and *not try* to go out? Because you *freely decided* to stay. Similarly, Christ freely chose, in submission to the Spirit, to resist temptation even though it was impossible for Him to sin; however, His divine awareness didn't overwhelm or impose itself on His human awareness.[19]

> Jesus could be truly tempted and tested, provided that he did not know that he could not sin. If he had known that he could not sin, it would be difficult, if not impossible, to make sense of genuine temptations; they would be reduced to make-believe, a performance put on for the edification of others. It was quite a different situation to be incapable of sin and not to know that.[20]

But if Jesus knew He stood in God's place as the great "I am" (John's Gospel) or the final judge (Matt 7:23), how could He *not* know sinning was impossible? The simple answer is that, though standing in God's place, He, as part of His mission, *was* ignorant about His return *and* other matters.

Rather than playacting, Christ suffered real temptation because He gave up temporary access to the knowledge that He couldn't sin. Through moment-by-moment submission to His Father's will and His being "led by the Spirit" (Luke 4:1 HCSB), He also sets an example for us to be "led by the Spirit" (Rom 8:14). Some Christians think, *Of course, Jesus didn't sin; He was God!* Yet His overcoming temptation wasn't automatic because He was divine but because He steadfastly

---

[18] Ibid., 185.
[19] Morris, *The Logic of God Incarnate*, 149–50.
[20] O'Collins, *Christology*, 271.

committed Himself to His Father's will and relied on the empowering Spirit.

Though an amazing *mystery*, the doctrine of the incarnation isn't a *contradiction*. In this mystery a fully divine, fully human Jesus possesses a certain dual awareness. In one, He is fully knowing; in another He is voluntarily limited in His knowledge so that He could *truly* endure temptation, identifying with us in every way except without sin.

Final Considerations

The incarnation of Christ serves as a caution to us: we must begin with Scripture rather than with some (perhaps) Greek philosophical abstractions about a generic "Unmoved Mover" or "First Cause"; otherwise, we may run the risk of beginning with a deity that more closely resembles that of Greek philosophy or Enlightenment Deism than the Triune God of the Christian faith. Even though there is a rightful place for arguments for God's existence, the discussion must move beyond this point to asking the personalizing question: "If some good, wise, powerful Creator exists, has He made Himself more clearly known, and, if so, how should I respond to Him?" The Scriptures emphatically state that God has revealed Himself in Jesus of Nazareth. This God is not necessarily the kind of God that, say, Plato or Aristotle would expect. Rather, Jesus shows up on the scene doing the sorts of things Yahweh is supposed to do—manifesting the presence of Yahweh, bringing forgiveness and deliverance from exile, and so forth. He does something unexpected, even though the Old Testament anticipates it: He stoops exceedingly low to identify with us and to rescue us, and in doing so He displays His greatness. Jesus of Nazareth, who said that the one who sees Him sees the Father (John 14:9), invites us to look to Him to see just what kind of God Yahweh is. Jesus' incarnation and crucifixion are profound indicators of what God is like.[21]

Earlier we looked at the Christ-hymn in Philippians 2, where Paul draws on Isa 45:22–23; 52:13; 53; 57:15—passages that stress how

---

[21] See N. T. Wright, "The Truth of the Gospel and Christian Living," in *The Meaning of Jesus: Two Visions*, M. Borg and N. T. Wright (San Francisco: HarperCollins, 1999), 214–15; see also chapter 5 in N. T. Wright, *The Challenge of Jesus* (Downers Grove, IL: InterVarsity Press, 1999).

God, though high and lofty and worship-worthy, dwells with the contrite and lowly in spirit. Here I should mention the *kenosis* theory or "kenotic Christology" (from the Greek word *kenōō*/"empty" in Phil 2:7, where God the Son "emptied Himself [*auton ekenōsen*]"). This view generally emphasizes the Son of God's temporarily surrendering certain divine attributes such as omniscience or omnipotence between the virginal conception and the resurrection (although since the incarnation, God the Son remains incarnate forever).[22] However, I believe that we have embedded in the Old Testament itself themes of God's "self-emptying" or self-humiliation coupled with His exalted status. These themes are brought together and cohere remarkably in the New, particularly in the person and work of Jesus of Nazareth. In this Christological hymn Paul is saying that the career of the Servant of the Lord—including His suffering, humiliation, death, and exaltation—is the manner in which the sovereignty of the one true God becomes evident to the world. It is precisely in the Servant's humiliation that God's greatness is most clearly revealed to the nations. In contrast to the kenotic theory, Yahweh is humble in His nature. This humility is not simply manifested in the Son of God's self-emptying, but, as I have argued elsewhere,[23] it is characteristic of God even apart from Jesus' earthly career.

Having said this, I want to discuss briefly how the New Testament expands on the twin themes of God's humility and exalted status. In John's Gospel, the words and themes of humiliation/suffering and exaltation are actually aligned closely: the Servant of Yahweh is exalted and glorified *in* and *through* His humiliation and suffering. John refers back to the Septuagint (Greek Old Testament [LXX]) of the Suffering Servant passage in Isa 52:13 ("Behold, My servant will prosper; He will be high and lifted up and greatly exalted" [my translation]). The verbs "lifted up" [Greek verb: *hypsoō*] and "glorified/exalted" [Greek verb: *doxazō*]) are brought together in John's Gospel to refer to Jesus' death on the cross. Note the following verses (my emphasis):

---

[22] On some of the issues surrounding kenotic Christology, see C. S. Evans, ed., *Exploring Kenotic Christology: The Self-Emptying of God* (Oxford: Oxford University Press, 2006).
[23] P. Copan, "Divine Narcissism? A Further Defense of God's Humility," *Philosophia Christi* n.s. 8 (January 2006): 313–25.

As Moses *lifted up* the serpent in the wilderness, even so must the Son of Man be *lifted up*. (John 3:14)

Jesus said, "When you *lift up* the Son of Man, then you will know that I am He, and I do nothing on My own initiative, but I speak these things as the Father taught Me." (John 8:28)

And Jesus answered them, saying, "The hour has come for the Son of Man to be *glorified*. Truly, truly, I say to you, unless a grain of wheat falls into the earth and dies, it remains alone; but if it dies, it bears much fruit." (John 12:23–24)

"And I, if I am *lifted up* from the earth, will draw all men to Myself." But He was saying this to indicate the kind of death by which He was to die. (John 12:32–33)

Therefore when [Judas] had gone out, Jesus said, "Now is the Son of Man *glorified*, and God is glorified in Him; if God is glorified in Him, God will also *glorify* Him in Himself, and will *glorify* Him immediately." (John 13:31–32)

John is using a double meaning of the verb "lift up": it is being used both literally (the crucifixion elevated one above the earth [cf. 12:33]) and figuratively: in the humiliation of the crucifixion, we note Jesus' simultaneous elevation to the status of divine sovereignty over the cosmos. The cross is *already* Jesus' exaltation or glorification.[24] So in the incarnation of Christ—particularly the shameful, humiliating crucifixion—we see God's greatest achievement, His supreme moment of glory: God is willing to descend to humiliating death (being physically lifted up on the cross) to display unsurpassable greatness (being spiritually lifted up, being glorified).

In the incarnation, the God-man becomes the perfect Mediator between humankind and God. Indeed, the essence of sin is humans attempting to take the place of God whereas the essence of salvation is God taking the place of man.[25]

[24] For further elaborations on these themes, see R. Bauckham, *God Crucified: Monotheism and Christology in the New Testament* (Grand Rapids: Eerdmans, 1998).
[25] J. Stott, *The Cross of Christ* (Downers Grove, IL: InterVarsity Press, 1987), 160.

Chapter 16

DOSTOYEVSKY, WOODY ALLEN, AND THE DOCTRINE OF PENAL SUBSTITUTION

Steve L. Porter

Introduction

I n Fyodor Dostoyevsky's classic work *Crime and Punishment* the character Raskolnikov commits a murder and is almost driven insane by getting away with it. Raskolnikov only comes to find peace of mind in owning up to the wrong he committed and willingly taking on the punishment that was his due. Dostoyevsky's plot turns on the notion that wrongdoing deserves punishment and that receiving the punishment one deserves is good not only for society and the victim but also for the wrongdoer. But much changes when we turn from Dostoyevsky's mid-nineteenth century Russian context to a late twentieth century, North American retelling of *Crime and Punishment* in the movie *Crimes and Misdemeanors* written and directed by Woody Allen. Allen's movie takes place in a historical and cultural context in which not getting caught, or barring that, having one's felony reduced to a misdemeanor is the name of the game. True to this setting, the murderer in Allen's film, Dr. Rosenthal, is able to find peace of mind in getting away with his crime and avoiding punishment altogether. In Allen's tale punishment is more of an obstacle to be avoided than a fitting consequence to be received.[1]

---

[1] For a comparison of Dostoyevksy's and Allen's stories, see E. Chances, "Moscow Meets

The difference between these two stories is extremely relevant when it comes to the doctrine of penal substitution, for it seems that most of the contemporary objections to the view that Christ suffered the punitive consequences of human sin on behalf of sinners are fueled by the fact that we in the West find ourselves more in the world of Dr. Rosenthal than Raskolnikov. The doctrine of penal substitution does not make sense to many of us because, unlike Raskolnikov, punishment in general no longer makes sense to us. The idea that the infliction of punishment is required for our offenses, let alone that punishment is good for all involved, is a bit fuzzy in many minds. Indeed, a recent philosophical publication argues that the practice of legal punishment should be abolished altogether.[2] While few would go that far, the emergence of such a point of view is indicative of an increasing tendency to see an emphasis on punishment as in some sense outdated or inhumane. The common idea is that we, let alone God, have moved beyond such primitive and violent ways of dealing with our anger. The importance of surfacing this shift in intuitions regarding punishment is to highlight the difficulty that the doctrine of penal substitution will have in receiving a fair hearing in such a Rosenthalian moral climate.

If the moral concepts that once served to make sense of the doctrine of penal substitution are no longer as predominant as they once were, then this will have implications for how the gospel might best be communicated in our contemporary setting. Moreover, it helps to explain why there has been a recent resurgence of objectors to penal substitution.[3] The question that is pressed is whether the theory of penal substitution is, shifting moral intuitions aside, an adequate explanation of the cross of Christ.

Manhattan: The Russian Soul of Woody Allen's Films," *American Studies International* 30/1 (April 1992): 65–78.

[2] D. Boonin, *The Problem of Punishment* (Cambridge: Cambridge University Press, 2008).

[3] For some recent objectors, see J. B. Green and M. D. Baker, *Recovering the Scandal of the Cross: Atonement in New Testament and Contemporary Contexts* (Downers Grove, IL: IVP, 2000); S. Chalke and A. Mann, *The Lost Message of Jesus* (Grand Rapids: Zondervan, 2003); S. Chalke, "The Redemption of the Cross," in D. Tidball, D. Hillborn, and J. Thacker, eds., *The Atonement Debate: Papers from the London Symposium on the Theology of Atonement* (Grand Rapids: Zondervan, 2008), 34–45; J. B. Green, "Must We Imagine the Atonement in Penal Substitutionary Terms? Questions, Caveats, and a Plea," in Tidball et al., eds., *The Atonement Debate*, 153–71.

Certainly the primary arena in which this question should be decided is biblical studies. And yet critics of penal substitution often question the doctrine's moral tenability before questioning its biblical credentials. For instance, Keith Ward writes, "One must therefore reject those crude accounts of Christian doctrine which . . . say that Christ has been justly punished in our place so that he has taken away our guilt and enabled God to forgive us. Almost everything is ethically wrong about these accounts."[4] Or as Paul Moser puts it:

> Unfortunately, some of the Christian tradition has offered a twisted reading of Jesus' role in divine forgiveness. The misguided reading implies that God's forgiveness of humans required that God punish and kill the sinless Jesus as the "just payment" for human sins. The source of this morally distorted claim isn't in the New Testament but rather is in later theology that suffers from a wooden misreading of Isaiah 53:10.[5]

For many objectors the moral implausibility of the doctrine either precedes or eclipses discussion of the biblical evidence. It will be difficult, no doubt, to openly consider the requisite biblical texts on this matter if it has already been determined that the whole notion of penal substitution is morally reprehensible.[6]

Hence, the first goal of this essay is to clarify and defend the plausibility of the moral framework required to ground penal substitution. But defending the moral plausibility of penal substitution stops short of determining whether penal substitution is a correct explanation of what transpired on the cross. So the second goal of this essay is to offer an argument that penal substitution is the best explanation of why Christ voluntarily went to His death. Both of these arguments leave untouched the biblical investigation, which remains the ultimate

---

[4] K. Ward, *Ethics and Christianity* (London: Allen & Unwin, 1970), 240.

[5] P. K. Moser, *The Elusive God: Reorienting Religious Epistemology* (Cambridge: Cambridge University Press, 2008), 174. See also P. K. Moser, "The Crisis of the Cross: God as Scandalous," in J. Gracia, ed., *Mel Gibson's Passion and Philosophy* (La Salle, IL: Open Court, 2004), 204–17.

[6] I have yet to find an opponent of penal substitution who finds the doctrine morally sensible and only thinks it biblically unsupported. Rather, the claim is typically that the doctrine is morally inadequate, and only then the claim is made that it is not taught in Scripture. This is not to say that the moral adequacy of the doctrine is irrelevant to the exegetical analysis but rather to highlight the importance of defending the moral coherence of penal substitution as part of an overall biblical-theological defense of penal substitution.

authority in deciding the legitimacy of penal substitution.[7] Before
turning to these two arguments, it is important to clarify what is (and
is *not*) being defended under the banner of penal substitution.

The Nature of Penal Substitution

I am *not* defending a characterization of penal substitution that goes
something like this: God was so angry because of human sin that He
had to inflict His violent wrath on somebody, and since He couldn't
punish guilty sinners, He took out His anger on His innocent Son instead. It is unfortunately somewhat easy for penal substitution to come
to be understood in this manner. For one, far too many human persons
fit such a characterization of anger and punishment, making it easy to
project this understanding onto God. But such an expression of anger and punishment is inappropriate at the human level, let alone the
divine level. What this characterization of penal substitution misses is
that God's anger/wrath is preceded and undergirded by His love and
wisdom, and so the transfer of the punishment for human sinners to
Christ is not out-of-control violence but rather loving and wise (cf.
1 Cor 1:23–25; John 5:8). Furthermore, this characterization erroneously splits the Trinity. On any thoughtful theory of penal substitution,
there isn't one person of the Trinity (the Father) looking to punish another person (the Son). Instead, the entire Godhead—Father, Son, and
Holy Spirit—acts to bring about atonement for sin in a loving, wise,
good, and just manner through the incarnate Christ's person and work.
Certainly some explanation is still required as to how a penal substitute
is loving, wise, good, and just, but there will be no ready answer to that
if the above mischaracterization is our starting point.

I am also *not* defending a view of penal substitution that reduces
Christ's salvific work to the cross alone or to only one aspect of what
the cross accomplished.[8] Jesus' central message was that the loving reign

---

[7] Some recent biblical investigation of penal substitution can be found in D. Tidball, *The Message of the Cross* (Downers Grove, IL: InterVarsity, 2001); I. H. Marshall, "The Theology of
the Atonement," in Tidball et al., eds., *The Atonement Debate;* C. E. Hill and F. A. James III,
eds., *The Glory of the Atonement: Biblical, Historical and Practical Perspectives* (Downers Grove,
IL: InterVarsity Press, 2004); S. Jeffery, M. Ovey, and A. Sach, *Pierced for Our Transgressions:
Rediscovering the Glory of Penal Substitution* (Nottingham, UK: InterVarsity Press, 2007).

[8] Perhaps no one has sought to make this point more clear than Dallas Willard. For instance,

of God is available to human sinners through His incarnate life, death, resurrection, ascension, sending of the Spirit, ongoing intercession at the right hand of the Father, and eventual ushering in of the kingdom in its fullness. Having one's sins forgiven is one essential part of being reconciled with God, but there is certainly more to God's reign enveloping human life than mere forgiveness of sins. There is confession, repentance, and forgiveness, but there is also abiding in Him, walking in and being filled with His Spirit, dying to self, learning to obey His commands, and so on. There is no question that salvation is more than the cross and the cross is more than penal substitution. Other models of the atonement (e.g., *Christus victor*) have biblical support and flesh out other dimensions of the cross and salvation.[9] Furthermore, certain cultures may more readily identify with nonpenal aspects of the atonement—whether these relate to Jesus' removing shame and impurity, bestowing a status of honor and purification—or to Jesus' superior power over evil forces at work. The atonement's bearing on considerations of *(im)purity, (dis)honor,* and *fear/power* in, say, Eastern or African cultures may resonate more powerfully than a penal model.[10] And yet, while we certainly don't want to reduce salvation and the cross to penal substitution, let us not make the opposite mistake of going too far to the other extreme and overly minimizing the role of the cross in salvation and/or the presence of a penal substitutionary element to the cross.

Of course, it is one thing to clarify what penal substitution is *not,* and it is another to specify what penal substitution is. While there have been numerous explications of the doctrine, the central claim is that in His voluntary suffering and death, Christ takes on the penal consequences of human sin on behalf of human sinners. It is precisely the plausibility of this general claim, however the details may be spelled out, that needs to be defended morally.

see D. Willard, *The Divine Conspiracy* (New York: HarperCollins, 1998), 42–50.

[9] For an array of complementary meanings of the cross, see C. E. Gunton, *The Actuality of the Atonement: A Study of Metaphor, Rationality and the Christian Tradition* (Edinburgh: T & T Clark, 2004). Consider also, J. B. Green, "Kaleidoscopic View," in J. K. Beilby and P. R. Eddy, eds., *The Nature of the Atonement: Four Views* (Downers Grove, IL: InterVarsity Press, 2006), 157–201.

[10] For a discussion on this, see chapters 10 and 11 in N. Jabbour, *The Crescent Through the Eyes of the Cross* (Colorado Springs, CO: NavPress, 2008).

The Moral Plausibility of Penal Substitution

In order to establish the moral framework that grounds the central claim of penal substitution it will be argued that (1) punishment is an appropriate human response to intentional human wrongdoing and (2) it is good in some circumstances for humans to exact that punishment. We will then proceed to argue from the human context to the divine context: (3) punishment is an appropriate *divine* response to human wrongdoing, (4) it is good in some circumstances for *God* to exact that punishment on human wrongdoers, and (5) the goodness of such punishment can still be achieved by God's taking that punishment upon Himself in the person of Jesus Christ.[11] Let's look at these premises in turn.

The first premise of the argument is: (1) punishment is an appropriate human response to intentional human wrongdoing. The support for this premise depends on what is meant by punishment. Allow me to suggest the following definition: punishment is the forcible withdrawal of certain rights and/or privileges in response to the intentional misuse of those rights and/or privileges. When we punish, we take away from the wrongdoer, by force if needed, the right and/or privilege to interact freely with persons or the possessions of those persons when the wrongdoer has intentionally abused that right and/or privilege. For instance, if you loan me your car and I intentionally crash it, it would seem that not only do you have the right to demand that I pay for the damages (what we typically call "reparation"), but you also have the right to withhold from me the privilege of borrowing your car again (what is here termed "punishment"). Or if little Johnny pushes his playmate Susie down "just because," Johnny's mother has the right to demand an apology from Johnny (what might be termed "confession") and withdraw from Johnny the privilege of playtime (this would be the "punishment").

The basic idea of punishment is that it is permissible to withdraw a right and/or privilege from an offender when that right and/or privilege has been intentionally abused by the offender.[12] While you certainly

---

[11] Another example of arguing from human moral notions to the divine context when it comes to the atonement is R. Swinburne, *Responsibility and Atonement* (Oxford: Clarendon, 1989).

[12] This definition is meant to be a definition of "retributive" punishment. The basic idea of

could withhold punishment and lend me your car again and while the mother could withhold punishment and let Johnny continue to play with Susie, there is something equally fitting (if not *more* fitting in these cases) about exacting the punishment that is due. Offenders (particularly in severe cases) do not deserve to continue to have the rights and/or privileges that they have abused, and it seems that they deserve to have those rights and/or privileges withdrawn.[13] There are certainly special circumstances in which the punishment otherwise deserved should not be exacted (e.g., mental incapacity), but what is being argued here is that punishment is an appropriate response in principle to intentional offenses. Common intuitions such as these are what give credence to claim 1 that punishment is an appropriate human response to intentional human wrongdoing.

But even if this is right, why think punishment should ever be exacted? While it is permissible to punish, is it not better (even virtuous) simply to forgive without demanding punishment? You might demand reparation for the damage I caused to your car but mercifully extend to me the privilege to borrow your car again. Or the mother might accept a contrite confession from Johnny and choose not to withdraw him from playtime. What can be said in favor of claim 2, that it is good in some circumstances for humans to exact the appropriate punishment? For one, when punishment goes unaddressed, there is a potential of trivializing the wrongdoer and the wrong done as well as the potential to express further devaluing of the victim.[14] On the other hand, when

retributive punishment is that punishment is permissible despite positive or negative consequences that might proceed from the punishment. This is not to say that positive or negative consequences should not be taken into account but that the initial justification of punishment does not depend on an assessment of those consequences. For the retributivist there is something inherently appropriate about punishment in response to wrongdoing irrespective of the consequences. For a contemporary defense of retributivism, see J. Jacobs, "Luck and Retribution," *Philosophy* 74 (1999): 535–55.

[13] Distinctions are made when it comes to retributive punishment between strict and moderate forms of retributivism. A strict theory would require that the punishment deserved is always exacted in full while a moderate form of retributivism would only maintain that it is permissible to exact the punishment deserved. On a moderate retributivism one could forego punishment altogether or reduce the penalty. For more on these distinctions, see J. R. Lucas, *Responsibility* (Oxford: Clarendon, 1993), 281.

[14] This has been termed the "expressive value" of retributive punishment. See J. Hampton, "The Retributive Idea," in J. G. Murphy and J. Hampton, eds., *Forgiveness and Mercy* (Cambridge: Cambridge University Press, 1988), 111–61; J. E. Hare, *The Moral Gap* (Oxford: Clarendon, 1996), 243–59.

punishment is exacted, the wrongdoer and the wrong done are treated with utter seriousness, and the punishment objectively expresses the value of the victim in contradistinction to the devaluing expressed by the wrong done to the victim. When you refuse to let me borrow your car in response to my abuse of that privilege, you take me and my act seriously and I am given the opportunity to take my offense toward you more seriously than I otherwise would. The gravity of treating you and your property responsibly is objectively expressed in punishment, and this can be subjectively appreciated by both the victim and the offender. Or when mother suspends Johnny's playtime, the value of his playmate Susie and the importance of treating her in accordance to her value is objectively affirmed. If playtime goes on more or less as is (even with the apology), the lack of punishment can communicate to Susie that Johnny's treatment of her is not that big of a deal and Johnny can get the impression that his choices in relationships with others are not so significant after all. Of course, it doesn't follow from this that punishment appropriate to the offense should always be exacted, but it does seem to support claim 2, that it is good in at least some circumstances for humans to exact the punishment deserved.[15]

All that has been done so far is to argue that punishment between human persons is appropriate and that for human persons to exact such punishment is good in some cases. But what can be said in favor of claim 3, that punishment is an appropriate *divine* response to human wrongdoing? If punishment is understood as the forcible withdrawal of certain rights and/or privileges in response to the intentional misuse of those rights and/or privileges, then the first question to ask is whether humans have misused any rights and/or privileges over which God has some claim. Of course, the prevailing Christian response is that humanity's gravest offense is against God Himself (e.g., Ps 51:4). We have been given the incredible privilege to live our earthly lives in loving dependence on God so that we might flourish in relationship with one

---

[15] Of course there are other potential goods that exacting punishment could bring about, but for the purposes of this paper, these will not be treated. For more extensive treatment, see S. L. Porter, "Rethinking the Logic of Penal Substitution," in W. L. Craig, ed., *Philosophy of Religion: A Reader and Guide* (Edinburgh: University of Edinburgh Press, 2002), 596–608; S. L. Porter, "Swinburnean Atonement and the Doctrine of Penal Substitution," *Faith and Philosophy* 21:2 (April 2004), 228–41.

another as stewards over the created order. No doubt we have each in our own ways abused this privilege, failing to trust wholly in God and subsequently failing to flourish in our relationships with one another and as stewards over the earth. The crucial question is whether our abuse of the privilege of human life and the opportunity for communion with God is such that we deserve to have those good gifts withdrawn. In other words, do we humans *deserve* a second, third, fourth, fifth, etc., chance in living human life as we were intended? It is clear from the Christian point of view that by God's mercy and grace we have been given more chances, but it is *merciful* and *gracious* precisely because we do not *deserve* it. The privilege of growing in communion with God and living out that loving communion with others on earth has been so intentionally abused by human persons (time and time again) that we, individually and collectively, do not deserve to have that privilege extended any longer—which is to say, we deserve to have the privilege withdrawn. But if that is the case, then claim 3 would follow: punishment is an appropriate *divine* response to human wrongdoing.

If one has come this far, then the question becomes: What is God going to do with the punishment human sinners deserve? Clearly it could be argued that God's moral nature, God's holiness and justice, demands that the punishment be exacted. But here, in claim 4, I would like to argue something slightly different: it is good in some circumstances for God to exact the punishment deserved from human sinners.[16] Why might it be good that God withdraw the privilege of having the opportunity to live life on earth in growing communion with Himself (what might be called the privilege of physical and spiritual life)? Wouldn't it be better, and more in keeping with His mercy, if He continued to offer the opportunity for physical and spiritual life even though we continue to abuse this opportunity? The ultimate answer is that it *is* more in keeping with God's mercy for Him continuously to extend the offer of physical and spiritual life to human persons who do not deserve it.

---

[16] It is not that the stronger claim is indefensible. Rather, I find a moderate theory of retributive punishment more in keeping with the biblical record and with compelling moral intuitions. While God has the right to punish sin in full, in some cases He either withholds that punishment for a time, limits the punishment, or forgoes punishment altogether. This also seems to be the way human persons punish—that is, we don't always exact from the offender the full penal debt. There is greater room for grace and mercy on a moderate retributivism.

But at least one danger of so doing is analogous to what was considered before. That is, when punishment goes unaddressed, there is a potential diminishing of the wrongdoer's responsibility and of trivializing the wrong done as well as the potential to express further devaluing of the victim. On the other hand, when punishment is exacted, the wrongdoer and the wrong done are treated with utter seriousness, and the punishment objectively expresses the value of the victim in contradistinction to the devaluing expressed by the wrong done to the victim. In this case punishment that is not exacted has the potential to trivialize the human person and his abuse of God's offer of physical and spiritual life as well as the potential to express further devaluing of God Himself. When God demands that the punishment be exacted, He makes clear that He takes human persons and their acts seriously and objectively reaffirms the value of the Godhead that is devalued in human sin. It seems that, as claim 4 notes, it is good in some circumstances for God to exact the punishment deserved from human sinners.

Such goods are likely only some of the many benefits that would be achieved by exacting the punishment human persons deserve. But absent the articulation of these other benefits, one might think that if these were the only goods that would be achieved by exacting the punishment due sinners, then God out of His mercy would forego the punishment due human sinners. But what if there were a way for Him both to accomplish these goods (as well as other putative goods) and to forego the punishment due human sinners? That is, what if there was a way that, as claim 5 suggests, the goodness of punishment can still be achieved by God Himself taking that punishment on Himself?

The demand that human persons lose the opportunity for physical and spiritual life is tantamount to a demand of physical and spiritual death. Of course, physical and spiritual death is what humans deserve for their abuse of God's offer of physical and spiritual life (e.g. Gen 2:17; Rom 6:23). We do not deserve the physical life we have been given here on earth, and we do not deserve the spiritual life we have been given to live in communion with God. Indeed, we deserve to have our physical and spiritual life taken away. The consequence of physical and spiritual death would take sinners and their sin with due moral seriousness and would objectively reexpress the value of the Godhead in response to the devaluing of the Godhead expressed by sin. And yet the exaction of such a penalty would mean the loss of life for human sinners. So God mercifully takes on the punishment we deserve in the incarnate Christ's voluntary submission to physical and spiritual death on the cross.[17] God as the victim of wrongdoing has the right to demand the exaction of the punishment due in a manner proportional to the wrong done. The goodness of the punishment is still seen in that Christ's going to the cross *for our sins* takes sinners and their sin with utter seriousness and objectively reexpresses the value of the Godhead in response to the devaluing of the Godhead expressed by human sin. By looking to the cross, we too can perceive the importance God attaches to us, to the gravity of our offense, and to the right valuing of the Godhead.[18]

While much more could be said, it has been argued here that a moral framework makes morally plausible the claim that Christ suffered the penal consequences of human sin on behalf of sinners.

The Actuality of Penal Substitution

While some might agree that God has the right to punish sinners with physical and spiritual death, that certain goods would be achieved by the exaction of such punishment that wouldn't otherwise be achieved, and that it is much the better that this good be achieved by a just transfer of the penal consequences to Christ on the cross than that human persons suffer these consequences, it may nonetheless be questioned whether this is what was actually going on in the historical crucifixion of Christ. It bears repeating that this is where the biblical evidence is crucial. Given the moral coherence of penal substitution, does Scripture indicate that such a transaction is taking place in

---

[17] For more on the coherence of penal substitutes, see D. Lewis, "Do We Believe in Penal Substitution?" in *Philosophical Papers* 26 (1997): 203–9.

[18] It might be wondered how the humiliation of Christ on the cross actually expresses the value of the Godhead. Once we understand that Christ is suffering the just penalty of human sin on the cross (i.e., physical and spiritual death) in order to demonstrate that sin against God is not a trivial matter, we are also in a position to see that the value of the Godhead makes the exaction of punishment good. Just as Susie's value is expressed in the exaction of the punishment Johnny deserves, God's value is expressed in the exaction of the punishment humans deserve. Of course, in the latter case God in Christ suffers the punishment humans deserve. Nonetheless, the Godhead's value is being expressed once it is understood that Christ is taking the place of human sinners.

Christ's suffering and death? While I am sympathetic to the biblical arguments in support of penal substitution, here I would like to explore a slightly different argument for the actuality of penal substitution.

The argument can be put as follows:

1. Christ voluntarily died on the cross.
2. It is either foolish or suicidal for Christ voluntarily to die on the cross unless some great good can only or best be accomplished by so doing.
3. Any great good one might suggest for Christ's death besides vicarious punishment seems to be of the kind that could have been accomplished without His death.
4. The one great good that can only or best be accomplished by Christ's voluntary death on the cross is that, by so doing, He took on the physical and spiritual death due human sinners.

Therefore, the doctrine of penal substitution is the only adequate explanation of Christ's voluntary death on the cross.

Let us turn to a consideration of these premises. First, I take it that premise 1, Christ voluntarily died on the cross, is rightfully assumed by all who accept that Jesus was God incarnate. Christ sets his face to Jerusalem and does not attempt to escape His death when He was obviously able to do so (Matt 16:21). Indeed, in the garden of Gethsemane, we see that both Christ and His heavenly Father see the cross ("the cup") as ultimately unavoidable (Luke 22:42).[19] Now presumably the cross was avoidable in all sorts of ways. Christ could have ascended into the heavens prior to His execution. He could have mysteriously slipped away from the soldiers as He had from other violent crowds in the past. By His own admission, He could have brought His rule and reign into the present with overwhelming authority and power (Matt 26:53). But He doesn't. The question is, Why does He voluntarily go to His death?

One thing we know for sure is that He must have had a good reason. Premise 2 is a specification of the more general claim that it is either

---

[19] There are alternative interpretations of what "the cup" refers to in this passage, but I take the crucifixion as well as the events leading up to the crucifixion to be the most plausible referent. See C. S. Keener, *A Commentary on the Gospel of Matthew* (Grand Rapids: Eerdmans, 1999), 637–38; M. J. Wilkins, *Matthew: The NIV Application Commentary* (Grand Rapids: Zondervan, 2004), 841–43.

foolish or suicidal to die voluntarily unless there is some great good that can only or best be accomplished by voluntarily dying. We think it either foolish or suicidal when a person jumps in front of a speeding train proclaiming love for a friend. Unless, of course, the friend (or someone else) is in front of the speeding train and jumping in front of the train was the only way to save that person. To offer a different example, if we find out the moral reformer knew the gunman was lying in wait and that she could have easily avoided the bullets but instead wanted to go down in a dramatic fashion, the reformer's death loses its meaning. By all means, stay alive if you can, unless going to your death is the only or best way to accomplish some great good. So too, Christ must have had a great good in mind that could only or best be accomplished by voluntarily dying. Surely His death was not suicidal or foolish.

And yet, what could that great good be that could not be accomplished in a less costly manner? The third premise claims: Any great good one might suggest for Christ's death besides vicarious punishment seems to be of the kind that could have been accomplished without His death.

Now setting forth an exhaustive listing of all possible reasons for Christ's voluntarily death is impossible, but examining a few prominent suggestions will make the point. For instance, some propose that Christ went to His death because it was the natural consequence of a perfect human life lived in an imperfect world. Since Christ freely went to His death, the idea becomes that for Him to avoid the likely outcome of His incarnate existence would have been to take the easy way out. The problem here is that while a perfect human in an imperfect world will be regularly threatened with violence, this does not seem to be an adequate reason to allow oneself to be killed. This is akin to a political reformer's allowing himself to be assassinated by his opposition because "they will kill me eventually so I will go along with their murderous plot." No, the reformer should stay alive as long as possible, dodging bullets if need be, and if the reformer had it within his power to avoid death altogether, that would be the better. We would never call the reformer who seeks to avoid his likely death a coward, so why think that it would be cowardly for Christ to avoid His likely death? All of this to say: if there wasn't some other reason why Christ should lay down His life, violent death being the natural outcome of a perfect human life seems insufficient.

But what about the great good of the resurrection? Christ's death is obviously a necessary condition for His resurrection. The idea here seems to be that the only way for Christ to have demonstrated His power over death was for Him to be resurrected from the dead and so this justifies His voluntary submission to the cross. But could not Christ have shown His power over death by raising numerous others, like Lazarus, from the dead? There seems to be no question among those who witnessed Christ's resurrecting others that He had power over death (e.g. John 12:10–11,17–19). While the demonstration of Christ's resurrection power is a great good, it does not appear that it is only or best achieved through Christ's own voluntary death. There are less costly ways for Christ to make His power equally well-known.

Nonetheless, if Christ Himself had not died and risen again, not as much attention would have been drawn to His message, or His message would not have been authenticated. No doubt the resurrection did accomplish both of these great goods, but the question is whether this would have been sufficient reason for Christ voluntarily to lay down His life. It seems incumbent on Christ to draw attention to and authenticate His message without voluntarily dying if that were feasible. Once again, do we admire the activist who draws attention to his cause by being an accomplice in his own death when there are other means of drawing equal attention that do not involve his death? It seems that for Christ there were other means. For instance, if Christ had ascended into the heavens right off of Golgotha, that surely would have created a stir. He could have returned after His precrucifixion ascension in much the same way as the Gospels record His postresurrection appearances. Certainly such an ascension and reappearance (while not quite a death and resurrection) would have caused Christ to stand out and would have clearly authenticated His divine status. Since these goods could be achieved in a manner that avoided Christ's death, the goodness and wisdom of His voluntary death is left unexplained.

Another possibility is that the cross shows us that the way of Christ is the way of humility, death to self, and nonviolence.[20] We see on the

---

[20] For a detailed presentation of this theme, see M. J. Gorman, *Cruciformity: Paul's Narrative*

cross that when God could have struck back, He did not. But once again we can have our cake and eat it too, for certainly Christ's teachings and life prior to the cross amply testify to His way of humility, death to self, and nonviolence (e.g. Matt 5:38–42). If we found that a moral reformer voluntarily submitted to her violent death when she could have avoided it in order to drive home these lessons, we would question the wisdom of that reformer. In other words, we could take Christ's death out of His incarnate life and still have a clear example of His way of humility, death to self, and nonviolence. Certainly His death adds something to His modeling a spirituality of descent, but if this were the only reason voluntarily to lay down one's life, it does not appear to be sufficient.

One might think that all of the above and much more are accomplished via the cross, but no matter what is offered, the general response will still hold. For whatever reason is proposed as the justifying reason for Christ's voluntary death, the response will be: that could have been accomplished equally well without a violent death. Therefore, for Christ voluntarily to lay down His life was either suicidal or foolish. In other words: (3) Any great good one might suggest for Christ's death besides vicarious punishment seems to be of the kind that could have been accomplished without His death.

Surely Christ's death was neither suicidal nor foolish, so He must have had a justifying reason to choose the cross. But the only reason we regularly accept as justifying a voluntary death is that by so dying one or more other human lives are spared: the person who jumps on the grenade to save others, the person who goes through a risky surgery to donate an organ that someone else needs to live, the person who accepts a dangerous mission knowing that death is likely in order to save many others from harm. These examples are neither suicidal nor foolish but rather move us deeply when we hear of them. Truly, "no one has greater love than this, that someone would lay down his life for his friends" (John 15:13 HCSB). Though, as has been shown, such sacrificial love is only authentically loving when by laying down your life your friends are thereby enabled to live.

The doctrine of penal substitution meets this condition. It explains Christ's voluntary death by claiming that the only or best way to save

Spirituality of the Cross (Grand Rapids: Eerdmans, 2001).

human lives from physical and spiritual death is for that physical and spiritual death to be taken on by the person of Christ: (4) The one great good that can only or best be accomplished by Christ's voluntary death on the cross is that by so doing He took on the physical and spiritual death due human sinners.

The only great good that can justify a voluntary death is if that death saves other lives, and the only theory of the atonement that makes sense of why the *death* of Jesus would save other lives is the theory of penal substitution. So the argument draws us to the conclusion that penal substitution is the only adequate explanation of why Christ would have voluntarily gone to the cross.

Conclusion

So while the doctrine of penal substitution may be a difficult teaching in our Rosenthalian moral climate, there does not appear to be any other adequate explanation of Christ's voluntary death on the cross. Moreover, we have seen that there is a plausible moral framework that makes sense of the doctrine. Christ's taking on the penal consequences of human sin is not the only purpose of His person and work, and salvation in Christ is not simply a means for persons to escape punishment for sin. "Christ in you" is "the hope of glory" (Col 1:27 HCSB). Nevertheless, Christ's taking on the penal consequences of human sin as a means for persons to escape punishment for sin ushers in the availability of the loving rule and reign of God in Christ by the Spirit in a manner that is rightful and fitting. Through Christ's death as punishment for our sins, we have the opportunity to see the importance God places on reconciliation with humanity, the seriousness with which He takes human sin, the great value of the Godhead, and the gracious and merciful love of God, who is willing to do all of this in our stead.[21]

---

[21] It is important to remember that the reality of the cross is a transformational reality. For a discussion of the transformational implications of a penal substitutionary view of the cross, see J. Coe, "Resisting the Temptation of *Moral* Formation: Opening to *Spiritual* Formation in the Cross and the Spirit," *Journal of Spiritual Formation and Soul Care* 1/1 (2008): 55–78. I am grateful to the Seal Beach Philosophy Group (Jason Baehr, Josh Blander, Tom Crisp, Michael Pace, Dan Speak, and Greg TenElshof) for discussion and encouragement on this chapter.

Chapter 17

HELL: GETTING WHAT'S GOOD MY OWN WAY

Stewart Goetz

Consider one way people think about the doctrine of hell. They assume the principle of an eye for an eye and a tooth for a tooth found in Deut 19:21 and look for an immoral deed or deeds for which the proportionate and just punishment is hell.[1] To illustrate the idea they have in mind, suppose that there is a man named "Smith" who makes another individual named "Jones" unhappy for every moment of the latter's 70-year life and that Jones never "gets even" with Smith, who lives out his years with more than his fair share of happiness. On the eye-for-an-eye principle, God should make Smith unhappy to the same degree and for as long as Jones was unhappy, which was for 70 years. Suppose now that Smith not only made Jones unhappy for 70 years but also made a million other people unhappy for various lengths of time. On the eye-for-an-eye principle, God should sum up the years of unhappiness caused by Smith and make him unhappy to the same degree as everyone else and for the same cumulative amount of time.

I will leave it to the reader to consider other examples like the one I have just elaborated. Some believe that a problem with thinking of hell in accordance with the eye-for-an-eye principle is that no matter how much unhappiness Smith causes it will always be finite in amount and he will deserve to be unhappy for only a finite period of time. There

[1] M. M. Adams summarizes such authors in her "Hell and the God of Justice," *Religious Studies* 11 (1975): 433–47.

seems to be no way to make sense out of the idea of someone's going
to hell forever if it is thought of in terms of the eye-for-an-eye principle. This implication has led to thought about whether the eye-for-
an-eye principle is itself a principle of punishment that is second-best
in nature. After all, even in this life there is no way of guaranteeing
that the person whose punishment is the loss of an eye or a foot will
be deprived of the same amount of good as his victim who lost an eye
or foot. Eyes and feet are sources of pleasure, and it is questionable
to think that the amount of pleasure one person gets from his intact
eyes and feet equals the amount of pleasure that another gets from
his. Even if there were some way to ascertain how much pleasure the
victim would lose from the loss of his eyes and feet, we have no way of
making sure that we could produce an equal amount of loss of pleasure
in the person being punished. Moreover, there is no evidence of the
literal application of the eye-for-an-eye principle in the Old Testament
except in the form of life for life, and many biblical scholars believe
that the Israelites used the eye-for-an-eye principle to express the abstract idea of commensurability and to discourage abuses of justice. If
these scholars are right, the eye-for-an-eye principle is not the perfect
principle of justice in the literal sense of its application but rather a
good way of limiting injustice in a world where there never is or can
be perfect justice.

Are there principles other than "an eye for an eye" in terms of which
to think about the doctrine of hell? Some have suggested that what a
person deserves for wrongdoing is a function of the offended party's
worthiness of honor.[2] Because God is infinite, He is worthy of infinite
honor (whatever that might mean), where God's honor consists in His
creatures being subject to Him or to His will. A person incurs infinite
guilt by a single act of refusing to be subject to God or to His will. But
could such an act justify God's consigning someone to hell forever? It
is hard to see how it could. Surely one such act or some finite number
of such acts could not rob God of an infinite amount of honor.

Does the idea of hell become any more intelligible if we think of
it in terms of God's happiness instead of His honor? It is hard to see
how it does. After all, while a creature's wrongdoing might make God

[2] Ibid.

unhappy, it is difficult to believe that it can produce in Him an infinite amount of unhappiness such that the creature deserves to be sent to hell to suffer an infinite number of years of unhappiness. Moreover, many believe that it is impossible for a creature to make God unhappy because He is not subject to changes of passion of any kind (God, it is said, is impassible).[3] Hence, no one could be sent to hell for making God unhappy.

Is hell, then, not something a person deserves because of any amount of harm that is actually done to other fellow creatures or to God but something that is deserved because of what a person intends (or tries) to do? But what might a person intend to do that would deserve an eternity of hell? Can a person intend to make someone else (another human being or God) unhappy forever? It is difficult to understand what a person might be thinking who believed that this was within the scope of his power. After all, a person can only intend to do what he believes he can do, and given he understands that he cannot prevent someone else from choosing to lay hold of perfect happiness, he likewise understands that he cannot intend to make someone else unhappy forever.

Is there any principle in terms of which hell is just? I believe there is, and while my purpose in this chapter is not to reconstruct C. S. Lewis's position on hell, I will at many points draw on his insights into the matter in developing my own account of hell. Christians sometimes ask me who I think was closest to getting it right about issues that are important to the Christian faith. I always answer "C. S. Lewis," and I have found his treatment of the doctrine of hell more persuasive than that of anyone else.

When Lewis put pen to paper about hell, he said that he detested the doctrine from the bottom of his heart. He also stated that he believed it. His reasons for doing so were deeply rooted in Western philosophy and Christian thought about the concepts of what is good, freedom of the will, and the meaning or purpose of life. I begin with the idea of what is good.

---

[3] See G. L. Prestige, *God in Patristic Thought* (London: SPCK, 1952), 6ff.

Hell and the Good

While it might come as a surprise to some readers, there is an overwhelming consensus in Western philosophical thought (perhaps such agreement also exists in Eastern thought, but I am not qualified to say) that what is good, and only what is good, is ultimately *attractive* to human beings. One thing this entails is that what we *desire* is ultimately always something that is good for its own sake. Because of this truth about what is good, we are able to make sense out of the idea of immoral or morally bad/wrong action. Whenever someone acts immorally, he ultimately does so in his pursuit of what is good for its own sake.

Just as what is good and only what is good ultimately attracts, so also no one ever pursues what is bad for its own sake. Everyone ultimately seeks to avoid what is bad for its own sake because everyone *desires* to avoid what is bad for its own sake. Lewis noted that we come closest to the idea of someone pursuing what is bad for its own sake in cruelty. Even here, however, he stressed that those who are cruel are so for the sake of some good they are pursuing:

> But in reality we have no experience of anyone liking badness just because it is bad. In real life people are cruel for one of two reasons—either because they are sadists, that is, because they have a sexual perversion which makes cruelty a cause of sensual pleasure to them, or else for the sake of something they are going to get out of it—money, or power, or safety. But pleasure, money, power, and safety are all, as far as they go, good things. The badness consists in pursuing them by the wrong method, or in the wrong way, or too much. I do not mean, of course, that the people who do this are not desperately wicked. I do mean that wickedness, when you examine it, turns out to be the pursuit of some good in the wrong way. You can be good for the sake of goodness: you cannot be bad for the mere sake of badness. . . . No one ever did a cruel action simply because cruelty is wrong—only because cruelty was pleasant or useful to him. . . . In order to be bad

he must have good things to want and then to pursue in the wrong way.[4]

Elsewhere, Lewis adds: "I think *all* pleasure simply good: what we call bad pleasures are pleasures produced by actions, or inactions, which break the moral law, and it is those actions or inactions which are bad, not the pleasures."[5]

How is the matter of what is good relevant to the doctrine of hell? In the following way: If someone goes to hell, it cannot be because that person chooses to go to hell. No person can choose to go to hell because hell is by hypothesis bad and no one can pursue what is bad for the sake of its badness. Thus, if there is an explanation for why people go to hell, it cannot be or include that they go to hell because they choose to go there.

Hell and Free Will

In the previous paragraph I mentioned the idea of choice. If one is to construct an adequate treatment of the idea of hell, one must address the issue of the freedom of the will. There is more than one concept of free will, but that which is most relevant to the topic of hell is what philosophers call "libertarian free will." If a person has libertarian free will, then that individual has the power to choose. In order to exercise his power to choose, a person must have a reason or purpose to do so. For example, when I was considering going to graduate school, I had a reason to attend and made a choice (exercised my power to choose) to do so. What is sometimes not understood, however, is that when a person makes a choice for a reason, he must also have a reason to choose otherwise. Thus, when I was considering graduate school, I not only had a reason to attend but also had a reason not to do so and was free to choose not to attend for that reason. When an individual is in a situation where he has a reason to do something and no reason not to do that thing and no reason to do something else, he cannot choose for that reason to do what he does. Rather, he simply goes ahead and

[4] C. S. Lewis, *Mere Christianity* (New York: Macmillan, 1943), 34–35.
[5] C. S. Lewis, *The Collected Letters of C. S. Lewis*, vol. 2 (San Francisco: HarperSanFrancisco, 2004), 462–63 (emphasis his).

deterministically intends to do what he does because he had no reason to do otherwise.

To say that a person was free to choose otherwise means that he was not determined to choose as he did. In other words, libertarian free will entails the falsity of determinism as it relates to an individual's choice. Thus, when I chose to go to graduate school, nothing determined that choice. Philosophers sometimes say that the choice was indeterministically made. Thus, if someone goes to hell because of a choice he makes (again, this is not a choice to go to hell), he must not have been determined to make that choice.

Hell and the Purpose of Life

Finally, it is necessary to treat briefly the idea of the meaning or purpose of life for an individual. What is the meaning or purpose of an individual's life? Once again, the Western philosophical tradition has for the most part agreed that the meaning of life is happiness. The Christian luminary St. Augustine asked: "For who wishes anything for any other reason than that he may become happy? . . . It is the decided opinion of all who use their brains that all men desire to be happy."[6] As the *Catechism of the Catholic Church* (45) says, "Man is made to live in communion with God in whom he finds happiness."[7] And Lewis wrote that "God not only understands but *shares* . . . the desire for complete and ecstatic happiness. He made me for no other purpose than to enjoy it."[8] Lewis believed that our desire for goods in this life was a pointer to the desire for the perfect happiness of life with God in heaven, where the latter desire is for the maximization of that of which we can have but a foretaste in this world. Lewis maintained that the desire for perfect happiness was itself evidence for the existence of the afterlife:

> [W]e remain conscious of a desire which no natural happiness will satisfy. But is there any reason to suppose that reality offers any satisfaction to it? "Nor does being hungry prove that

[6] St. Augustine, *The City of God*, trans. M. Dods (New York: Modern Library, 1993), IV, 23; X, 1.

[7] *Catechism of the Catholic Church* (New York: Doubleday, 1995).

[8] Lewis, *The Collected Letters of C. S. Lewis*, vol. 2, 123 (emphasis his).

we have bread." But I think it may be urged that this misses the point. A man's physical hunger does not prove that man will get any bread; he may die of starvation on a raft in the Atlantic. But surely a man's hunger does prove that he comes of a race which repairs its body by eating and inhabits a world where eatable substances exist. In the same way, though I do not believe (I wish I did) that my desire for Paradise proves that I shall enjoy it, I think it a pretty good indication that such a thing exists and that some men will.[9]

Hell, the Self, and Happiness

Given that which is good, the existence of libertarian free will, and the purpose of an individual's existence, which is happiness, how do we explain the possibility of a person's going to hell? The beginnings of an answer are found in the fact that each of us is a substantial self that exists in its entirety at any moment that it does exist and is capable of persisting or enduring as that same substantial self across or through time. For example, though I now have different traits of personality than I had when I was much younger, I am the same self as I was then in the sense that the self that once had personality trait T1 is the same self as that which now lacks that trait and has a different personality trait T2. A story that illustrates this truth recently attracted national attention.[10] A woman named Sara Jane Olsen was released from prison for good behavior after serving only six years of her 14-year sentence. What is particularly interesting about Ms. Olsen is that in 1975 she was a member of a radical group of the 1970s called the Symbionese Liberation Army (SLA). After participating in various acts of violence with the group in California, she subsequently reinvented herself by changing her name, marrying a doctor in Minnesota, and becoming the mother of three children. When she was finally tracked down, arrested, and pleaded guilty in 1999 for her involvement in the violent acts in the 1970s, those who knew her in Minnesota could not believe that she had been a member of the SLA all those years ago in

[9] C. S. Lewis, *The Weight of Glory* (New York: Harper Collins, 2001), 32–33.
[10] "Sara Jane Olson, Former SLA Member, Released from Prison," *The New York Times*, March 21, 2008.

California. Olsen, however, never denied that she was the same self that persisted through the change from a 1970s countercultural radical to a law-abiding spouse and mother at the turn of the twenty-first century.

Now given that a person is aware that he is a substantial self that persists self-identical through time, he comes to distinguish between his short- and long-term well-being or happiness. Often these do not conflict. For example, the teenager who enjoys athletics and avidly participates in them is not only promoting his short-term well-being but is also furthering his long-term potential for happiness by strengthening his heart and muscles and keeping his weight within reasonable limits. Sometimes, however, a person's short-term and long-term happiness conflict in the sense that pursuit of the former undermines the likelihood of the latter. All of us are encouraged not to smoke, abuse alcohol, or use recreational drugs, no matter how happy they might make us in the short run, because addictions develop that more often than not adversely affect our long-term well-being.

Now if our ultimate or long-term happiness is in the afterlife with God who is the source of both, then our awareness of the potential for a conflict between that happiness and our short-term well-being begins with the realization that we are not the only ones with short- and long-term goods. Though it is all too easy for each of us to think of himself as more important than the next person, and sometimes to wish that others who want a good that we desire were not around, the truth of the matter is that each of us is basically one subject among others of the same kind and stature and with needs for many or all of the same goods. All other things being equal, if my having food and shelter is good for me, then it is also good for someone else. If my experiencing hunger is evil, then so is anyone else's experience of hunger. If my family's not having adequate clothing and shelter is evil, then so is any other family's lack of these things. In virtue of the fact that each of us is one among equals with the same purpose for existing, we are subject to the moral imperatives not to steal, not to lie, not to commit adultery, etc. When we exercise restraint and choose to act in accordance with these moral imperatives, we act justly. Justice in this world is ultimately concerned with the deserved experience or lack of experience of goods such as health, food, clothing, shelter, friendship, etc., and requires the exercise of restraint in pursuit of those goods and allowing others their deserved opportunity to pursue them. When we fail to exercise restraint and this opportunity deserved by others is undermined or denied, we act unjustly. As Lewis wrote, "Morality, then, seems to be concerned . . . with fair play and harmony between individuals."[11]

Choices and Life Plans

As I have pointed out, each of us is a substantial self that persists self-identical across or through time. Because we are this kind of being, we not only have a short- and a long-term good and the possibility for a conflict between them, but also we make choices and, thereby, plans about how we will pursue what is good over time. We are agents who regularly choose and, thereby, form intentions in advance about more or less complex plans concerning our futures, where these plans guide our later actions. It is instructive to think of the more expansive or conduct-controlling plans as *life plans*. According to the philosopher Robert Nozick,

> To intend that my life be a certain way, I must have an intention . . . that focuses upon my life as a whole. . . . The strongest sort of intention about one's life is a *life plan*, an individual's set of coherent, systematic purposes and intentions for his life. . . . A life plan specifies the intentional focus of a person's life, his major goals (perhaps partially ordering them), his conception of himself, his purposes, what if anything he dedicates or devotes himself to, and so forth. . . . [A] life plan focuses on a person's whole life or a significant chunk of it as a life.[12]

If we combine the idea of a life plan with a libertarian conception of freedom, we end up with the idea that agents settle on life plans by making choices. Consider two choices of life plans. The first is a

---

[11] Lewis, *Mere Christianity*, 57.
[12] R. Nozick, *Philosophical Explorations* (Cambridge, MA: The Belknap Press, 1981), 577 (his emphasis).

choice of an alcoholic who has chosen never again to touch the demon of drink. Such a choice entails much about his future behavior, which might include no longer having alcohol in his house, no longer frequenting his old haunts, no longer associating with old friends, regularly attending AA meetings, and so forth. The person who makes this choice is planning to avoid as best as he can future situations in which he might be tempted to drink. Through no fault of his own, he might find himself in the kind of situation that he sought to avoid and be forced to make a choice he hoped never again to have to make, but a choice to foreswear drink is a choice of a life plan to guarantee as best as he can that he will not be tempted in this way.

The second is a choice of a line of work, profession, or vocation. The fact that I awoke this morning to walk to my office, teach classes, and write this essay indicates that some time ago I made a choice about a plan for a career that we can think of as a *career* choice. This choice imposed constraints on the kinds of actions I would perform on a day-to-day basis in the future. My career choice entailed that I would rise at a certain hour each morning, routinely carry out certain kinds of work-related activities, return home at a certain time each afternoon, etc. Had I instead made a different career choice, it would likely have imposed different constraints on the kinds of actions I would have had to carry out on a day-to-day basis. Whatever career choice I might have made, the fact that I made such a choice would have introduced a large amount of regular activities into my daily life, which were intended without being repeatedly chosen.

Though a career choice is broad in terms of its scope of influence over the activities that are carried out daily, it is not the most wide-ranging choice of a life plan an individual makes. A career choice is nested within even wider-ranging choices of life plans. For example, in light of the points made about the meaning of life as happiness, an agent's most broadly influential choice about a life plan is about *when* he will maximize his happiness and the kind of action he will adopt in pursuit of that happiness. Because happiness is a person's ultimate *good*, I will term this most wide-ranging choice an ultimate *good-seeking* choice. The following quote from the philosopher Owen

Flanagan about a choice of Augustine's nicely illustrates the kind of choice I have in mind:

> St. Augustine was the ultimate party animal until his early thirties, at which point he changed his ways and became an exemplary moral person, a great philosopher, a bishop, and eventually a saint. We might say that Augustine was ruled by his passions until he saw the light in his early thirties. But according to the [libertarian] picture, we would not mean that he *couldn't* control himself. We would mean that he chose not to control himself or chose to control himself badly.[13]

What Flanagan is suggesting about Augustine's life is something like the following. At a certain point early in his life, Augustine made an ultimate good-seeking choice that entailed he would not restrain himself from pursuing certain means to maximizing his short-term happiness. Then some years later he made a different ultimate good-seeking choice that implied he would restrain his pursuit of goods that promoted his short-term happiness, where exercising this restraint involved his avoiding the performance of certain kinds of actions. Augustine's own account of this latter ultimate good-seeking choice supports Flanagan's description of it. While Augustine says that he was *converted* to God, in whom he believed he would find long-term, perfect happiness, it is clear from his summary of the events leading up to that conversion that he understood that this ultimate good-seeking choice entailed that he would no longer seek to satisfy certain desires for goods that would promote his short-term happiness:

> But now . . . as I heard how [two men] had made the choice that was to save them by giving themselves up entirely to your care, the more bitterly I hated myself in comparison with them. . . . [N]o more was required than an act of will. But it must be a resolute and whole-hearted act of the will. . . . I was held back by mere trifles, the most paltry inanities, all my old attachments. They plucked at my garment of flesh and whispered, "Are you going to dismiss us? From this moment we shall never be with you again, for ever and ever. From this

[13] O. Flanagan, *The Problem of the Soul* (New York: Basic Books, 2002), 58.

moment you will never again be allowed to do this thing or that, for evermore."[14]

It is plausible, then, to understand Augustine's conversion as an ultimate good-seeking choice in which he chose a life plan that he believed would maximize his later experience of happiness (this belief is implicit in Augustine's comment that the choice of the two men would save them), where that choice entailed a commitment on his part to restrain himself from pursuing his short-term happiness in certain ways. As Lewis pointed out, there is nothing amiss with a person who is concerned about his ultimate, long-term happiness. Indeed, there is something amiss if a person is not concerned about it:

> If there lurks in most modern minds the notion that to desire our own good and earnestly to hope for the enjoyment of it is a bad thing, I submit that this notion . . . is no part of the Christian faith. Indeed, if we consider the unblushing promises of reward and the staggering nature of the rewards promised in the Gospels, it would seem that Our Lord finds our desires not too strong, but too weak. We are half-hearted creatures, fooling about with drink and sex and ambition when infinite joy is offered us, like an ignorant child who wants to go on making mud pies in a slum because he cannot imagine what is meant by the offer of a holiday at the sea.[15]

Though Augustine's ultimate good-seeking choice involved a conversion to Christianity, there is nothing essentially Christian about the idea of an ultimate good-seeking choice that requires restrained pursuit of short-term happiness for the sake of that which lies in the future. This is because *any* individual, *qua* human being, has a desire for his short-term happiness. Given his desire for happiness in the short term, he has a reason to act for the sake of (to promote) his own immediate well-being. If, however, such an individual also believes that other persons exist who have a similar desire for their own short-term happiness, then he will believe that were he to act in certain

---

[14] St. Augustine, *Confessions*, trans. R. S. Pine-Coffin (New York: Penguin Books, 1961), VIII, 7, 8, 11.
[15] Lewis, *The Weight of Glory*, 26.

ways he would undermine their opportunity to satisfy their desire for their own short-term well-being, an opportunity to which they have as much right as he has to his own. As a result of what he believes about the potential impact of his actions on the immediate well-being of others, he comes to have moral beliefs about certain kinds of actions that he should not perform. The upshot of this line of reasoning is that a person, as a human being, comes to possess beliefs about permissible and impermissible ways of pursuing what he believes is good and will promote his short-term happiness, where he views the former ways of pursuing what is good as just and the latter ways as unjust. Given these ideas about just and unjust ways of pursuing what is good, a person forms ideas about two corresponding life plans, one which consists of restraint in pursuit of what conduces to his short-term happiness and the other which does not.

An ultimate good-seeking choice of the former kind of life plan, which is the kind Augustine made in his early thirties, is what I will call an ultimate just-good-seeking choice, while an ultimate good-seeking choice of the latter way of life is what I will term an ultimate unjust-good-seeking choice. In simplest terms an ultimate just-good-seeking choice is a choice to live a life of restraint in pursuit of what is good, while an ultimate unjust-good-seeking choice is a choice not to exercise this restraint.

Might not, however, a person's moral beliefs be erroneous? And if they might, can a person really be morally responsible for having made an ultimate just- or unjust-good-seeking choice on the basis of those moral beliefs? After all, if an individual's moral beliefs are seriously misguided, then what he subjectively regards as just and unjust might not be objectively so. Hence, it is possible for a person to make an ultimate choice of a life plan that he believes (subjectively) is just when in reality (objectively) it is (in whole or in part) unjust and for a person to choose a life plan that he thinks (subjectively) is unjust when in reality (objectively) it is (in whole or in part) just.

While the distinction referred to in this objection is a real one, it is not relevant to the issue at hand. What is important is the fact that a person makes an ultimate just- or unjust-good-seeking choice in light of his beliefs about what is just and unjust, regardless of whether those beliefs are true or false, and he understands that he is obligated to make an ultimate just-good-seeking choice in light of those beliefs by virtue of what is appropriately called his conscience, where his conscience is an inner voice or judge that pronounces a verdict of innocence or guilt upon him depending on whether he makes an ultimate just- or unjust-good-seeking choice. St. Paul frequently appealed to this notion of conscience, as in the following comments in his letter to the Romans: "When Gentiles who have not the law do by nature what the law requires, they are a law to themselves, even though they do not have the law. They show that what the law requires is written on their hearts, while their conscience also bears witness and their conflicting thoughts accuse or perhaps excuse them" (Rom 2:14–15 RSV). The philosopher Immanuel Kant also recognized the importance of conscience:

> [T]he accusation of conscience cannot be . . . readily dismissed, neither should it be; it is not a matter of the will. . . . Conscience is an instinct to judge with legal authority according to moral laws; it pronounces a judicial verdict, and, like a judge who can only punish or acquit but cannot reward, so also our conscience either acquits or declares us guilty and deserving of punishment.[16]

Life Plans and Ultimate Destinations

It is now time to tie the idea of life plans and ultimate just- and unjust-good-seeking choices to the matter of heaven (perfect happiness) and hell (the lack of perfect happiness). The link is as follows: those who make an ultimate just-good-seeking choice are plumping for the long-term good of heaven (or, more precisely, the new heaven and new earth), while those who make an ultimate unjust-good-seeking choice are plumping for the short-term good at the expense of forfeiting heaven. In simplest terms ultimate justice is the idea of a separation of persons on the basis of their ultimate choices about life plans into two camps or modes of existence where this separation leaves both parties to do as they have chosen. Heaven is occupied by those

---

[16] I. Kant, *Lectures on Ethics*, trans. by L. Infield (New York: Harper Torchbooks, 1963), 131.

who have made an ultimate just choice of a way of life, and hell is inhabited by those who have made an ultimate unjust choice of a way of life.[17] Thus, heaven and hell must ultimately be understood in terms of how a person chooses to live his life in pursuit of what is good. Does an individual choose a way of life of restraint and deference to others who are created by God in the short term for the purpose of experiencing perfect happiness in the long term? Or does he choose a way of life of a lack of restraint and deference to others in the short term for the purpose of maximizing his happiness in the short term?

Those who make the former kind of choice know all too well how others who make the latter kind of choice want to have nothing to do with them. Those who make the choice to exercise restraint in pursuit of what is good are thought of by those who do not make it as boring, prudes, goody-goodies, etc. Indeed, those who make this choice are often despised by those who do not make it. Moreover, those who do not make this choice also want to have nothing to do with God and despise Him for the same reason. Given that they can't be happy in the short term in the presence of either those who have chosen to exercise restraint or God, they couldn't be happy with either of them in the afterlife, and God will ultimately justly give them their wish to be left alone to live with others who have ultimately chosen to live the same unjust way of life with all of its sorrows and pains. As the *Catechism of the Catholic Church* (1033) states, hell is the "state of definitive self-exclusion from communion with God and the blessed." Lewis makes the same point:

> Either the day must come when joy prevails and all the makers of misery are no longer able to infect it: or else for ever and ever the makers of misery can destroy in others the happiness they reject for themselves.[18]
>
> [T]he damned are, in one sense, successful, rebels to the end; that the doors of hell are locked on the *inside*. . . . In the

---

[17] An ultimate unjust choice of a way of life is sometimes described as either the sin of pride or the choice to be God over one's life. Neither description is objectionable because each entails a choice to reserve the right to pursue the good sooner rather than later at the expense of the well-being of others. Each description entails a choice to reserve the right not to exercise restraint in the pursuit of what is good.

[18] C. S. Lewis, *The Great Divorce* (New York: Harper Collins, 2001), 136.

long run the answer to all those who object to the doctrine of hell, is itself a question: "What are you asking God to do?" To wipe out their past sins and, at all costs, to give them a fresh start, smoothing every difficulty and offering every miraculous help? But He has done so, on Calvary. To forgive them? They will not be forgiven. To leave them alone? Alas, I am afraid that is what He does.[19]

There are only two kinds of people in the end: those who say to God, "Thy will be done," and those to whom God says, in the end, "Thy will be done."[20]

In explaining why it is reasonable to believe in the existence of hell, I have not claimed that libertarian free will is an intrinsic good (good for its own sake) and that its existence justifies the existence of hell. I do not believe that libertarian free will has intrinsic value. Indeed, I believe that it lacks intrinsic value. Rather the great intrinsic goods of perfect happiness and justice justify the existence. St. Paul said about perfect happiness "that the sufferings of this present time are not worth comparing with the glory that is to be revealed to us" (Rom 8:18 RSV). And given the goodness of perfect happiness, it would be unjust if one were to receive it regardless of what kind of ultimate choice one made to live a way of life. And the making of an ultimate just- or unjust-good-seeking choice of a way of life requires the existence of libertarian free will.

---

[19] C. S. Lewis, *The Problem of Pain* (New York: Harper Collins, 2001), 130.
[20] Lewis, *The Great Divorce*, 75.

Chapter 18

WHAT DOES GOD KNOW? THE PROBLEMS OF OPEN THEISM

David P. Hunt

Introduction

C hristians have traditionally understood God's omniscience to include complete knowledge of the past, present, and future. This
understanding is now under fire from a movement known as Open
Theism (or Openism for short). Openists hold the classic Arminian
position that human beings, despite the damage done by the fall, are
endowed with *genuine* free will (and not just some simulacrum of freedom that's compatible with causal or theological determinism), and
they think of God as temporal, dynamic, venturesome, and genuinely
responsive to creatures—a view that will also be acceptable to many
Arminians, depending on how it is cashed out. Calvinists, of course,
will reject both parts of this picture. But what should make Open
Theism controversial for Christians of almost every theological stripe,
whether Arminian or Calvinist, is the openists' claim about what supposedly *follows* from this view of man and God: *that God does not have
complete knowledge of the future.*

Openists allow that God knows a good deal about the future. What
they deny is that He knows so-called "future contingents." A contingent event is one that doesn't have to occur; things could have turned
out differently. Open theists, like other Arminians, believe that the

future contains such events. In particular, human agents sometimes choose between alternative courses of action, each of which is genuinely open to the agent. According to Openism, God does not know such choices in advance. In sum, when the future *can* go in more than one way (and it sometimes can), God doesn't know which way it *will* go.

This represents a significant departure from the classical theist understanding of divine knowledge. While not, in my judgment, *heretical*, it is certainly *heterodox*. It should therefore be subjected to careful scrutiny. There is even some urgency to this task: because Openism's denial of exhaustive foreknowledge is attached to a picture of God that many find appealing, its influence is growing not only among ordinary believers but also among professional philosophers.[1] The crucial arguments for Open Theism are in the end philosophical in nature; identifying and responding to these arguments will therefore occupy much of our attention. But we must also look at the case for (and against) Open Theism from Scripture and theological tradition.

As this essay appears in a book largely devoted to responding to Christianity's critics, I am in no way implying that proponents of Open Theism are not Christians! This chapter, as with other chapters in this section, responds to subbiblical perspectives on the divine nature (in this case, omniscience) that have been held both by professing Christians as well as those outside the church.

Open Theism and Divine Omniscience

Before beginning this examination, we need to be clear about what exactly open theists are saying about divine foreknowledge. The obvious difficulty is that a God who is ignorant of future contingents knows *less* than a God who isn't so ignorant, making the openist God appear less

---

[1] The movement's manifesto, which brought it to the attention of the larger Christian community, is *The Openness of God* (Downers Grove, IL: InterVarsity Press, 1994), cowritten by C. Pinnock, R. Rice, J. Sanders, W. Hasker, and D. Basinger. Controversy has dogged the movement ever since. In 1999 the Southern Baptist Convention adopted a resolution against Open Theism, and in 2001, at its annual meeting, the Evangelical Theological Society did the same; two years later a move to expel two of its members for advocating Open Theism narrowly failed. A measure of its growing support in philosophical circles is the Open Theism and Science Conference hosted by Azusa Pacific University in April 2008.

impressive and Godlike than His more traditional rival. Some openist efforts to clarify their position on this score are genuinely helpful while others are not. Let's look first at a couple that are not.

Gregory Boyd, a leading defender of Openism, attempts to turn the tables on the critic by claiming that the openist God actually knows *more* than the God of Classical Theism (hereafter, the "classical God"). Boyd thinks the critic overlooks all the possible ways the contingent future *might* go. Since these possible futures are all but infinite in number, this is a vast trove of knowledge, and it's available to the openist God.

So far so good. What is puzzling is Boyd's claim that the openist God would therefore know *more* than the classical God. This implies that the classical God would *not* know these truths. But why suppose this? The future contingents known by the classical God, being contingent, *can* happen otherwise; it's just that they *won't*. Unless Boyd can show why the classical God would mistakenly regard the contingent future as *non*contingent, this God must know not only how things *will* turn out but also all the possible ways they *might* have turned out if they hadn't turned out *that* way.

Boyd also tries to shift attention away from God's limited knowledge by reconceiving the problem. If God knows less, it's because there's less to be known, and there's less to be known because *that's the kind of world God chose to create.* God could have created a world in which the future is completely settled in advance and therefore completely knowable; instead, He chose to create a world in which the future is not completely settled and therefore not completely knowable. For this reason Boyd claims that the dispute between openists and classical theists isn't really about God's *knowledge* but about the doctrine of *creation*.

But which dispute is Boyd talking about? The dispute over creation is with *Calvinists*. What is the nature of the dispute with traditional Arminians? The latter *agree* with open theists that God created a world with future contingents. They have no dispute with openists over creation; theirs is clearly a dispute over *what God knows*.

With these red herrings out of the way, we can look at some genuine clarifications of the openist position. With all due respect to Boyd, the dispute *is* over God's knowledge, and it's a dispute in which the openist God *knows less*. How then do openists explain their position so that their conception of God doesn't seem inadequate or impoverished? Openists have endorsed three basic lines on this question.

1. There are no such truths to be known (Boyd, Sanders). That part of the future that is contingent does not yet have a fixed truth-value so there is nothing yet there for knowledge to grasp. Failing to know future contingents, like failing to know the prime numbers between 13 and 17, is therefore a virtue in God, not a vice.[2]

This move preserves divine omniscience. An omniscient being is one who knows all truths. There may be fewer truths for God to know, but He does know *all* of them.

2. There are such truths, but they are logically unknowable (Hasker, Basinger). Knowledge comes with conditions. A *lucky guess*, for example, may be true, but it can't be credited to the believer as *knowledge*. The contingent future, because it is not yet fixed one way or the other, cannot be known by anyone, even God—perhaps *especially* by God since His knowledge must be infallible.[3]

This move abandons omniscience. If there are truths that God doesn't know, for whatever reason, then He isn't omniscient. But perhaps this isn't so serious. After all, if God's *omnipotence* isn't compromised by His inability to *do* what is logically impossible, perhaps His *cognitive power* isn't compromised by His inability to *know* what is logically unknowable.

3. There are such truths, God can know them, but He freely refrains from doing so in order to secure the sorts of goods openists think are at stake (Willard). If tomorrow Jones faces a significant fork in life's road, God *can* foreknow Jones's choice, but doing so would

---

[2] This is at least implicit in G. Boyd's contribution to *Divine Foreknowledge: Four Views*, eds. J. K. Beilby and P. R. Eddy (Downers Grove, IL: InterVarsity Press, 2001); it also seems to fit best with the various things J. Sanders says—e.g., in *The God Who Risks: A Theology of Divine Providence*, rev. ed. (Downers Grove, IL: InterVarsity Press, 2007), chap. 6. For a clear endorsement of this position, see D. Tuggy, "Three Roads to Open Theism," *Faith and Philosophy* 24 (January 2007): 28–51. Another way to deny that there are any true future contingents for God to know is to hold that all genuine future contingents are *false*. For a defense of this variation of strategy one, see A. R. Rhoda, G. A. Boyd, and T. G. Belt, "Open Theism, Omniscience, and the Nature of the Future," *Faith and Philosophy* 23 (October 2006): 432–59.

[3] W. Hasker, *God, Time, and Knowledge* (Ithaca: Cornell University Press, 1989), chap. 10; D. Basinger, "Can an Evangelical Christian Justifiably Deny God's Exhaustive Knowledge of the Future?" *Christian Scholar's Review* 25 (1995): 133–45.

presettle the question of which way Jones will go. If it's important to God that this question *not* be presettled because it's important that Jones have both directions genuinely open to him, then God might decline to know Jones's choice until it's made.[4]

This also abandons omniscience, but the parallel with omnipotence might again be invoked to argue that God's greatness is not thereby diminished. God still has unlimited cognitive power; He just chooses not to exercise it. We don't think God is less powerful because He refrains from exercising all the power He possesses; so why think He would be less knowledgeable just because He refrains from knowing all the things He can know?

In sum, openists give different accounts of *why* God doesn't know future contingents, and this leads them to different conclusions about whether God is omniscient. What all three forms of Openism have in common, however, is that God *learns* things over time that He didn't know earlier: as time progresses, there are (1) more truths to be known, (2) more truths that are knowable, or (3) more truths that God allows Himself to know. This common Openist view that God's body of knowledge *grows* over time is sometimes referred to as "dynamic omniscience."

What Do the Scriptures Teach?

For readers who assume that Classical Theism is securely grounded in Scripture, it may come as some surprise to learn that openists regard this as their strong suit. On the one hand, the Bible is filled with passages depicting God as learning things (Gen 22:12; 2 Chron 32:31), changing His mind (Exod 32:14; Num 23:19; Jer 18:10; 26:13), reacting with surprise and disappointment (Gen 6:6; 1 Sam 15:10; Isa 5:2; Jer 3:7), and in other respects behaving in just the ways one would expect if the openists are right about His lacking exhaustive foreknowledge. On the other hand, passages invoked for Classical Theism often contain less than meets the eye: Isa 41:22–23 makes knowledge of the future the mark of a prophet but nowhere states that God's disclosures to true prophets include the *contingent* future, while Isa 46:9–10,

---

[4] D. Willard, *The Divine Conspiracy* (New York: HarperCollins, 1998), 244–53.

where God "declare[s] the end from the beginning, and from ancient times things that are not yet done" (KJV) is explicitly about His own future actions, *not* the contingent future. Perhaps the best extended proof text for the traditional view is the paean to God's incredible knowledge in Psalm 139, which contains a number of passages that are highly suggestive of exhaustive foreknowledge; still, these aren't sufficiently unambiguous to settle the issue, given all the passages that appear to point straightforwardly in the other direction.

Openists have a theory about why most Christians nevertheless believe that the Scriptures teach exhaustive foreknowledge: (1) Traditional nonopenists start out with an a priori criterion of what is worthy of God (*dignum deo*); (2) they then identify verses that are most sympathetic to this a priori conception of God, employing them as *control texts* for understanding other biblical passages; (3) openist-friendly passages are subjected to an *accommodationist hermeneutic* which assigns them a nonliteral sense; (4) the result of this expedient is *strained exegesis*.

I deny that these four points give open theists the advantage.

1. Openists have their own conception of what is *dignum deo*, and they don't hesitate to draw on it when the Scriptures are silent. For example, if the openists are right that the Bible doesn't clearly teach exhaustive omniscience with respect to the future, it's no less true that it doesn't clearly teach exhaustive omniscience with respect to the *past and present*; yet openists accept the latter. Why? Presumably because ignorance of any detail of the past and present would not be *dignum deo*.

2. Classical theists have control texts in terms of which they can read the openists' favorite passages, but openists have their own control texts for reading the classical theists' favorite passages. What alternative is there when the Scriptures pull in different directions? The question is not *whether to use control texts*; it's *which* control texts and *why*.

3. It would be astonishing if God *didn't* accommodate Himself to our condition in the Bible. If this exegesis can be abused, the lesson is not to abuse it. Moreover, the openists themselves must allow for anthropomorphisms (various biblical passages attribute to God eyes,

ears, mouth, face, hands, arm, backside). Why do they draw the line where they do?

4. The charge of "strained exegesis" is overblown; moreover, openists have their own problems with strained exegesis. Since openists rest so much of their case on their superior exegetical position, let's look at some examples. I'll begin with a couple of openist-friendly passages that classical theists can supposedly evade only through "strained exegesis."

a. In Isa 5:4 we are told that the Lord expected (domesticated) grapes from a vineyard that instead yielded wild grapes. Gregory Boyd cites this as a case in which God didn't know beforehand what would happen. But how exactly does the fact that God *expected* grapes support Boyd's claim? If I tell a group of grade-school boys that I *expect* them to behave, does this show that I *believe* they will behave? Not at all. I may, at the same time as I *expect* them to obey, also believe that they will fall short of my expectations. (I've had experience with this particular group before!) If God expected grapes *in this sense*, His expectation provides no evidence whatsoever that He didn't also foreknow that the vineyard would yield wild grapes instead. To support Boyd's claim, God's expectation of grapes must be a *belief* that the vineyard would yield grapes. But in that case, God not only didn't know what the future held in store; He held a *false belief* about the future. No open theist, however, would accept such a conclusion. Open theists, then, should join classical theists in seeking a plausible reading of this passage in which God's expectation of grapes is not construed as a *belief* about the future. But that means the passage is useless as a proof text for Openism.

b. John Sanders believes that "conditional prophecies" undermine the doctrine of exhaustive foreknowledge: "How can a conditional promise, say to Saul (1 Sam 13:13), be genuine if God already foreknows the human response and so foreknows that God will, in fact, never fulfill his promise?"[5] What exactly is the problem here? Suppose it's true that if a certain nation does evil, God will destroy it; and if it turns from evil, God will spare it (Jer 18:7–10). Suppose further, as classical theists maintain, that God already knows what He will do and

---

[5] Sanders, *The God Who Risks*, 133.

that He knows He will destroy it. Sanders doesn't see how God could reveal the second conditional (that if it turns from evil, God will spare it) while knowing this unconditional truth about the future (that He will *not* spare it but will in fact destroy it). But why? These are both *truths,* so God wouldn't be lying. Sanders thinks it would nevertheless be *disingenuous*: it's only if God does not know what will actually ensue that He can be "sincere when uttering conditional statements." But I'm not sure why. The destruction of this nation is a bad result; God wants it to be spared (and so should we). Then it's important that we know: "If you repent, I spare! If you don't repent, I destroy!" This is *motivating* knowledge. And why not *also* reveal that destruction, rather than mercy, is what will in fact occur? Here's a reason. Since we are prone to fatalistic fallacies, we are strongly tempted to reason like this: It's no use trying to turn from our evil (thereby securing mercy rather than destruction) since destruction (alas!) is what *will* occur. That's *unmotivating* knowledge for irrational (fatalist-susceptible) creatures like ourselves, and God wisely declines to reveal it.

Let's now look at a couple of classical theist-friendly passages and the openist response to them.

c. The night following Jesus' betrayal, Peter came to three forks in the road at which he could either avow or deny his affiliation with Christ, and each time he took the road of denial. Jesus' prediction earlier that evening that Peter would deny Him three times is therefore a prima facie example of divine foreknowledge of future contingents. What resources can openists bring to bear on this and similar examples?[6] In the first place, it might be a *disguised conditional:* if you don't straighten up, Peter, this is how it will play out (exactly three times!). Second, Christ might not have been expressing a definite belief about the future but only an assessment of the *probabilities* of the predicted event's occurring, given His knowledge of the past and present. Or third, Jesus might have known that God intended to *ensure* that things turn out this way so that (as Boyd speculates) "three times Peter's true character was squeezed out of him."[7] Besides the individual

---

[6] The three resources that follow are the ones Sanders summarizes in *The God Who Risks*, 138–39.

[7] Beilby and Eddy, eds., *Divine Foreknowledge: Four Views*, 21.

problems to which each of these is prone, there's the overarching problem that none of these is even remotely a "straightforward" reading of the texts rather than a wholly speculative account driven simply by the requirements of the openist position on foreknowledge.

d. In John 18:4 (NRSV) we read, "Then Jesus . . . came forward and asked them, 'Whom are you looking for?'" This is just the sort of passage openists cite on behalf of their position. If Jesus knew whom they were seeking, He wouldn't have asked; since He did ask, He didn't know. Anyone whose Christology requires that Jesus already knew the answer will have to engage in "strained exegesis" to explain how He could ask such a question without being disingenuous. For example, they might claim that Christ is not asking the question *for His own sake* (e.g., to find out something of which He's ignorant) but *for their sake*; it's an accommodation to the mob's ignorance of the fact that He already knows rather than a reflection of His own ignorance.

Is it possible to determine whether such charges of "strained exegesis" are just and to do so in a neutral way without a prior commitment to one side or the other? I believe it is. Discerning readers may have noticed that this was supposed to be an example of a classical theist-friendly text; even more discerning readers may have noticed that I misquoted the text. It actually reads: "Then Jesus, *knowing all that was to happen to him*, came forward and asked them, 'Whom are you looking for?'" So Jesus did the very thing openists would ordinarily regard as demonstrating His ignorance, while in fact "knowing all!" If this doesn't settle the case definitively in Classical Theism's favor, it at least shows that the Scriptures themselves approve of the exegesis that openists label "strained."

Who's got the Bible on their side is a big topic which can hardly be settled from just four texts. I believe, however, that the lessons just learned from these texts would be borne out by other texts we could have examined with sufficient time. Classical theists should admit that there are passages whose straightforward reading favors Open Theism. But that's as far as the concessions should go. The alternative classical reading of these texts is *not* strained, and it's the openist reading of certain *other* texts that *is* truly strained. When all the scriptural data are taken into account, the openists' charge of "strained exegesis" bounces back on them.

What About the Tradition?

Before getting to the philosophical debate, I want to comment briefly on another touchstone: the theological tradition. Not all readers can be expected to care, or care to the same degree, about what the tradition has to say on the matter. I do care; certainly the openists care.

The tradition is important to openists in two respects. In the first place, openists need to explain the tradition's endorsement of exhaustive foreknowledge, despite what they take to be the plain teaching of Scripture. They do this by alleging that the tradition was corrupted by pagan thought. Openists therefore look to the tradition for evidence of this corruption. In the second place (and running somewhat at cross-purposes with the first point), openists hope to uncover early openist voices—a "pilgrim church" of open theists who remained faithful to biblical Openism. If successful, this move might dampen criticism that Openism is a theological innovation.[8]

Regarding the first point, it is beyond dispute that the Fathers were, to varying degrees, *influenced* by the pagan philosophical heritage. (For anyone who doubts this, I suggest reading a few treatises from Plotinus's *Enneads*, followed by Augustine's *Confessions*.) Whether this influence amounts to corruption depends on whether, owing to this influence, the church fathers reached the *wrong conclusions*. This point, then, depends on the success of the openists' scriptural arguments (which we've already covered) and philosophical arguments (which we'll come to next).

As for the second point, the effort to identify a "pilgrim church" of openists is embarrassingly short on results. Exhibit A in the openist case is Chalcidius, who wrote that God "knows necessary truths necessarily and future contingent truths contingently." A number of comments are in order here.

---

[8] Both sorts of interest in the tradition are on display in Sanders's contribution to *The Openness of God* and in chapter 5 of his *The God Who Risks*.

1. *That's it:* there is no Exhibit B (at least until the nineteenth century). Many early figures qualify as proto-Arminians but none rejects exhaustive foreknowledge.

2. Chalcidius (c. 400) is a rather late witness to Open Theism, much too late to represent an early, uncorrupted, preheretical church. (Think how many heresies emerged to confuse believers during the first four centuries.)

3. We just don't know much about him; though probably a Christian, even this isn't certain.

4. Interpreting Chalcidius as a proto-openist may also involve wishful exegesis: it's not at all clear that the phrase quoted above means what the openists want it to mean. Any Arminian, believing that God has knowledge of future contingents, should agree that God has this knowledge contingently. If the foreknown event is contingent, it might not have been true; if it might not have been true, God might not have known it; and if God might not have known it, the fact that He *does* know it is a *contingent* fact.

5. The strangest thing about the openist love affair with Chalcidius is that he's supposed to be someone who—unlike such theological giants as Augustine, Gregory of Nyssa, and so on—had the discernment to resist the corrupting effects of pagan philosophy. This is strange because the little we know about Chalcidius implicates him thoroughly in pagan philosophy. Chalcidius was a Platonist; he translated Plato's *Timaeus* and wrote a treatise engaging Stoic arguments on fate. If the Fathers were touched by Platonism, this alleged openist was thoroughly implicated in it! Exhibit A is a bust.

Conclusion: The tradition goes decisively against Open Theism. Openists should frankly acknowledge that their position on divine foreknowledge is a theological innovation and focus on arguing that it's an innovation whose time has come.

Four (Bad) Philosophical Arguments for Open Theism

While the tradition is hardly sacrosanct, one should at least have *good reasons* for departing from it. I have argued that Scripture does *not* provide good reasons for departing from the traditional doctrine of divine foreknowledge. At the same time, I don't believe the Scriptures alone absolutely require the classical position. If there were strong nonscriptural reasons for rejecting Classical Theism—say, if Classical Theism just *didn't make sense*—then I don't believe there would be insuperable obstacles to reading the Scriptures as openists propose. I do think that the case for Openism comes down to reasons for thinking that Classical Theism, in one way or another, just doesn't make sense; that is, it comes down to *philosophical* objections to Classical Theism. Four are particularly important.[9] I cannot hope to do justice to all four in this brief chapter, but I can perhaps say enough about each to persuade the reader that the traditional Christian commitment to exhaustive divine foreknowledge is not in serious jeopardy.

1. God Can't Know the Contingent Future Because It's Not Yet True

Statements about future contingent events aren't true until the events occur; since the occurrence of these events isn't *true* in advance, God can't *know* them in advance.

This reason for embracing Openism flies in the face of both logic and common usage. Let's begin with logic. Either I will call my mother tomorrow, or I won't call my mother tomorrow. One or the other of these statements about the future must be true. The principle that either a given statement or its denial is true is called the "Law of Excluded Middle." But this first brief on behalf of Openism requires that this law be abrogated. That's a heavy cost, and the vast majority of logicians would decline to pay it.

Ordinary usage and common sense also reject it. We make claims about the contingent future all the time, and we assume that such claims are sometimes true. Consider the following:

1. This coin will land heads on the next toss.
2. My wife will vote for candidate X in tomorrow's election.

---

[9] Actually five, by my count, are particularly important, but space considerations compelled me to drop the one that is least prominent in openist literature. The essence of the objection is this: the more of the future one knows, the less of the future is open to one's agency ("one cannot deliberate over what one already knows is going to happen"); this is no less true of God than of human agents, but then maximal foreknowledge would render God maximally impotent. For more on this objection and my own suggestion for how to handle it, see my contribution to Beilby and Eddy, eds., *Divine Foreknowledge: Four Views*, 91–96.

3. The U.S. will elect its first female president in 2016.

The openist may object to taking such claims at face value on the grounds that the future is *not yet real* and that claims about it are therefore *not yet true*. But this objection would be received with bemusement by anyone engaged in the actual practice of making claims about the future. If I bet that this coin will land heads and it does land heads, then *I was right*; you can't take my money on the grounds that there are no true future contingents, I bet on one, and so *I was wrong*.

This attempt to renege on a bet, like the openists' denial of truth-values to future contingents, rests on a misunderstanding of what future-tense statements are all about. This misunderstanding is perhaps best exposed by comparing the future tense with the past tense. If statements about the future are not yet true because the future is *not yet real*, then statements about the past should be no longer true because the past is *no longer real*. But that's nonsense. Consider the following:

4. Caesar was assassinated in 44 BC.
5. In 1492 Columbus sailed the ocean blue.
6. Yesterday I promised my wife I'd wash the car.

These statements are true in virtue of what happened in 44 BC, AD 1492, and yesterday; none is true in virtue of anything that is happening now (if Caesar were being assassinated now, then he *wasn't* assassinated in 44 BC). Yet each of these is true *now*. (Imagine trying to get out of washing the car on the grounds that, because statement 6 is past, it is no longer true!) These statements are *about* the past (not the present) but are being *made* now. That's the nature of statements about the past. Likewise, supposing that my wife does vote for candidate X tomorrow, it is *now true* that she will vote for X tomorrow. This obviously does not mean that she is now voting for X; the polls haven't opened yet! This statement is *about* the future (not the present), but it is being made *now*. That's the nature of statements about the future.[10]

There is one important difference between statements about the past and statements about the future. The contingent future can only

---

[10] For a clear discussion of why truth should not be denied to future contingents, see W. L. Craig, *The Only Wise God: The Compatibility of Divine Foreknowledge and Human Freedom* (Eugene, OR: Wipf & Stock, 2000, chap. 4.

rarely be *known* by human beings, and even when it can be known (as I might know whom my wife will vote for tomorrow), it cannot be known with certainty. But this is simply irrelevant to the question whether there are future-contingent *truths*. "This coin will land heads on the next toss" is true just in case that's what happens; its truth does not depend in any way on whether anyone can also *know* this truth in advance. If God can't know these truths, it must be for some reason *other* than the absence of any truths there to be known. But what could that reason be, given that God is unsurpassably great?

2. God Can't Know the Contingent Future Because Then It Wouldn't Be Contingent

A contingent event is one that can go either way; but if God already knows which way it will go, it *can't* go the other way because *God can't be mistaken.* So this foreknown event is not contingent after all; nor can any infallibly foreknown event be contingent. Consider my wife's vote tomorrow. God knew before she was even born whether (and if so, how) she would vote. When tomorrow arrives, can she do anything other than exactly what God has always believed she would do? Of course not. But then she's not free in what she does.

Entire books have been written about this problem, and I don't think anything I could say within the space available to me here would be adequate. I will therefore restrict myself to two *in*adequate points—inadequate in that they don't pretend to show *what* is wrong with this argument, only *that* there is something wrong with it.

In the first place, readers should know that the vast majority of Christian philosophers, past and present, have rejected this argument. Openists are in a minority here. That doesn't mean they're wrong—the truth isn't determined by majority vote—but it does mean that readers ill-equipped to follow the abstruse twists and turns of the philosophical debate shouldn't endorse the openist position just because an openist apologist claims that it's a good argument.

There is no consensus, among the majority who reject the argument, over the exact point at which the argument goes wrong. I have my own favorite response to the argument, which follows Augustine's analysis of the problem in his *On Free Choice of the Will*.[11] But discussion of the argument over the centuries has turned up *many* different points at which it can be challenged. Defenders of traditional foreknowledge can regard this as an embarrassment of riches. What are the chances that *all* of these challenges are mistaken? A further point concerns the historical figures most closely associated with these various critiques. They include Aristotle, Augustine, Boethius, Thomas Aquinas, Duns Scotus, William of Ockham, and Jonathan Edwards. What is interesting about this list is that all of these figures are Christians, except Aristotle. And which step does Aristotle reject? The very step that most openists reject: that there are future-contingent truths. This is at least ironic, given the openist charge that classical theists are the ones corrupted by pagan philosophy!

The second reason readers should distrust this argument as a ground for Open Theism has to do with the fact that we are sometimes justified in thinking that a position is mistaken even when we don't know *how*. An example is Zeno's paradoxes. One of the more famous of these is a "proof" that Achilles cannot win a footrace against a tortoise if the tortoise is given a head start, no matter how small. We *know* that this can't be right—we see faster things passing slower things all the time—but Zeno gives a clever argument for his conclusion, and it's actually hard to refute. In the face of this argument, one is perfectly within one's rights in saying: "I know that argument is mistaken even though I don't see *how*."

The argument that God's knowledge of the future would render the future noncontingent is another case of this sort. Here's why. Take an action that satisfies to the highest degree *your* favorite criteria for free action, whatever they may be. If *anything* is a free action, *that* is. Now *add* an infallible foreknower to the scenario. How can the introduction of this foreknower, just by itself, change the status of the action so that it is no longer free? There are conditions that clearly *would* warrant such a reassessment—for example, if it were added that the agent was acting under posthypnotic suggestion or was being controlled like a marionette by tiny invisible wires. But the idea that the

---

[11] Augustine's analysis appears in Book III, chapter 4. I argue on behalf of Augustine's solution in my "On Augustine's Way Out," *Faith and Philosophy* 16 (January 1999): 1–26.

mere presence of an infallible foreknower could make this kind of difference is utterly implausible. Readers therefore have good reason to be confident that this argument goes wrong, even if they're unable to determine exactly *where* it goes wrong.[12]

3. Even if God Knew the Future, Such Knowledge Could Not Help Him

Many supporters of traditional foreknowledge may fear that abandoning this doctrine would disable God in some way, depriving Him of a crucial providential resource. Openists hold that this fear is baseless. "The doctrine of divine foreknowledge . . . is of no importance whatever for the religiously significant concerns about prayer, providence, and prophecy," William Hasker writes.[13] "If simple foreknowledge [of future contingents] did exist, it would be useless."[14] There is therefore no real theological cost to giving up the traditional doctrine.

Note that there would still be one significant theological advantage to exhaustive foreknowledge, even if Hasker and other openists are right about its uselessness: it would make God *smarter*, and thus *greater*, than if He lacked it. But leave this to one side.

If God already knows what's going to happen, how can He *use* that knowledge to enhance His providential oversight? He couldn't use it to *change* the future because the future would then be different than He "knew" it would be, and that's clearly impossible. So what good is it to know the future? Wouldn't such knowledge turn God into a passive spectator of events rather than an active agent?

To refute a universal claim, it is enough to provide a single counterinstance. Suppose then that a warrant will be issued next week for the arrest of an underground church leader. The classical God knows about this decision by the authorities well in advance; the openist God does not. It's also clear that this gives the classical God an *advantage*. This fact can be obscured if one looks for this advantage to God's ability to prevent the authorities from issuing the warrant in the first place.

---

[12] Readers interested in pursuing this objection further and thinking hard about some of the argument's premises, while avoiding the technicalities of an article or book written for an audience of professional philosophers, may find what they are looking for in my contribution to Beilby and Eddy, eds., *Divine Foreknowledge: Four Views*, especially 72–91.

[13] Hasker, *God, Time and Knowledge*, 55.

[14] W. Hasker, *Providence, Evil and the Openness of God* (London: Routledge, 2004), 104.

God can, of course, prevent the issuance of the warrant; but then His foreknowledge would not have included its issuance! Given that He foresaw the warrant being issued, He can't *use that* knowledge to bring it about that the warrant *isn't* issued. What He *can* do, however, is just what *you* would do if you knew about the arrest order in advance and wanted to help the underground church leader: He can warn him. And this is something the openist God, who lacks knowledge of future contingents, cannot do.

A number of questions can be raised about this case. For example, mightn't God's intervention and the church leader's response to it, coming before the foreknown event, *interfere* with it in some way? Answer: Whether it can, it *won't*. Since what God foreknows is what *will in fact* happen and is consequently the result of everything leading up to it, if God's warning to the underground leader results in his taking action that leads the authorities to act sooner, then their acting sooner is precisely what God foresaw in the first place. It remains the case that whatever God foresaw happening (and what He foresaw is what *will in fact happen*, given everything leading up to it), He can use that knowledge in ways not available to the openist God.

This is all I can do with the short space available. But I trust this is enough to convince the reader that the prospects for the providential usefulness of divine foreknowledge are more promising than they may have appeared.[15]

4. If God Knew the Future, the Problem of Evil Would Be Harder to Resolve

The problem of evil is tough enough as it is; we shouldn't take theological positions that make it even tougher. But that's just what the traditional doctrine of exhaustive foreknowledge does. It's harder to explain and justify evils God knows about *in advance*. John Sanders, for example, speaks movingly of the death of his brother in an auto accident and the false comfort of Christians who assured him that it was

---

[15] I go into these matters in more detail in my "Divine Providence and Simple Foreknowledge," *Faith and Philosophy* 10 (July 1993): 396–416, and in my contribution to Beilby and Eddy, eds., *Divine Foreknowledge: Four Views*, 96–101.

all part of God's providential plan. By denying divine foreknowledge, one can avoid making this problem even harder than it has to be.

A number of things are wrong with this move. For one thing, if this were an acceptable way to address the problem of evil, why stop with foreknowledge? Why not reduce God's power and goodness as well? Replace Jehovah with Zeus, and the problem of evil might disappear altogether.

More importantly, I don't believe that the problem of evil is made any easier by denying traditional foreknowledge. (It's an easier problem for Zeus, but that's for reasons other than Zeus's lack of exhaustive foreknowledge!) Many of the concrete cases that try believers' faith, like the death of Sanders's brother or the cancer death of my one-year-old nephew, are not explained by denying divine foreknowledge. The openist God, omniscient with respect to the past and present, had more than enough knowledge to save my nephew, but He didn't do so. Foreknowledge plays no role in generating this puzzle, and adding foreknowledge does not make the puzzle harder.

Why did God allow my nephew, or Sanders's brother, to die? I don't know, and I don't know anyone who does. Since I don't know what the reason is, I'm in no position to say that it's a reason that would be available on the assumption that God lacks exhaustive foreknowledge but *un*available on the assumption that God's omniscience encompasses future contingents. No open theist, to my knowledge, has even begun the task of showing this. Solving the problem of evil for the God of Open Theism is already so difficult that any solution, supposing one to exist, might turn out to be adequate for the God of Classical Theism as well—in which case evil would provide no ground for preferring the former over the latter.

Conclusion

I conclude that there is no good reason for Christians to embrace Open Theism. The openists' claim to a clear-cut exegetical advantage is a chimera. Openism *is* an innovation, ungrounded in the tradition. And the philosophical arguments that are supposed to give Open Theism a logical edge over Classical Theism are highly dubious.

CONTRIBUTORS

Paul Copan
(Ph. D. in philosophy, Marquette University) Professor and Pledger Family Chair of Philosophy and Ethics at Palm Beach Atlantic University

William Lane Craig
(D.Theol., Ludwig-Maximilliéns-Universität München, Germany; Ph.D., University of Birmingham England) Research Professor of Philosophy at Talbot School of Theology in La Mirada, California. Fellow of the Alexander von Humboldt-Stiftung. Prior to his appointment at Talbot he spent seven years at the Higher Institute of Philosophy of the Katholike Universiteit Leuven, Belgium

Craig A. Evans
(Ph.D., Claremont) Payzant Distinguished Professor of New Testament at Acadia Divinity College in Nova Scotia, Canada

Gregory E. Ganssle
(Ph.D., Syracuse) Senior fellow at the Rivendell Institute and lecturer in the department of philosophy at Yale University

Stewart Goetz
(Ph.D., Notre Dame) Professor of Philosophy at Ursinus College

Gary R. Habermas
(Ph.D., Michigan State University) Distinguished Research Professor and Chair of the Department of Philosophy and Theology at Liberty University, teaching primarily in the Ph.D. program in Theology and Apologetics at Liberty Baptist Theological Seminary.

David P. Hunt
(Ph.D., Vanderbilt University) Professor of philosophy at Whittier College in Whittier, California. Adjunct professor at Talbot School of Theology in La Mirada, California

Mark D. Linville
(Ph.D. in philosophy, University of Wisconsin-Madison) Adjunct professor of philosophy at Clayton State University

Elsa J. Marty
(M.A. candidate, University of Chicago Divinity School) Co-author of the *Historical Dictionary of Philosophy of Religion* (Scarecrow Press, forthcoming)

Michael J. Murray
(Ph.D., Notre Dame) Arthur and Katherine Shadek Professor of Humanities and Philosophy, Franklin and Marshall College

Steven Porter
(Ph.D. in philosophy, University of Southern California; M.Phil. in philosophical theology, University of Oxford) Associate Professor of Theology and Philosophy, Institute for Spiritual Formation, Talbot School of Theology and Rosemead School of Psychology, Biola University. Managing editor, *Journal of Spiritual Formation and Soul Care*

Victor Reppert
(Ph.D. University of Illinois at Urbana) Adjunct professor of philosophy at Glendale Community College, Grand Canyon University, and Ashford University

James Daniel Sinclair
James D. Sinclair is a senior warfare analyst with the United States Navy. He has authored numerous papers for symposia such as the Military Operations Research Society and the Combat Identification Systems Conference. He holds a Master's degree in Physics from Texas A&M University where he studied Supersymmetry and Cosmology. He has recently finished a project of interviewing many of the world's premier cosmologists on the subject of the origin of the universe.

Robert H. Stein
(Ph.D., Princeton Theological Seminary) Senior Professor of New Testament Interpretation, The Southern Baptist Theological Seminary

Charles Taliaferro
(Ph.D., Brown) Professor of Philosophy, St. Olaf College

Daniel B. Wallace
Professor of New Testament Studies, Dallas Theological Seminary. Executive Director, Center for the Study of New Testament Manuscripts

Michael J. Wilkins, Ph.D.
(Ph.D., Fuller Theological Seminary) Distinguished Professor of New Testament Language and Literature, and Dean of the Faculty, Talbot School of Theology, Biola University

Ben Witherington III
(Ph.D. Durham) Amos Professor of NT for Doctoral Studies, Asbury Theological Seminary, Wilmore, Kentucky. Doctoral Faculty St. Mary's College, St. Andrews University, Scotland

AUTHOR INDEX

287

SCRIPTURE INDEX